FOLK LIFE AND CULTURE

OF

O D I S H A

FOLK LIFE AND CULTURE

OF

O D I S H A

by

Bhagabana Sahu

2015

Kaveri Books

New Delhi - 110002

First Published in 2015

ISBN: 978-81-7479-170-2

Published by

Kaveri Books

4832/24, Ansari Road
New Delhi-110002 (India)

Tel: 011-23288140, 23245799
E-mail : kaveribooks@vsnl.com
E-mail : kaveribooks@gmail.com
Website: www.kaveribooks.com

Typeset in AGaramond Font at
Delta Book World, New Delhi - 110 002.

PRINTED IN INDIA

Acknowledgement

I have the pleasure to acknowledge with thanks my indebtedness to a galaxy of persons for their assistance and help for the preparation of this work. Among them Prof. R.C.Misro, Professor of History, Berhampur University, Berhampur stands first. Having acted as my guide and supervisor he has helped me a lot in enriching the standard of the work. I am highly indebted to him.

I express my deep sense of gratitude to Prof. Jayanta Kumar Mohapatra, former Vice-Chancellor of Berhampur University, Berhampur for his immense help and encouragement at the different stages of the preparation of this thesis.

I also take the opportunity of expressing my sincere thanks to Prof. L.N.Raut, Prof. S.C.Padhy, Prof. M.Padhy of the P. G. Department of History for their inspiration and Prof. D.P. Patnaik, P.G.Department of Odia, Berhampur University for providing few photos for this book.

I am very much grateful to the authorities of Orissa State Archives of Bhubaneswar; H.K.Mahatab State Library, Bhubaneswar; Jaydeva State Museum, Bhubaneswar; National Library, Kolkata; Conmerra Library, Chennai; Tamilnadu State Archives, Chennai; Andhra Pradesh State Archives, Hyderabad;

different District Collectorates' Record room and the various village libraries of south Odisha for the help they rendered in consulting records, manuscripts, books and newspapers required for the purpose.

I owe my gratitude to Sri Gouri Shankar Misra, Retd. D.I. of Schools and a keen researcher in History for his fatherly blessings and inspiration throughout the period of the preparation of this thesis.

I would also like to express my sincere feelings of obligation to my wife Dr.(Mrs.) Manorama Dash, my son Sibun, daughters Sradhasree and Soumyasree without whose cooperation this work would not have been completed. Lastly, I express my thanks to M/s Kaveri Books, New Delhi, for the publication of the book in the record of the time.

Bhagabana Sahu, D. Litt

Preface

This work is the first of its kind to bring to light the various aspects of the folk culture of south Odisha in a comprehensive, critical and compact manner during the colonial era from historical point of view. The period covered is, in fact, the most significant and formative from the administrative and political point of view. The period witnessed the British conquest of Odisha, the Resistance Movement, the Socio-Religious Reform Movement, growth of renaissance and Odia Nationalism, Utkal Union Movement for the unification of all Odia speaking areas and the freedom struggle for the independence of India.

The southern part of modern Odisha comprising of seven districts viz. Ganjam, Gajapati, Rayagada, Koraput, Nabarangapur, Malkangiri and Kandhamal originally formed a part of the ancient kingdom of Kalinga which was supposed to have been founded in the 9th century B.C. Hemmed in on the side by the sea, and on all other sides by ranges of mountains and dense forests, and intersected by innumerable rivers, south Odisha, has developed a distinct pattern of life, art and literature of her own. Her gods, goddesses and temples, her social structure, her dance and music and festivals have all developed fascinating individual variants which mark them out as distinct entities in similar categories in India.

Several factors are attributed to shape south Odisha's folk cultural heritage. The geographical situation of the region is the prime factor to rear up of such a culture. Lying between north and south India across a natural highway along the eastern coast of India, south Odisha acts like a bridge between the Aryan culture of north and Dravidian culture of south. The socio-cultural life of this region thus form a highly interesting amalgam evolved out of Dravido-Aryan elements with delightful assimilations from the life of the tribals and not so much affected by the external influences of Islam and Christianity as other parts of India.

Rural background of south Odisha was another factor that led it to retain the unique folk traditions of this region. It is basically a land of villages having about 30,000 villages big or small. They have retained the folklore traditions alive and intact till today.

The conservativeness of the people was another factor that led to the growth of folk culture in this region. The people of south Odisha were very much conservative, superstitious and ignorant. They were averse and apathetic to modern ideas and western influences for a long time.

Puranic traditions and existence of *Bhagabata Tungis* also supplied good incentives for the people of south Odisha to rear up folk culture in a perfect manner. In almost all the villages of south Odisha the *Purana Panda* recited *puranas* in every evening hours either in the *Bhagabata Tungis* or in the temple precincts or in the verandahs of the munificent persons.

The creative power of the people and the literary background of south Odisha was another factor which made the folk culture of south Odisha a prominent one. The famous poets of Odia literature, like Kabisamrat Upendra Bhanja, Kabisurya Baladeva Ratha, Gopalakrushna Patnaik, Tripati Gayaka Ratna, Hanumana Rayaguru, Bhakta Ramadas, Kabuli Narusu, Padmanava Narayan Dev(King of Paralakhemundi), Banamali Patnaik, Kabichandra Raghunath Parichha, Kishora Chandra Rajendra (King of Chikiti), Goswami Krishna Chandra Das, Raghunath Singh Deo, Krishna Singh(King of Dharakote), Kishore Chandra Harichandan Jagadev(King of Surangi), Rama Chandra Sur Deo(King of Tarala),

Srinivas Rajamani(King of Manjusha), Krishnamohan Patnaik, Mohan Goswami, Vikram Deo Varma(King of Jeypore), Dinabandhu Harichandan, Chandra Chudamani Harichandan of Surangi; Tarini Charan Patra of Kabisuryanagar and Bharat Choudhry of Brahmanachhai; Kesaba Das of Tentuapada; Kanhu Das of Mangalapur; Narasingha Matha of Karakhandi; Pitambar Das of Tanhara(Pitala) were born in this region of Odisha who created a renaissance in the history of *Odissi Champu, Chhanda,Purana* and folk songs of Odisha.

The existence of *Akhadas* in several villages of the region helped a lot to maintain the tradition of folk dance, music and songs. Even today, the musical instruments and equipments preserved in the *Akhadas* serve as the place of rehearsal organized by the locally recruited *Gurus.*

The beauty and bounty of the region also contributed a lot to develop a fascinating and distinct culture of her own. Endowed with rare scenic beauty by its soaring mountains, terraced valleys, lush green forests, murmuring streams and waterfalls, sweet sounds of singing birds, golden sea-beach with rolling blue lagoons, amazing charm of the lake Chilika, picturesque landscape, and rich tribal life of this part of Odisha is a veritable paradise of nature lovers. These elements of purely indigenous culture contributed immensely for maintaining the folklore traditions alive and vibrant.

The political patronage of the *Rajas* and *Zamindars* of south Odisha was another factor which helped the growth of folk-lore traditions vibrant. Folk dances were generally patronized by the *Rajas, Maharajas,* and *Zamindars* as well as by the affluent sections of the society for centuries. Most of the *Zamindars* of south Odisha not only patronized the folk dances and *natakas* but also composed and staged in their palace *rangalayas.*

Political patronage alone cannot build up a cultural edifice, the spiritual faith of the people is something higher and nobler. South Odisha was the pivot of many cults, creeds and religious saints. It has the largest number of Jagannath temples and *Sakti*

Pithas of Odisha and given birth to many *Sadhus* and *Santhas* like Arakhita Das, Ram Das, Keshava Das, Pitambar Das, Raja Lakshmi Narayana Dev, Raja Krushna Singh, Narasingha Matha and others.

South Odisha is more backward and rural then the Odisha proper. It is predominantly an agricultural region. The Odias live in villages that were interestingly different in pattern from those in the neighbouring states. There are, generally, two rows of thatched houses standing shoulder to shoulder, with a street running in between, and with a temple and a tank at one end and a *Bhagavata Ghara* or a village *Akhada* at the other. The village homes are invariably decorated with mural paintings of some sort, and have a shady garden at the back. The *Bhagavata* of Jagannatha Dasa and the village priest still wield considerable influence on the social and individual life of the average Odia in the village. Even today, the *Bhagavata* of Jagannatha Dasa is recited daily, either in the common *Bhagavata Ghara* or in the Hindu families of most of the villages.

South Odisha occupies a prominent place in the folk culture of India. South Odisha in general, and the district of Ganjam in particular is regarded as the cradle of the folk-dances of Odisha. The geographical location, the topographic feature, the religious and literary background, the beauty and bounty of the nature all have jointly contributed significantly towards the culmination of its unique pattern of folk culture.

South Odisha is perhaps next to Kerala in the richness of folk dance and theatre traditions. The folk dance and music, folk-songs, folk-tales, folk-beliefs, folk-medicines and methods of treatment, folk-festivals, folk-art and crafts of south Odisha were so lively and colourful that they could captivate the minds of all the art-loving people. The folk-songs, folk-tales, folk-riddles, proverbs and ballads of this region were not only simple in its form and composition but also carries the deep message of human values. But, it is a matter of great regret that the folk-dances and theatres, folk-songs and tales, folk-arts and crafts which were a great source of entertainment and livelihood for the rural folk, and also helped in spreading the messages of morality, truthfulness, victory of righteous over evil forces, cooperation and harmony in the society are on the verge of decline and death. So necessary steps may be taken to revive these folklore traditions, to record and preserve them either by the Government or by the Private munificence in the form of DVD and e-library for the posterity. Otherwise, the tradition of the centuries and wealth of the society will be vanished within a few decades.

The researches on folklore of Odisha are very rare. There are no systematic researches in this field. It is most unfortunate that no adequate light has yet been thrown on the folk culture of Odisha especially of its southern region. There are some passing references in respect of folklore in the works of John Beams, Elwin Verrier, U.N.Duttagupta, etc. Scholars like Raghavananda Das, Gopal Chandra Praharaj, Nilamani Bidyaratna, Aparna Panda and Bhagaban Hotta have given a mere cursory reference to the folk culture of Odisha. There are yet a few other scholars like Chakradhar Mohapatra, Kunja Bihari Dash, Shyam Sundar Mohapatra, Hemant Kumar Dash, Dhiren Patnaik, etc., who have brought certain aspects of folk culture in their scholarly works written in Odia but an exhaustive and analytical study complete in all respects pertaining to the various aspects of folk culture of south Odisha was a desideratum. Hence, this humble attempt is the first attempt to present the various and variegated facets of the folk culture of the south Odisha in the subsequent pages. If the present work usefully supplies this long-felt want, I shall consider my labour amply rewarded.

The study is mainly based on primary sources collected from the different archives, libraries, collectorate record rooms, village *pathagaras* and *akhadas* and through the means of field study, interview with the *Gurus* and artists of folk dances and *natakas.* Checking and cross checking of source materials were done before utilization and interpretation. The modern scientific historical research methodology was adopted very minutely for the preparation of this thesis. Thus, both analytical and descriptive methods have been adopted to complete this work.

The work has been arranged in seven chapters besides an introduction and conclusion to portray a clear picture of the folk culture of south Odisha during the 19th and first half of 20th century. First chapter gives a graphic account of the history of south Odisha from ancient period till the integration of the princely states of Odisha in 1948. Second chapter throws a flood of light on the folk-tales and their relevance to the society. The third chapter deals with the different folk-songs of south Odisha and their utility for the reconstruction of the history of south Odisha. Fourth chapter is devoted to discuss the different folk-dances and theatres prevalent in the region during the period under review. In the fifth chapter there is the delineation of south Odisha's folk observations (*Oshas* and *Vratas*), folk festivals, and folk beliefs. An attempt has been made to draw a clear picture of folk arts and crafts in the sixth chapter. Chapter seven is devoted to analyse the folk medicine, folk method of treatment and their social applications in a rational manner. The concluding chapter includes the major findings of the earlier chapters.

Contents

Abbreviations

AAR.	-	Annual Administrative Report
ACCN.	-	Accession
AHRS.	-	Andhra Historical Research Society
BAR.	-	Bengal Administration Report
BRP.	-	Bengal Revenue Proceedings
CPC.	-	Calendar of Persian Correspondances
CRR.	-	Chhatrapur Revenue Records
JASB.	-	Journal of Asiatic Society of Bengal
JBORS.	-	journal of the Bihar and Orissa Research Society
OHRG.	-	Orissa Historical Research journal
OHR.	-	Orissa Home Records
ORR.	-	Orissa Revenue Records
OSA.	-	Orissa State Archives
RCFBO.	-	Report of the Commissioners appointed to enquire in to the Famine in Bengal and Orissa.
ROK.	-	Report of Lieutenant S.C.Macpherson, Assistant Agent to the Governor, Fort St. George in Ganjam, on the Kandhs of the Records of the Goomsur Maliahs.
SRMJ.	-	Selection from the Records of the Madras Government
SRG.	-	Selection from the Records of the Bengal Government for the Suppression of Human Sacrifice.
TNA.	-	Tamilnadu State Archives.

List of Colour Plates

Plate 15: *Soura* wall painting showing the worship of ancestors.

Plate 16: A view from Thakunani yatna of Benhampun.

Plate 17: Folk-art *Nabagunjara* with fantastic composition of nine animals i.e. the head of a cock, the hump of a bull, neck of a peacock, leg of a tiger, horse, elephant, balley of cow, hood of a serpant and the hand of a woman holding a flower.

Plate 18: Scene of a Natha Yogi.

Introduction

The Subaltern study as well as the history of rural folk has emerged as a recent trend of historical research. Now-a-days, it has drawn the attention of teachers, research scholars and intellectuals of the whole world to highlight the different aspects of the culture of the rural mass.

The study of folk culture, particularly of a region, is of prime importance because "the history of a nation or country cannot be comprehensive or exhaustive without the proper study of its component parts. The history of the component units subscribes much to the main-stream of national history. The richer the regional history, national history becomes more extensive and comprehensive".[1] In this perceptive, the study of the different aspects of the folk culture of south Odisha during 19th and 20th centuries seems to be quite imperative and relevant.

Several factors are attributed to shape south Odisha's folk cultural heritage. The geographical situation of the region is the prime factor to rear up of such a culture. Lying between north and south India across a natural highway along the eastern coast of India, south Odisha acts like a bridge between the Aryan culture of north and Dravidian culture of south. The socio-cultural life of this region thus form a highly interesting amalgam evolved out of Dravido-Aryan elements with delightful assimilations from the life of the tribals and not so much affected by the external influences of Islam and Christianity as other parts of India.[2] These elements of purely indigenous culture contributed immensely for maintaining the folk-lore traditions of south Odisha alive and vibrant.

Cultural and religious synthesis of Odisha is another factor to rear up of such a folk culture. The symbol of this purely indigenous cultural synthesis is the shrine of Lord Jagannath.[3] Starting as an unknown deity of the *Sabaras* in the dense forest; Jagannath manifested Himself as one of the greatest Gods of the whole world. Jagannath has been regarded as the presiding deity or *Rastra Devata* of the Odia people. The world famous temple of Lord Jagannath at Puri has influenced the life of the Odia people to such an extend that their dance, drama, music, art, fasts, festivals and food habits all evolved around it.[4]

Rural background of south Odisha was another factor that led it to retain the unique folk traditions of this region. It is basically a land of villages which is still predominantly an agricultural tract having about 30,000 villages big or small. South Odisha did not possess a single city or town worth the name during the period under review. Even Berhampur, Paralakhemundi, Chatrapur, Bhanjanagar, Gunupur, Rayagada and Jeypore were only partly urban.[5]

The conservativeness of the people was another factor that led to the growth of folk culture in this region. The people of south Odisha were very much conservative, superstitious and ignorant. They were averse and apathetic to modern ideas and western influences for a long time. Therefore, their development and transformation was very slow. It indirectly helped them to retain their folklore traditions alive and vibrant for a long time.

The isolation of the region was another factor for maintaining their folk culture intact for a long time. The whole province was geographically isolated from the rest of India and even the Odisha proper. It had no roads, no railways, and no navigable canals till the end of the 19th century. The people were shut up in a narrow province between pathless jungles and an impracticable sea.[6] There was not a single road in existence in the modern sense of the term. The only one road which connected south Odisha with Cuttack passed over large unbridged rivers and was unmetalled.[7]

John Beams has rightly remarked that "Owing to the isolation in which their country has remained for so many ages, the peasantry of Odisha has retained old world ideas and fancies to a greater extent than any other Aryan people of India. They are shy of imparting these ideas to strangers, and a man might live among them for years without finding out the singular views and original processes of reasoning on which many of their habits are based. This shyness arises, I suppose, from the gradual infiltration of modern ideas. The men are beginning to be ashamed of these antiquated fancies, and though in their hearts believing in them, would rather not talk about them".[8]

Puranic traditions and existence of *Bhagabata Tungis* also supplied good incentives for the people of south Odisha to rear up folk culture in a perfect manner. In almost all the villages of south Odisha the *Purana Panda* recited *puranas* in every evening hours either in the *Bhagabata Tungis* or in the temple precincts or in the verandahs of the munificent persons. The rate of literacy was very low in these villages. However it is beyond the haze of doubt that an illiterate man who listens to these *puranas* may not be literate but it is certain that he becomes a learned man.

The creative power of the people and the literary background of south Odisha was another factor which made the folk culture of south Odisha a prominent one. The famous poets of Odia literature, like Kabisamrat Upendra Bhanja, Kabisurya Baladeva Ratha, Gopalakrushna Patnaik, Tripati Gayaka Ratna, Hanumana Rayaguru, *Bhakta* Ramadas, and Kabuli Narusu of Badakhemundi; Padmanava Dev, Banamali Patnaik, Kabichandra Raghunath Parichha of Paralakhemundi; Kishora Chandra Rajendra of Chikiti; Goswami Krishna Chandra Das and Raghunath Singhdeo and *Raja* Krishna Singh of Dharakote; Srinivas Rajamani, Krishnamohan Patnaik and Mohan Goswami of Manjusa; *Raja* Vikram Deo of Jeypore; Dinabandhu Harichandan, Mukunda Harichandan and Chandra Chudamani Harichandan of Surangi; Tarini Charan Patra of Kabisuryanagar and Bharat Choudhry of Brahmanachhai; Kesaba Das of Tentuapada; Kanhu Das of Mangalapur; Narasingha Matha of Karakhandi; Pitambar Das of Tanhara(Pitala) were born in this region of Odisha who created a renaissance in the history of *Odissi Champu, Chhanda,Purana* and folk songs of Odisha.

The Existence of *Akhadas* in several villages of the district helped a lot to maintain the tradition of folk dance, music and songs. Even today, the musical instruments and equipments preserved in the *Akhadas* serve as the place of rehearsal organized by the locally recruited *Gurus.* These *Gurus* often moved from village to village to teach different folk dances and *natakas.* Efficient *Gurus* are felicitated with *Kundalas, Suna-Khadus* and *Pattavastras* for their contributions to the folk dances of the area.

The large number of tribal population also contributed immensely to make south Odisha the cradle of folk songs and folk dances. "*Adivasi* not only comes in as a character in poetry and *Puranas* from the earliest times, but also has played a glorious role as literary creator".[9]

The beauty and bounty of the region also contributed a lot to develop a fascinating and distinct culture of her own. Endowed with rare scenic beauty by its soaring mountains, terraced valleys, lush green forests, murmuring streams and waterfalls, sweet sounds of singing birds, golden sea-beach with rolling blue lagoons, amazing charm of the lake Chilika, picturesque landscape, and rich tribal life of this part of Odisha is a veritable paradise of nature lovers. All these gifts of the nature helped a lot to maintain such a culture in this part of India. Therefore, a great writer amptly remarks that, "Orissa's hills and dales tell stories, its trees and creepers sing and its people dance to the tune of the music".[10]

The political patronage of the *Rajas* and *Zamindars* of south Odisha was another factor which helped the growth of folk-lore traditions vibrant. Folk dances were generally patronized by the

Rajas, *Maharajas*, and *Zamindars* as well as by the affluent sections of the society for centuries. Most of the Zamindars of south Odisha patronized the *Prahallada Nataka, Radhaprema Leela, Bharat Leela, Rama Leela, Krishna Leela, Dasakathia* etc. They not only patronized the folk dances and *natakas* but also composed and staged *Prahallada Natak, Radhaprema Leela, Bharat Leela, Rama Leela, Krishna Leela, Dasakathia* etc. Madan Mohan Singdeo, the *Raja* of Dharakot, built a stage known as *Kesari Rangamanch* and helped a team of artists to display *natakas* like *Prahallada natak, Probodha Chandrodaya* etc. Krupasindhu Narendra Deva, the *Raja* of Mahuri (Brahmapur) used to organize numerous *natakas* through a party at Brahmapur. Ramakrushna Chhotaray, the *Raja* of Jalantara (now in Andhra Pradesh) was credited with the composition of the original version of *Prahallad Natak*. Kishore Chandra Harichandan Jagadeva, the Raja of Surangi wrote another version of *Prahallada Nataka, Chandana-Pala* and *Kishorechandra- Pala*. Biswambar Rajendra Deo, the *Raja* of Chikiti (1851-55) wrote *Krishna Leela* and *Raghunatha Vilas*. Padmanava Narayana Dev (1872-1914) who belonged to the royal family of Paralakhemundi was a great patron of dramas, *natakas* and folk dances. His works include *Chandravati Swayambar, Bana Darpadalan, Dana Parikshya, Srimad Bhagabatamahatmya* and *Prahallad Natak*.

The famous *Rajas* and Zamindars of south Odisha like the *Rajas* of Chikiti, the *Rajas* of Badakhemundi, the Rajas of Paralakhemundi, the *Rajas* of Kodala-Athagadh, *Raja* of Jalantara, Rajas of Dharakote, *Rajas* of Surangi etc. not only patronised the *Gurus* of folk dances but also established the *manchas* and *akhada-gharas* for the spread and popularity of these dances.

Political patronage alone cannot build up a cultural edifice, the spiritual faith of the people is something higher and nobler.[11] South Odisha was the pivot of many cults, creeds and religious saints. It has the largest number of Jagannath temples and *Sakti Pithas* of Odisha and given birth to many *Sadhus* and *Santhas* like Arakhita Das, Ram Das, Keshava Das, Pitambar Das, Raja Lakshmi Narayana Dev, Narasingha Matha and others. All the folk dances, songs, musics and festivals are centering round this Jagannath Cult or *Sakti* Cult. Under this background the folk traditions of south Odisha are to be studied.

According to Mozharul Islam, "If culture is the product of the intellectual faculty of man, folklore is the result of his urge for creativity and impulsive love for beauty. In one, he finds his intellect and sense of refinement released, in the other his creative ideas are expressed and shaped, his aesthetic impulse speaks. By doing so, man also nourishes his culture through folklore. Folklore is thus the product of culture; a component part of culture."[12]

The folk lore of south Odisha has to be explored and appreciated with this picture of the villages in the background. It is strange that folklore has withstood the realignment and reassessment of the social norms of the different strata of the village population and for this we have to give the entire credit to the womenfolk. But for them folklore might have disappeared. It is the women folk who have sustained the Folk-tales, folk songs, proverbs, riddles and folk arts and crafts.

The main concern of the study is to discuss the various and variegated facets of folk life and culture of south Odisha during the colonial era. The study is confined to the folk life of the villages of south Odisha without touching the sophisticated life style of the elites of towns and cities. "Folk" means, people or community having common occupation, language, religion and region. "Lore" means knowledge in practice. Thus, folklore means community learning and practicing. Folklore is the traditional or popular culture. It is as old as the history of mankind. Folk is an old English word. In German language its synonym is Volk. W. J. Thomas, was the first person who coined folklore in 1846.[13] Folklore consists of unrecorded knowledge on oral tradition, customs and materials used by the traditional communities or individuals.

City dwellers cannot be grouped as folk and they cannot have folklore of their own. When a country is industrialized, cities and towns spread, folklore has its natural death there.[14]

The content of it is enormous and may differ from one region to another region. It is an important part of culture of a community. The International Encyclopedia of Social Sciences says folklore comprehends all knowledge that is transmitted by word of mouth (oral tradition) and all crafts and techniques that have learnt by imitation or by examples as well as the products of these crafts.[15]

Folklore includes folk living style, folk customs, folk beliefs, folk medicines, folk arts and crafts, tools, costumes, music, dance, ballads, songs, dramas, festivals, rites, gestures and folk speech. It includes tales, legends, myths, proverbs, riddles, poetry, food items, dress, housing pattern etc. We may not know the author's name of folk lore items. It is also the collective heritage of the community. Folklore is the pulse of the community. Herskovits has said that, "Folklore is an important mechanism to maintain the stability of culture of communities. It is the creation of the mental world of non-literate or formality untrained or unschooled or non-learned and scientifically unstructured community". There is significance of folklore as they are part of the memory collection and re-invention in performance.

Thus, folk culture means the culture of the unsophisticated and illiterate common mass of the villages. It is quite different from the sophisticated culture or the elite culture of the towns and cities. Folk culture is also known as little tradition and sophisticated culture is known as great tradition.[16]

The researches on folklore of Odisha are very rare. There are no systematic researches in this field. Among the galaxy of scholars who have made some contribution to the study of Folklore of Odisha were John Beams, Upendra Narayana Datta Gupta, Elwin Verrier, Gopal Chandra Praharaj, Nilamani Bidyaratna, Raghabananda Das, Aparna Panda, Bhagaban Hota, Chakradhar Mohapatra and Kunja Bihari Dash.

John Beams was the first person who worked on the Folklore of Odisha in 1872. While he was the Collector of Baleswar he collected a number of folk songs and spells with the help of Fakir

Mohan Senapati and contributed an interesting article entitled "Folklore of Orissa" in the *Indian Antiquary* in its March volume of 1872 published from Bombay. But it was very small, unscientific which included only a few folk songs and spells of Odisha. In 1872, G.E.Grover published his book *Folk Songs of South India* which included a few tribal songs of Odisha. Sir Richard Temple was the first person to give a detailed classification of the motifs of Indian folklore in the following manner.

"The studies in one folklore lack a definite policy, which would enhance scientific research. Some renowned scholars like Temple, Grierson, Crooke S.C.Mitra, K.P.Mitra and Elwin have made valuable contributions no doubts, but in their works the references to Odisha or south Odisha are quite meagre. The work so far done is only of the nature of a foundation".

In 1876, Kapileswara Bidyabhusana Nanda Sharma collected different proverbs of Odisha and published it in the form of a book. Gopal Chandra Praharaj's attempt for collecting folk songs, riddles, proverbs and Folk-tales of Odisha was praise-worthy. He had a vision to publish these in six volumes. His *Utkala Kahani* was the first Folk-tales of Odisha. But he only published two volumes and his project remained incomplete. In 1903, Nilamani Bidyaratna who was working as the manager of Bhimadeba Press at Badakhemundi published a book only on Odia proverbs and idioms. In 1914, Raghavananda Das and Bhagaban Hotta published *Prabadamala* in Odia. In this aspect the efforts of Aparna Panda of Paralakhemundi was most welcome. He published *Dhagamalika* in 1923 from Gajapati Press, Paralakhemundi. In 1923 Upendra Narayana Duttagupta published *Folk-tales of Orissa* from Calcutta. Chakradhara Mohapatra struggled very hard for collecting folk songs from the different villages of Odisha. His collections were published in the form of a book entitled *Utkala Gaunli Gita* in 1959 from Cuttack. But in the field of folklore research, the contribution of Kunja Bihari Dash is significant. He published two books in Odia such as *Palligita Sanchayana*, *Lokagalpa Sanchayana* and "Folklore of

Orissa" in English but his books did not include all the aspects of folk culture and mainly confined to the north Odisha. In this regard the efforts of Elwin Verrier were praise-worthy. He composed a number of books on the folklore and folk myth of Odisha like- *Bondo Highlander, Songs of the Forest, Tribal Myths of Orissa,* and *Folktales of Mahakosala.* But, these books are mainly deal: with the folk myths of the tribes of Odisha. Besides that, *Brata Sahitya* of Arabinda Patnaik (Odia), *Lokanataka* of Hemanta Kumar Das (Odia), *Loka Sahitya O Loka Sanskruti* of Krushna Chandra Pradhan gives us some information on folk festival, folk dances and folk literature in Odia. But an exhaustive and analytical study complete in all respects pertaining to the folk cultures of south Odisha was a desideratum. It is hoped that the present study will fulfill the desire of the people who love to know the accurate picture of the different aspects of the folk culture of south Odisha in detail.

The period covered is, in fact, the most significant and formative from the administrative and political point of view. The period witnessed the British conquest of Odisha, the Resistance Movement, the Socio-Religious Reform Movement, growth of renaissance and Odia Nationalism, Utkal Union Movement for the unification of all Odia speaking areas and the freedom struggle for the independence of India.

This study is the first of its kind to discuss the different aspects of the folk culture of south Odisha in a critical, compact and comprehensive manner from historical point of view. The study is significant in many respects. Firstly, this region was the cradle of various folk dances, folk songs, folk music, folk art, folk festivals, folk beliefs, folk medicines, riddles and idioms of Odisha. Secondly, the great poets and litterateurs of Odia literature like *Kabisamrat* Upendra Bhanja, *Kabisurjya* Baladeba Rath, *Kabi* Gopal Krushna Patnaik, *Bhaktakabi* Ramdas, *Santhakabi* Arakhita Dash were born in this region. They played a great role in enriching the Odia language, literature and cultural values. Thus, this region more particularly the district of Ganjam was the cultural fort of Odisha. There were many *zamindars* and *Rajas* of south Odisha who patronized the poets, folk dances, folk artists, and influenced the socio-cultural life of the people of this region. Despite its feudal legacy this region flourished in the sphere of folk culture and folklore traditions. Thirdly, the people of this region showed remarkable courage for the organization of the Odia Movement for the unification of all the Odia speaking areas and the creation of the separate province of Odisha. Truly speaking, Odia Movement was blooming and nourishing under the lap of the leaders and *zamindars* of this region. Fourthly, the people of this region had the proud privilege of staging heroic struggle against the British Government and making significant contribution in the India's grim struggle for freedom. They composed many folk songs, idioms, proverbs to create and spread the nationalist ideas and patriotic flavour.

The study is mainly based on primary sources collected from the different archives, libraries, collectorate record rooms, village *pathagaras* and *akhadas* and through the means of field study, interview with the *Gurus* and artists of folk dances and *natakas.* Checking and cross checking of source materials were done before utilization and interpretation. The modern scientific historical research methodology was adopted very minutely for the preparation of this thesis. Thus, both analytical and descriptive methods have been adopted to complete this work.

For the presentation of the different aspects of the folk culture of south Odisha, the thesis is organized and arranged in eight chapters. First chapter gives the historical background of south Odisha from the fall of Hindu Kingdom of Odisha to the integration of the princely states and the creation of the greater Odisha state in 1948. A detailed account of the nature and composition of the folk people, their way of life has been described vividly in the second chapter. Third chapter throws a flood of light on the Folk-tales and their relevance to the society. Attempt has been made to portray the different folk songs of south Odisha and their utility in the fourth chapter. Fifth chapter is devoted to discuss the different dances and theatres prevalent in the region during the period under review. In the sixth chapter there is the delineation of south Odisha's folk observations (*Oshas* and *Vratas*), folk festivals, and folk beliefs. An attempt has been made to draw a clear picture of folk arts and crafts in the seventh chapter. Chapter eight is devoted to analyze the folk medicine, folk method of treatment and their social applications in a rational manner. A gist of the entire thesis containing the main findings is appended as the epilogue to draw a conclusion.

References

1. B.C.Ray (ed.), Proceedings of Orissa History Congress, Berhampur Session, 1977, Presidential address.
2. M.Mansinha, *A History of Oriya Literature*, New-Delhi, 1962, p.2.
3. *Ibid.*, p.2.
4. *Bhagabana Sahu*, Socio Economic and Cultural History of Orissa, Cuttack, 2002, p.33.
5. *Ibid.*, p.4.
6. RCFBO-1866, vol.I, Calcutta, 1866, p.21.
7. J.K.Samal, Orissa Under The British Crown, New-Delhi, 1977, p.vi.
8. John Beams, "Folklore of Orissa", in: The Indian Antiquary, vol. xxi, June, 1872, pp.168-170.
9. M.Mansinha, *A History of Oriya Literature*, New-Delhi, 1962, p.1.
10. C.R.Das (ed.), Folk Culture, vol.I, Cuttack, 1978, p.1.
11. M.N. Dash (ed.), *Side Lights on the History and Culture of Orissa*, Cuttack, 1977, preface.
12. Mozharul Islam, *A History of folk-tale collections in India and Pakistan*, Dacca, 1963, p.24.
13. Sankar Sen Gupta, *Folklore and Folk Life of India*, Calcutta,
14. *Ibid.*, p.26.
15. W.R.Boscom, *Folklore and Anthropology*, no place, 1953, p.71.
16. R.Redfield, *Peasant Society and Culture- an anthropological approach to civilization*, Chicago, 1956, p.37.

1 Historical Background

The southern part of modern Odisha comprising of seven districts viz. Ganjam, Gajapati, Rayagada, Koraput, Nabarangapur, Malkangiri and Kandhamal originally formed a part of the ancient kingdom of Kalinga which was supposed to have been founded in the 9th century B.C.[1] The ancient political geography of this region was included in Khinjili *Mandala*, Kangoda, Trikalinga, and *Dakshina* Tosali.[2] The territory comprising the undivided district of Koraput was a part of ancient *Atavika* Kingdom referred to in the special Rock Edicts of Asoka. Asoka occupied Kalinga in 261 B.C. but, the land of the *Atavikas* which could not be conquered remained outside his empire. The fierce and war-like people of that territory were a constant source of anxiety for him and Asoka tried his best to appease them and make them his allies.[3]

Very little is known about the history of this region after Asoka till the rise of *Mahameghavahana* dynasty in 1st century B.C., when Kalinga regained her political predominance. Under Kharavela, Kalinga became one of the strongest powers in India and the *Atavika* land comprised an important part of her growing empire. The successors of Kharavela could not retain the independence of Kalinga for long. In the first century B.C. Odisha was conquered by Satavahanas of Andhra.[4]

After this, the history of south Odisha remained in obscure till the rise of the Matharas in the second half of 4th century A.D. Kalinga rose into prominence as an independent kingdom, when the kings of Mathara dynasty united a large portion of Kalinga from the Mahanadi in the north to the river Godavari in the south, and their rule lasted for about 150 years. Towards the end of the Mathara rule, Eastern Gangas, a branch of the famous Ganga dynasty succeeded to extend their political dominance over Kalinga. Their kingdom extended from Mahendragiri (one of the seven *Kula Parvatas* in India) in north to the river Godavari in the south. It clearly included Vizagapatnam district of Andhra Pradesh, Ganjam and Gajapati and the undivided district of Koraput.[5]

After the fall of the Eastern Gangas, the Sailodbhava dynasty ruled over this land-mass. They not only established a powerful kingdom in Odisha but also established colonies in South-east Asia. The famous Chinese pilgrim Hieun-Tsang who visited Odisha in 639 A.D. writes, "Kong-u-to (Kangoda) was a powerful kingdom with an area of 1000 Le in length which was approximately 150 miles. It had a capital city about 3 miles in circuit".[6] One of the Princes of the Sailodbhava dynasty sailed to Java and founded a new dynasty known as Sailendra dynasty there.[7] They were also the pioneers of temple building activities in Odisha. The earliest group of temples of Odisha belonged to them.

In the first half of the 8th century A.D, Bhaumakaras emerged as powerful rulers in Odisha after the fall of the Sailodbhavas. Bhaumakaras originally came from Assam and established themselves as paramount power in Odisha. They had a sound and well organized administrative system in Odisha. This dynasty is famous not only for building up of an empire but also for spreading Odishan culture and civilization throughout India and even too far off countries like China. Their rule may be regarded as the golden age in the history of Odisha.[8] After the fall of the Bhaumakaras, the Somavamsi-Kesari kings ascended the throne of Odisha by succeeding the issueless ruler of Bhaumakar dynasty in 936 A.D.[9]

With the accession of Somavamsis, there ushered an epoch-making era in the history of Odisha. They not only united Utkal, Kosala and Odra under one political umbrella but also built majestic temples like Lingaraj, Mukteswar, Raja-Rani and Brahmeswar. However, the Somavamsi rule was replaced by the rule of the Imperial Gangas. Their capital was at Kalinganagara identified with modern Mukhalingam in the Srikakulam district of Andhra Pradesh.[10]

The Gangas conquered a number of states both in north and south India and therefore, Odisha emerged as a mighty and far-flung empire during their reign. They ruled over Odisha for more than five hundred years with full grandeur and glory, and excelled the preceding Kesari rulers. With a series of conquests, they extended the boundaries of Odisha from Ganges in the north to the Godavari in the south and from Amarkantaka in the west to the Bay of Bengal in the east.[11] When the adjoining states were suffering under the Mohammedan invaders, the Odias were brave enough to invade and annex portions of adjoining states defeating the powerful Mohammedan rulers so much so that for many years, Muslim Sultans did not have the courage to enter into Odisha.[12]

But, during the reign of the last Ganga king Bhanu Deva-IV, Tughan Khan, the Governor of Bengal attacked Odisha and went back with a number of elephants. After the death of Bhanu Deva IV, his minister Kapileswar usurped the throne and founded a new dynasty known as Suryavamsi or the Solar dynasty by declaring himself as Gajapati Kapilendra Deva.

With the accession of Gajapati Kapilendra Deva there started a brilliant epoch in the history of Odisha. By a series of conquests he extended the kingdom of Odisha from river Ganges in the north to river Kaveri (Tanjore or Trichinapalli) in the south. As a great patron of arts and letters, he brought about a renaissance in Odia literature.[13]

However, Gajapati Prataparudra Deva, the grandson of Kapilendra Deva who ruled Odisha from A.D. 1497 to 1540 suffered great reverses at the hands of Krishna Dev Ray-the king of Vijayanagar Empire (Karnataka).[14] After the death of Prataparudra Deva, the administration of Odisha lapsed to a state of conflict and confusion. A military commander of Prataprudra namely Govinda Vidyadhara usurped the throne of Odisha in 1542 A.D. after killing his two sons. But soon dissensions seem to have arisen amongst the sons of Govinda Vidyadhara. Taking advantage of the chaotic condition of the country, the Chalukyas of the south availed the opportunity of invading this land. In 1559, Mukunda Deva of Chalukya dynasty who possessed the title of 'Mukunda Harichandan'(Also known as Telenga Mukunda Deva) usurped the throne and ruled over Odisha till 1568 A.D.[15]

Internecine feuds and animosities among the petty communities leading to political instability made Odisha fall an easy prey to foreign invaders. Mukunda Deva who became the king of Odisha in 1559 A.D. was the last independent Hindu king of Odisha. He played a crucial role in the strife-stricken political field of Odisha and retained the independence of the country despite numerous odds.[16]

After 1568 A.D. dark days loomed large and Odisha entered into a period of disaster and defeat. In 1568 A.D., Sulaiman Karrani, the Afghan Sultan of Bengal marched up to the banks of the Ganges and drove Mukunda Deva southwards where he was killed.[17] Thus, Odisha passed into the hands of the Afghans. When the capital of Odisha was overrun by the Afghans from the north, the southern part of it gradually slipped into the hands of the Muslims of Golconda.

In 1571 A.D., Ibrahim IV, of Qutbshahi dynesty of Golconda conquered the Chicacole *Circar.* Consequently, Ganjam which formed a part of the Chicacole *Circar* came under the rule of the Qutbshahis. It marked the beginning of the territorial dismemberment of Odisha, and Ganjam was, thenceforth, to remain apart from Odisha for nearly 365 years.[18]

Although, the entire district of Ganjam was nominally under the Muslim kings of Golconda, but actually the *Zamindars* of Ganjam owed their allegiance to the *Maharajas* of Khurda(Odisha). Thus, the districts of Visakhapatnam and Ganjam were in one unit under them and the Odia *Zamindars* used the *anka* years of the *Rajas* of Khurda.[19] This region remained under the Muslim control until 1753 A.D. when Salabat Jung, the Nizam of Hyderabad assigned the Northern Sarkars to the French. Yet, during all these years, Ganjam was able to retain much of its original culture till it was transferred to Odisha Division from Madras Presidency, and the subsequent formation of separate province of Odisha in 1936 A.D.

During the entire Muslim period, the history of the land witnessed many upheavals. The Qutbshahi dynasty of Hyderabad ruled over it from A.D. 1571 to 1687. In 1687 A.D. Aurangzeb, the Mughal Emperor of Delhi conquered Golconda and annexed the country to his empire. The newly conquered province was placed under the administration of *Subedar* (or *Subahdar*) of Deccan, who was afterwards designated as Nizam of Hyderabad.

The whole Chicacole *Circar* including Ganjam was administered by a Muslim *Foujdar* of Chicacole with the assistance of a Deputy at Ichhapur. Even after the death of Aurangzeb in 1707 A.D., Ganjam remained under the ruling family of Hyderabad which had assumed the virtual sovereignty over the tract. However, there was every possibility of a Maratha invasion from Cuttack who established their supremacy in 1751 A.D.

During the period of Anglo-French struggle for pre-dominance in Deccan, Muzaffer Jung, the *Subedar* of Deccan was killed while he was on the way to take possession of Golconda. In the meanwhile, Salabat Jung was proclaimed as Nizam of Hyderabad by the direct assistance of the French General De Bussy. As a mark of gratitude, Salabat Jung gifted four out of the five districts of Northern Circars to the French as the price for their help. Monisieur Moracin, the French Chief at Masulipattam, undertook the responsibility of the management of the region, consisting of Mustaphanagar, Ellore, Rajahmundry and Chicacole. The annual revenue of the region was thirty-one lakhs of rupees.[20]

In 1765 A.D., the Mughal emperor gifted the Northern *Circars* to the English by an Imperial *firman.* However, the British took the actual possession of the Northern *Circars* by concluding the Treaty of Hyderabad with Nizam Ali, the *Subedar* of Deccan on 12th November, 1766.[21] Accordingly, Nizam Ali, the *Subedar* of Deccan had directed all the *Zamindars* of the Northern *Circars* to pay their tributes and obedience to the British Company without raising any trouble or disturbances. Thus, the Northern *Circars,* in which south Odisha was a part, was ceded to the English in 1766 A.D. The Chicacole *Circar* which had been divided, under Mohammedan rule, into three divisions; Ichhapur, Chicacole and Kasimkota was named as Ganjam district in 1768 A.D., and Chicacole became one of its sub-divisions.[22]

Mr. Cotsford was the first Englishman appointed as Resident to take charge of Ganjam district in the year 1767. Similarly in 1769 Mr. John Andrews, then Chief at Masulipatnam was sent to Vizagpatnam and made the first Chief-in-Council of that district. The district of Ganjam was divided into 21 *zamindari* estates and 8 *Praganahs* (*purgunnahs*). The *zamindaries* of this tract were Chikiti, Mohuri, Dharakote, Badagada, Sheragada, Sorada, Ghumusar, Athagada, Khallikote, Palur, Biridi, Humma, Surangi, Jarada, Panalakhemundi, Badakhemundi, Sana Khemundi, Jallantar, Manjusha, Budarsing and Taralah. The last four *Zamindaries* are now in the Srikakulam district of Andhra Pradesh, while the rest of 16 are in the district of Ganjam. The eight *Praganahs* of the district were-Aska, Purbakhanda, Kurala, Ganjam, Mansurkota, Mantridi, Ichhapur and Baruva. The last two *Praganahs* are now in the Srikakulam district while the rest 6 are in the district of Ganjam.[23]

On the advent of the British, the different Odia-speaking areas came into their hands at different times and were placed under different administrative units. The Central Province was created with effect from 2nd November 1861, and Sambalpur was attached to this newly constituted province. The district of Ganjam, and Jeypore *zamindari* estate (in the district of Vizagapatnam) were attached to Madras Presidency; the district of Cuttack, Puri, and Baleswara remained under the Bengal Presidency; while a large tract remained under the Feudatory Chiefs who had once been the vassals of the kings of Odisha, and had become independent after the downfall of the central authority. It was natural on the part of the people of Odisha to lose courage as Odisha was practically dismembered.

Upon the retirement of Mr. Costford in 1773 A.D., the form of the government was changed, and Mr. Smith was appointed as Chief at Ganjam with a Council of three to assist him in the affairs of administration. In 1779, the Council was abolished and Mr. Morgan Williams was appointed as Resident. In 1782 the Office of Resident was again abolished and the Council was revived. It consisted of three members but was subsequently increased to five. Soon quarrel took place in the Settlement at Ganjam among the members of the Council which continued without intermission till 1786 A.D. and it became so notorious as to call for the interference of Government of Madras. In 1790 the Council was again abolished due to this quarrel and Mr. Cortsford was appointed as Resident. In 1794 the Office of the Resident and the Chief at all the Settlements, along the coast was abolished and the Office of Collector, which continues till today was established and Mr. Walter Balfour was appointed as the first Collector of Ganjam. In 1803 Chicacole division was incorporated with Ganjam and Mr. Cherry became first Collector.[24]

Social Structure

The geography and environment are intricately interwoven with the culture of a region. The land and climate, the flora and vegetarian, the navigational importance, the demography and health, the natural resources, the topography have a distinct and conspicuous role to shape the life style of the people of a region.[25] South Odisha was no exception to this universal phenomena.

Hemmed in on the side by the sea, and on all other sides by ranges of mountains and dense forests, and intersected by innumerable rivers, south Odisha, has developed a distinct pattern of life, art and literature of her own. Her gods, goddesses and temples, her social structure, her dance and music and festivals have all developed fascinating individual variants which mark them out as distinct entities in similar categories in India.[26]

Lying between north and south India across a natural highway along the eastern coast of India, south Odisha also displays in and through her native individuality an interesting synthesis of both Dravidian and Aryan cultures, with delightful assimilations from the life of the tribals who form not only a considerable portion of her population, but also an integral part of the economic and social life of the region.[27]

The region is divided into two parts i.e. plains and *maliahs.* The plains are the plain lands situated below the *ghats* and the maliahs are the hilly country above the *ghats.* The plains are inhabited mainly by the caste Hindus and scheduled caste people where as the maliahs or uplands are chiefly inhabited by *Kandhs, Sabaras* and the other aboriginal inhabitants.[28]

Broadly speaking the people of south Odisha could be grouped in to three classes according to religious faiths i.e. the Hindus, the Muslims and the Christians. The percentage of population of each religion to the total population of this region are 99.1%,0.24%,0.75%, for Hindus, Muslims and Christians respectively.[29] The Hindus consist of *Brahmanas, Kshatriyas, Vaisyas* and Sudras, the four castes under the traditional *Varnasramadharma.* They are again sub-divided each into a number of castes and sub-castes. There are also scheduled tribes who cannot be categorized with these castes, but are nevertheless an integral part of the Hindu community.[30]

The Hindu religion is pre-eminently ritualistic and the worship of gods is looked upon as the first duty of man. Oblation, a prayer and the recitation of the sacred hymns are also observed. The Hindus worship a number of gods and goddesses, but the primary gods and goddesses are Vishnu and His consort Lakshmi, Siva and His consort Parvati, Saraswati, Ganesh, Sri Ram and Hanuman. There are a large number of temples, old and new, scattered throughout the state. *Kirtans* and daily *pujas* in the temples and celebration of the big festivals in a large way are common. The social structure of the different regions of south Odisha did not undergo much change during the 19th and first half of the 20th centuries. There were however a distinct caste consciousness in the villages. The *Brahmanas,* the *Karanas,* the *Kshatriyas,* who formed the higher castes, occupied the better lands in the villages. The so-called lower castes namely the *Dhobas,* the *Hadis,* the *Dandasis,* the *Dombs,* the *Bauris* etc. lived on the fringes of the villages. They were the actual tillers of the soil but they were not, by and large, tenants and had to remain poor. The others, however, flourished at the expenses of these under privileged people.[31]

Muslims

Muslims who are numerically next to Hindus and Christians constituted less than 1% of the total population of the region. They performed *Namaj* (Prayer) 5 times a day. They gave *zakat* (alms) to the needy persons. They also observed *Roza* (fasting) for one month in the month of *Ramzan,* and made *Haj* or pilgrimage to Mecca.[32] But, they are mostly the inhabitants of the towns and urban centres.

Christianity

This religion is the second largest religion of south Odisha .The followers of this faith formed less than 1% of the population. Almost all the Christians are converts from the Hindu fold. There are both Protestants and Catholic sects of Christianity in south Odisha. They were engaged in extensive evangelical activities in this part of Odisha. They undertook relief operations in times of natural calamities like flood, famine, cyclone and epidemics.

Besides the people of three main religions i.e. Hindus, Muslims and Christians, the following socio-religious groups among the Hindus are also found in south Odisha. [33]

Mahima *Dharma*

The followers of Mahima *Dharma* or *Alekha Dharma* are found more or less in the different villages of south Odisha. They believe in one god i.e. *Parambrahma*, the Supreme Being. The name of this cult varies from place to place. In some parts of the region, it is known as *Alekha Dharma*. The word *Alekha* means one who cannot be described in *lekha* (writing). In some other parts, the people call it as *Kumbhipatiyas*. It is so because; the *Sanyasis* of this religion wear bark (*bakala*) of the *kumbhi* tree as their only garment. Similarly, it is also known as *Satya Mahima Dharma* and *Satya Sanatana Mahima Dharma* due to its propagation of *satya* or truth.[34] Monotheism, *Ahimsa* or non-violence; building of caste-less society; opposition to idol worship and Hindu mode of worship and rituals, sacrifice of animals, emphasis on *guru* worship, recitation of *Bhajanas*; morality; non-possession of wealth etc. are the main principles of Mahima cult.[35]

Brahmo Samaj

Among the people of this region, a microscopic section belongs to the 'Brahmo Samaj'. The Brahmos are monotheists. They do not believe in idol worship, sacrificial system, casteism, untouchability, dowry system, priest-hood, child-marriage, Polygamy and re-birth. They encourage inter-caste and widow marriage. They give much emphasis on the rights of the women and their education.[36]

Arya Samaj

A microscopic section among the Hindus follows the principles of the 'Arya Samaj'. Sribatchha Panda a great freedom fighter and a social reformer was the founder of the the 'Arya Samaj' branch of Odisha. He sacrificed a lot to spread this cult in this part of Odisha. He established an *Arya Kanya Gurukulashram* and *Gorakhya Ashram* (Cow Protection Centre) in the village Tanarada near Bhanjanagar. 'Arya Samaj' workers were active in preaching against untouchability, oppression of women and other social evils of Hindu society.[37]

Common Feature of the Castes

Some of the characteristics common to most of the castes are given below. Most of the working population is engaged in agriculture and allied pursuits. Thrift and economy are little practiced except by the *Kumuti* caste. The women are scantily dressed. They cover the bossom, but do not wear bodices. The poor class women wear a great amount of coarse brass bangles on each arm. Their wrists and hands are generally marked with a heavy substance like bracelets. There is a strong affection for applying turmeric paste on their face and body which is considered as an antiseptic paste to beautify their appearances. Until recently the girls (except *Kshatriyas, Karanas*) were married before puberty. The number of castes in south Odisha is very large. Among them the following are note-worthy:

1. *Badhei,* 2. *Bania,*
3 *Bhandari,* 4 *Brahmin,*
5 *Chitrakara,* 6 *Dera,*
7 *Gouda,* 8 *Gudia,*
9 *Kachara,* 10 *Karana,*
11 *Kansari,* 12 *Khandayata,*
13 *Khitivmasa* (or *Mativamsa*), 14 *Kshatriya,*
15 *Kumbhara,* 16 *Kumuti,*
17 *Kurmi,* 18 *Mali* (*Raula*),
19 *Nolia,* 20 *Paika,*
21 *Patara,* 22 *Sundhi* and
23 *Teli.*[38]

Schedule Caste

Besides these caste-groups, Scheduled Castes constituted about 15% population of the region. The Schedule Castes are as follows:

1. Adi Andhra, 2. Amat,
3. Barika, 4. Baghuti,

5. Bouri,
6. Bhoi,
7. Chamara,
8. Chandala,
9. Dandasi,
10. Dhivara,
11. Dhova,
12. Domb,
13. Ghasi,
14. Gonda,
15. Haddi,
16. Jaggili,
17. Kandara,
18. Kela,
19. Keuta,
20. Khadala,
21. Madari or Mediri,
22. Madiga,
23. Mala,
24. Mundapota,
25. Painda,
26. Pano,
27. Patratanti,
28. Relli,
29. Sountia,
30. Siyal and
31. Tiar.

A unique feature of south Odisha is the presence of a number of aboriginal tribes since ancient times. Odisha has the third largest tribal population in India next to Madhya Pradesh and Bihar. They are mostly concentrated in the districts of Ganjam, Gajapati, Koraput Nabarangapur, Malkangiri, Rayagada and Kandhamal districts of south Odisha. These Schedule Tribes are as follows,

Scheduled Tribes

1. Jatapu,
2. Kandh,
3. Koli(Malhar),
4. Konda-dora,
5. Koya,
6. Lodha,
7. Matya,
8. Munda,
9. Paraja,

10. Bonda,

11. Saura (Savara) and

12. Savara Lodha.[39]

The social structure of the different parts of south Odisha did not however undergo much change even during the political turmoils such as Resistance Movement, Odia Movement, Freedom Movement, change of Kingship, administration and the abolition of *zamindari* system. The agriculturists continued to own their lands and to raise crops and taxes through the headmen of the villages. The landless masses toiled on others' lands on a subsistence level.

Village Pattern

Village is known to be of great antiquity which came into existence when agriculture became the economic basis of subsistence of group life. The village has been from its very inception one of the primary units in which human activities are socially arranged. Thus the people throughout India have been mainly village folk.[40]

Villages were formed by a number of families residing at one place. Most of the villages came into existence as a result of movement of the members of the family, tribe or clan to a particular site because of such factors as pressure on land, or inimical atmosphere in the habitat or bad location of the houses or availability of better amenities.[41]

There were different types of villages in south Odisha such as: village situated near the city gate, cattleman's village, camp village, endowed village, village with market, village without market, border villages, partly deserted village, village occupied largely by people belonging to a single caste or following a single craft or profession.[42]

South Odisha is more backward and rural then the Odisha proper. It is predominantly an agricultural region. The Odias live in villages that were interestingly different in pattern from those in the neighbouring states. There are, generally, two rows of thatched houses standing shoulder to shoulder, with a street running in between, and with a temple and a tank at one end and a *Bhagavata Ghara* or a village *Akhada* at the other. The village homes are invariably decorated with mural paintings of some sort, and have a shady garden at the back. The *Bhagavata* of Jagannatha Dasa and the village priest still wield considerable influence on the social and individual life of the average Odia in the village. Even today, the *Bhagavata* of Jagannatha Dasa is recited daily, either in the common *Bhagavata Ghara* or in the Hindu families of most of the villages.[43]

The village homes are invariably decorated with *chittas* or ceremonial paintings of some sort, and have a shady garden at the back and a *guhala*- the cowshed, reserved at the frontal part of the house. The houses consist of three to four rooms which are small and badly ventilated. The verandah outside is used as a place for gossiping and in the warm weather forms a convenient sleeping place with the simple addition of a rush mat. When the family is divided the division takes place longitudinally. The walls are built of wooden lattice work plastered on both sides with a mixture of cow dung and mud. The mud floor is also plastered with clay and cow dung. The houses are of row type with common walls shared by two families adjacent to each other. The village site or *Basti* consists of two rows of houses with common *Danda* in between which intercepted with a *Chaupadhi* (community hall) or a temple. The *Danda* infront of each house is also dotted with *Khanis* (underground store for storage of paddy) where paddy is kept after harvesting season for about three to four months but again dug out before the rainy season to improve the taste of food grain and to save the grains from paste attack.[44]

Another feature of the village is a greater sense of affiliation and mutual support among certain castes and a sense of allergy, if not antagonism, to other castes. This is very unfortunate but it is there. For example, the *Karanas* and Brahmins do not feel very happy with each other. So are the *Kshatriyas* and *Sudras*.

The Odia and Telugu speaking population constitute bulk of the population of the region. The main tribal people of south Odisha are the *Kandhs* and the *Savaras.* They are mostly confined to the mountainous tracts, otherwise known as maliahs or the "Agency". The Telugus are an enterprising people and their colonies are chiefly found along the sea coast as far north as Balugaon to the southern border of Srikakulam.

Agriculture is the chief means of livelihood for 82% population of the region. That is why south Odisha's folklore draws sustenance mainly from the culture-complex based on agriculture. The villages, by and large, have no roads worthy of the name excepting cart-tracks till the end of the 19th century. Bullock carts and ponies were the usual mode of conveyance as late as the first quarter of the 20th country. Bicycles have become very common in the villages from the second half of the 20th century.

The villages, however, have very little of cultural activities. Libraries are scarce and community village hall exist only in big villages. Gossip and politicking usually fill up the leisure hours of both young and old males. Women have very few means of relaxation. There is a strong trend among the elite and affluent people to migrate to the urban areas leading to a lopsided growth of the towns. No literate or educated man normally wants to live in a village and this is also due to the economic factor as there are hardly any employment opportunities for the educated youth in the villages. The tools for agriculture are still primitive.

South Odisha was one of the rarely gifted regions to boast of its high density of tribal population. It had the third large concentration of tribals of India forming about one-fourth of the total population of the state.[45] They inhabit the picturesque hill-tops and thickly wooded lands of southern Odisha. Each tribe has its rich pattern of music and dance which are lively and artistic.

However, the settlement pattern of the tribals of south Odisha was of a linear type. The tribal villages occupied a vantage position on the slopes of the valley from where the people get a clear view of their fields made at the lower level of the hills. The village was established at a levelled ground flanked by the hill and the main road on the west and east respectively whereas the open fields forming the higher terraces were present on the other two sides. Only two rows of houses on either side of the central street was the average pattern of settlement.[46] The villages looked like a river amongst the hills.[47]

The *Kandhs* and *Sabaras*- who formed the bulk of the tribal population kept their houses neat and clean rather more than the Odias. The walls of their houses and their verandahs were ash-coloured presenting a charming sight. Their women folk kept their houses and surroundings spotlessly clean.[48]

The thatch of the adjacent houses merge in such a way as to give an impression of a long roof stretched from one end of the village to the other. The tribals lived in small and low wooden houses which they built themselves. The maximum height of the roof was 10 feet. One had to stoop to enter a house. The rooms did not generally have a window as a result the houses were not well ventilated.[49]

The month of *Chaitra* is full of the festivals of gods and goddesses. In *Yatras* and festivals, folk songs and folk-dances play a dominant part for the entertainment of the people. Even today most of the villages of the region have *Akhadas* which maintain the musical instruments and equipments, and serve as a place of rehearsal organized by the locally recruited *Gurus.* Efficient *Gurus* are felicitated with *Kundalas* and *Patavastras* for their contributions to the development of folk dances in the area.[50]

In the medieval period, every village in south Odisha had a library of palmleaf manuscripts known as *Bhagavata Ghara* where during leisure hours, poems were recited, songs were sung, and *Puranas* were discussed. The keen desire of the people to have the pride and joy of possessing knowledge and wisdom seems to have been killed forever through an imposed system of education under the British and by the capitalist-run press. The sanctity of the palm-leaf and the ancient iron stylus is still considered by the simple villagers as a sacred thing. A printed book, or even paper for that matter, was not acceptable on ceremonial occasions during the period under review.

The traditional distribution of occupation which constituted the four principal castes among the Hindus has been greatly altered. In this respect it may be stated that the *Varnasramadharma* has yielded place to the *Yugadharma*. The Brahmins have no longer a monopoly of learning and priesthood than the *Vaisyas* of trade, the *Kshatriyas* of governance or the *Sudras* of tilling the soil, and doing the service for the higher castes. But, there was however, a distinct caste-consciousness in the villages. The Brahmins, the *Karanas* and the *Kshatriyas* who formed the higher castes occupied the better lands in the villages and normally lived in separate zones known as *Badasahi* or *Badadanda*. The so-called lower castes lived on the fringes of the villages. They were the actual tillers of the soil but they were not, by and large, tanents and had to remain poor.

Today it can be seen that the traditional costumes and ornaments of the people of south Odisha have undergone a change because of the heavy impact of western education, television, cinema and popular visual publicities. In spite of the impact of the different entertainment media, the agricultural peasants of Odishan villages still skillfully retain some of their traditional performing arts and folk-culture intact.

South Odisha has a rich tradition of folk culture. The folk art and craft, folk-drama, folk dance and music were so lively and colourful that they could captivate the minds of all the art-loving people. These folk songs were not only simple in its form and composition but also carried deep message of human values. But, it is a matter of great regret that the folk dances and theatres, folk songs and tales which was a source of great entertainment and livelihood for the rural folk, and also helped in spreading the messages of morality, truthfulness, victory of righteous over evil forces, cooperation and harmony in the society are on the verge of decline and death. So necessary steps may be taken to revive these folklore traditions, to record and preserve them either by the Government or by the Private munificence in the form of DVD and e-library for the posterity. Otherwise, the tradition of the centuries and wealth of the society will be vanished with in a few decades.

References

1. T.J.Maltby, The Ganjam District Manual, Madras, 1918, p76-77.
2. P.Acharya, The Antiquity of the words Odisha and Odia, in: OHRJ, vol.II, September, 1953, pp.56-57.
3. A.K.Pattnayak, History of Rayagada, in: Cultural Heritage of Orissa, vol.IX, Rayagada District, Bhubaneswar, 2007, pp.46-47.
4. H.K.Mahatab, History of Orissa, vol.I, Cuttack, 1951, pp.343-346.
5. N.C.Behuria, Orissa District Gazetteers: Ganjam, Cuttack, 1992, pp.65-66.
6. K.C.Panigrahi, History of Orissa, Cuttack, 1981, p.63.
7. R.C.Majumdar, Ancient Indian Colonies in the Far East, vol.II (suvarna dvipa), Delhi, 1961, p.227.
8. H.K.Mahatab, op.cit., p.131.
9. U.K.Subuddhi, The Bhauma-Karas of Orissa, Calcutta, 1978, p.10.
10. S.N.Rajguru, History of the Gangas, vol.I, Bhubaneswar, 1958, Chapter-IV.
11. Walter Hamilton, Geographical, Statistical and Historical Description of Hindostan, vol.I, London, 1820, p.31.
12. Janardana Nanda, Orissa Calling, Nimapada, 1961, p.2.
13. Bhagabana Sahu, Cultural History of Orissa, 1435-1751, New-Delhi, 1997, p.1.
14. R.Subramanyam, Suryavansi Gajapatis of Orissa, Waltair, 1957, p.92.
15. H.Beveridge, Akbaranama of Abul Fazal, vol.II, Calcutta, 1912, p.381.
16. H.K.Mahatab, op.cit., p.6.
17. A.B.Mohanty, Madala Panji (Prachi Edition), pp.60-61.
18. T.J.Maltby, op.cit., p.80.
19. Odisha Sahitya Academy, Konark, vol.59, 1986, pp.33-34.
20. Guide to the Records of Ganjam District, Madras, 1934, Chapter II, Accn No.335-336, TNA.
21. C.U.Aitchison, Treaties and Engagements between the Hon'ble East India Company and the Native powers in Asia, vol.I, London, 1845, p.165.
22. W.W.Hunter, Imperial Gazetteer of India, vol.V, 1885, p.3.

23. T.J.Maltby, op.cit., pp.91-94.
24. Ibid.
25. Gopinath Mohanty (ed.), Cultural Heritage of Gajapati, Bhubaneswar, 2004, p.10.
26. Mayadhar Mansinha, A History of Oriya Literature, New-Delhi, 1962, p.1.
27. Ibid.
28. T.J.maltby, op.cit., p.1.
29. N.C.Behuria, Orissa District Gazetteers: Ganjam, Cuttack, 1992, p.168.
30. Ibid, p.169.
31. Ibid.
32. Ibid, p.168 and p.176.
33. Ibid, p.168 and p.174.
34. Bhagabana Sahu, Socio-Economic and Cultural History of Orissa, Cuttack, 2002, pp.133-134.
35. R.C.Misro, Mahima Movement and Bhima Bhoi: The saint poet's Distinct voice against Dominance and Hegemony (Dr. D.Janaki Endowment lecture) in: Proceedings of South Indian History Congress, 30th session, Kannur (Kerala), February, 2010, pp.605-619.
36. Bhagabana Sahu, op.cit., p.126.
37. Ibid.
38. N.C.Behuria, op.cit., p.168.
39. Ibid, pp.177-214 also N.Senapati(ed.), Orissa District Gazetteers: Koraput, Cuttack, 1976, pp.89-111.
40. A.L.Bashan, The Wonder that was India, London, 1954, p.189.
41. K.K.Thaplyal, Kautilya's Arthasastra, in: Village and Village Life in Ancient India, New-Delhi, 2004, p14.
42. Ibid, pp.16-17.
43. Mayadhar Mansinha, op.cit., p.4.
44. N.C.Behuria, op.cit., pp.220-221.
45. Govt. of Orissa, Tribal Heritage of Orissa, 1971, p.5.
46. Benerjee. Ethnographic Study of the Kuvi-Kandha, Calcutta, 1969, p.10.
47. E.T.Dalton, Tribal History of Eastern India, Delhi, 1973, p.295.
48. R.C.S.Bell, Orissa District Gazetteers: Koraput, Cuttack, 1945, p.61.
49. M.Ahmed, Lakhrish-A Village of Kandhs, Cuttack, 1961, Paras: 17-21.
50. N.C.Behuria, op.cit.

2

Folk Tales

In any region or country there happens to be chiefly two types of source material for literature, viz., the general literature and the folk literature. The tradition of the general literature is chiefly found to be in the written form, and is preserved in that form. But, the literature that was composed by the illiterate folk in the ancient and the medieval periods was meant not to be read, but to be listened, to be recited, and to be sung. This was known as oral literature or Folk literature.[1]

The oral literature of a country or a region belongs to its common man whose thoughts are expressed in the most native, down to earth and poetic way. It is archaic, archetypal and has neither any written text nor any claims on its authorship. The word 'oral' itself suggests that such literature is not chronicled. It originates from illiterate people in a language akin to them.[2] This type of literature is not a part of the literary history.

Oral literature is much older than a country's written literature. At a time when people used to live in integrated social groups, the oral literature of each community grew and developed. It is a product generally of the unlettered, classless community as a whole and not of any individual belonging to any particular community or group. It is generally believed that, initially oral literature is the creation of an individual and in process of recreation and constant variation it gradually becomes a group product. Oral literature is, therefore, a communicably re-created and oriented form which thrives in the life of the unlettered mass of the country.[3]

Though written literature has quite an old tradition and has been developing among the enlightened for more than a thousand years in *Odisha,* yet a very rich tradition of oral literature still exists here. In fact, it served as a storehouse of ideas and themes for written literature and, after the progressive enrichment of written literature, developed as a parallel to it, keeping all its freshness and liveliness. The key to the mystery behind this strange vitality of oral literature lies in the fact that it always re-creates and transforms itself. It never stands still anywhere or on any belief or theme.[4]

Early and late medieval *Odia* literature drew its inspiration mostly from the existing oral tradition. Modern literature grew only after the introduction of western education in the 19th Century.[5] This has been mostly responsible for breaking down the age-old tradition of life and literature of our country. In such a situation one can obviously see that this is posing a great threat to oral literature. But, taking into account its rich and varied tradition, we can discuss the various aspects of Oral literature which still constitute it.

Oral literature or folk literature can be broadly divided into six categories i.e.

1. Folk-tales,
2. Folk-songs,
3. Ballads,
4. Riddles,
5. Proverbs, and
6. *Dakabachanas.*

Among them Folk-tales are most popular, heart touching and vibrant.

Folk-Tales:

Folk-tale is an important part of the oral literature.[6] South Odisha like Odisha proper has a rich and glorious tradition of folk-tales which form a major part of oral literature. Folk-tale is known as *Loka-Kahani* or *Loka-katha* or *Loka-barta.* South Odisha is a wonderful treasure of folk-tales.

Story-telling is the oldest traditional folk art.[7] The telling of Folk-tales as in several other countries, continues to be the domain of mostly the older member of the *Odia* family. It is a common feature in many houses that grandmothers during their leisure hours generally in the evening or night surrounded by their grand children narrate these tales. The folk-tales with fancy and wonder as their main characteristic are listen to by children with great attention. They are enthralling not only to children but also to grown-ups.

It is an intellectual hobby of some villagers especially old man and women, who are endowed with great power of imagination, power of expression and dramatic action. A story teller is a man of genius possessing childlike simplicity, youthful spirit, sympathetic heart and power to evoke emotion in others. He must be a man of amiable disposition, sound character and commanding personality with thorough mastery over the language to convince the youth listeners of the truth of the incidents. The listeners must make their doubts. They must weep or smile, open their eyes wide in wonder or curiosity or jump up in great delight, that is, to be of one mind and spirit with the story-teller.[8]

In the villages of south *Odisha,* boys and girls assemble at the door of the story-teller, most often an old woman on whom rests the charge of keeping the child in good humour. The child has finished his play. As he has nothing else to do at home he might trouble his mother and other members. The best means devised to keep him quiet is story-telling. It makes him sit silently and patiently for hours, inculcates a habit of self-control, a habit to hear other's speak.[9]

The sun has set. Stars twinkle. Ploughmen take rest. The village appears calm, serene and sacred. The grandmother starts her story with the following meaningless lines.

> "Let me tell you a story,
> Let me tell you a story-
> What story? Of a frog,
> What frog? A wooden frog.
> What wood? An oilman's wood.
> What oilman? Who moves a pressing machine.
> What pressing machine? Of sugar cane.
> What sugar cane? A *'Kantari'* sugar cane.
> What *Kantari*? An old woman who knows charms.
> What old woman?
> Old wife of fisherman who dances with the basket of beaten rice".

After the recitation of the first song, the story teller asks the boy to choose the subject matter from among the following: about a king or a merchant or a tiger or a crocodile or a snake or a giant or a ghost. The boys and girls, who choose the folk-tale according to their taste and mood, differ great deal from one another in their choice; for, most of the stories were heard beforehand. If the issue remains undecided, the old lady uses her discretion and starts. "Once upon a time there was a king (or a merchant)." At each pause during narration, the listener has to say 'hum' (yes) to encourage the story-teller and keep it going.[10]

Folk stories are roughly classified into legends and Folk-tales. There has not been any regular attempt at collection of the thousands of legendary tales connected with historical personages, gods and goddesses and the building of the gigantic temples of Odisha .[11] Folk-tales have their roots in the hoary past when men acquired the power of articulate expression. He proudly gave out his heroic feelings in case of hunting a ferocious tiger or lion or killing his inveterate enemy or narrated his pitiable lot in course of storm, flood, and famine or earthquake. But, a folk-tale is a fully imaginary piece which may not bear any relation to the real fact of life.[12]

The Legends:

Here are some of the examples of the legends. A brief resume of all such legends popular in south Odisha are given below:

The Legend of Sibei Samantara:

The legend of Sibei Samantara is well known throughout Odisha. Sibei Samantara- the great architect of the emperor Narasingha Deb was given the responsibility of constructing the world-famous sun temple at Konarka. The place fixed for laying the foundation was in the deep waters of the river Chandrabhaga .The architect threw hundreds of cartloads of stones into the midst of the river but to no effect. They were all washed and swallowed by the current of the water. He, however, could not detect his own mistake and had to discontinue his work in despair. Once, while going home fully exhausted, he was invited by an old lady to dinner and was served hot porridge. Sibei began eating the hot dish from the middle and not from one side and consequently burnt his finger. In this way he could not satisfy his hunger. The old lady remarked that, he should not behave like Sibei Samantara, whom she could not recognize. On hearing this he asked her about Samantara's defects. She said that, despite his great wisdom and skill in architecture, he lacked common sense. He tried to lay the foundation from the middle and not from one side and became unsuccessful in his endeavour. Sibei, fully enlightened, tried again by the new method and his efforts were crowned with success.[13]

The Episode of Dharmapada:

Another legend connected with the construction of the world famous temple of Konark is the following. The temple could not be completed with strenuous efforts of twelve hundred architects who worked for twelve years. The Emperor of Odisha promulgated an order that they would all be beheaded if they were not able to complete the temple in one more day. Dharama, a boy of twelve years of age, who was in the womb when his father Bisu came to Konarka for construction, could however completed the temple to his great credit and thus saved the lives of twelve hundred architects.

Instead of rejoicing at this unexpected turn of events, the architects thought that to be defeated by a skillful boy of their community though a great glory, is fraught with grave danger. The emperor might on that account reward the boy and punished them all for worthlessness. They asked Bisu to choose one of the alternatives' either to discard the community or to sacrifice the son. Bisu choose the latter. Before that, Dharama convinced his father and volunteered to sacrifice his life for the nation, by jumping from the top of the Konark temple into the sea.[14]

The Story of Boula Cow:

There was a cow named Baula. She left the three day old calf in the cowshed and went to graze in the forest. A tiger suddenly appeared and wanted to make a meal of her. The cow made a pathetic appeal to him saying that she would come back after fidding the new born calf and then allow herself to be eaten up by him.

The tiger did not belief that a pray once slipping out of the hunter's clutches would ever come back. The cow convinced him that she would keep her promise at all costs. For, an individual, life is not greater than truth.The tiger released her on good faith. Boula went back to the homestead and told her calf with tearful eyes all that had occurred. Then she came back to the tiger, bidding farewell to friends who tried their best to dissuade her. The truthful cow turned a deaf ear to all entreaties and reached the tiger followed by her calf. The tiger's heart melted at the sight. It left the cow unhurt, but died quickly only to go to heaven.[15]

To make a tiger talk of god or *Dharma* may sound ludicrous. The moral it preaches is that, truth is greater than life; soul is still greater than body. Facts are really marked. The characters have living truth behind. The story is so pathetically told that people hearing it cannot restrain their tears.[16] This story has its counter-part in the Bhojpuri and Hindi ballads in northern India and in the Canaries in south India. In Bhojpuri, the calf accompanied Boula and addressing the tiger as uncle offer himself to be eaten of instead of his affectionate mother. This feeling of a cow towards the mother touched the heart of the tiger which let them go back home.

The name of the cow in Canaries is '*Punyakoti*' and that of the cowherd is '*Kalinga*'. The tiger pleased at the presence of the truthful cow said that *Punyakoti* had earned great virtue by keeping her promise. God would never forgive him if he would destroy the valuable life.[17]

The Story of Govinda Chandra:

The life story of Govinda Chandra - a king of Bengal is also sung by the *yogis* in ballad form. Mayanabati- a queen of *Raja* Manik Chandra became a disciple of Hadipa. She advised her son Govinda Chandra to become a monk. The prince after a great deal of argument with his mother, was convinced of the efficacy of a saintly life, left his ninety-nine queens, his handsome palace and all worldly enjoyment and followed his guard who placed him at the disposal of a prostitute and put his character and personality to severe test. He was successful and proved fit to take to life of a monk.

In the sixteenth century, Yasobanta Das one of the *Panchasakha's* of *Odia* literature wrote Govindachandra ballad in verses. The book give an account of the eighty-four *siddha yogis* viz. Hadipa, Tantipa, Gorakhanath, and Machhandranath etc. *Raja* Govinda Chandra's initiation and the various hard tests he had to pass through. The story was so popular that village poets, *yogis* and beggars sang it very often in the village streets on their own way. Teaching of Mayanabati in the village poet's songs is really commendable. "You use a crocodile as a boat to cross the ocean. Do not be led astray by glittering wealth of the world. All that is mirage. Woman is like a *Mahakal* fruit with a charming exterior, but when broken you will see nothing but charcoal. She looks attractive like a red '*simul*' flower in the spring. After some time you will see nothing but cotton flying away. The farewell of Govinda Chandra from his queens is so heart touching that soft hearted woman cannot but shed tears.[18]

The original source of this pathetic story is Bengal. It spread to Bihar, *Odisha,* U.P, North-West Frontier Province, Punjab, Sindh, Maharastra and other parts of India and acquired local variety, character and colour. The scene of Govinda relinquishing his ninety nine queens, luxurious palace and boundless property and moving about in a *yogi's* dress with a begging bowl drew tears from the eyes of the soft and meek village-women.

The name of Govinda's mother is Mayanabati in Bengal,but Mukutadei in Odisha . We find various oral compositions dealing with the same theme too, some of which have been partially corrected.

Mukutadei had to undergo hard sufferings for her barrenness. She was imprisoned in a stable by the angry king who provided her with scanty rations. The hardships being intolerable, she escaped to the forest and built a palace there with the help of her queen mother. The King once went on hunting, exceedingly tired and exhausted took shelter in the palace and could recognize the disgraced queen. The King became suspicious of her character and made her pass through severe tests, i.e., walking on the needles, sharp sword and burning charcoals. Then the queen overcomes all these tests thus proved her chastity to the satisfaction of the king who made her his chief queen.

After sometime had elapsed, a son was born to her. He was known as Govinda Chandra. He ascended the throne of his father and married ninety-nine queens. Once Mukutadei was pained to discover by consulting the stars that her son was going to live only eighteen years. She advised him to turn a monk to prolong the span of his life. The King at first reluctant to renounce the pleasure of love, royal wealth and power, ultimately complied with his mothers wish. He quitted the world and having received initiation at the hands of Hadipa, averted the doom.[19]

Story of *Bada Deula Tola* (Construction of the Temple of Lord Jagannath):

The story of the circumstances under which the temple of Lord Jagannath, was constructed, is very popular in Odisha. Due to an *Odia* poem, *Deulatola* or the construction of the temple of Lord Jagannath, a particular class of beggars used to recite this poem in the 1st decade of the 20th century. The date of this poem has not yet been determined. It narrates that Indradyumna, the king of a certain country, sent his *Brahmana* priest, Vidyapati, to find out a god, capable of bestowing salvation on his worshippers.Vidyapati left his home, wandered over many countries and at last reached Nilagiri which was the place of a *Savara*, Visvavasu by name. Vidyapati was tired which forced him to ask for food and shelter from this *Savara.* Visvavasu gladly received him as a guest and employed his young daughter to look after his comforts.

Entertained by the *Savari* girl Lalita, Vidyapati spent some days at Nilagiri. In the meantime he noticed his host going out every day in the morning and returning home after sunset. One day, he asked the *Savari* girl where her father had been going every day. In reply she said "The navel portion of the lord, Sri-Krishna, remained unhurnt in the pyre and it was carried to the sea. A remote ancestor of my father collected from the sea and installed it on the top of the hill called Nilagiri or blue hill. He called this relic *Nila-Madhava* and worshipped it. Handed down from generation to generation that worship was inherited by my father who has been performing it every day."[20]

On showing his eagerness to visit Nilagiri, Vidyapati was told that except the worshipper nobody was allowed to go there. After a few days, the girl fell in love with Vidyapati. The *Brahmana* agreed to marry her only if her father would consent to escort him to Nilagiri. The father consented on condition that the Vidyapati would travel blind fold, opening his eyes only at the destination. Vidyapati had to agree to this condition, but in order to mark the way for the use of the king, Indradyumna, in future he decided to cleverly wrap some mustard seeds at both ends of his cloth in such a manner as to sow these on his way to Nilagiri that the seeds would sprout and the mustard plants indicate the way later on.[21]

Vidyapati accompanied Visvavasu to Nilagiri the next day. On arrival at the destination his eyes were unveiled and he was surprised at the sight of the wonderful splendour of the god, *Nilamadhava.* Thereafter he returned and married the *Savari* girl. After some days he took leave of her and proceeded to his native land.

Vidyapati reached the Court of Indradyumna and narrated what he had seen on the Nilagiri. Then the king became eager to pay his homage to the god, *Nilamadhava,* proceeded with Vidyapati towards Nilagiri They arrived at the place of Visvavasu who, knowing the approach of the king concealed the god, before his arrival. When the king and Vidyapati proceeded to Nilagiri and found it devoid of the god, they enquired of Visvavasu and were told that the god had disappeared as he did not like to show his person to the king sinful as he was. Indradyumna then practiced *Yoga* to wipe off his sins. A few days after he heard a voice from the sky asking him to give up the *Yoga*-practice, make the image of the god out of the *Nimba* log *(Darubrahma)* that would be found floating in the sea and worship it for salvation.[22] There upon, the king looked round and found the log floating on the sea. It was carried to land, and when a suitable carpenter was being searched, the god appeared in the guise of a carpenter and promised to undertake the work of image-making on condition that he would work in a house with doors closed for a period of twenty-one days from the day of commencement of the work.

Arrangement was made accordingly and the work commenced. After the lapse of fifteen days, however, the king lost patience and broke open the doors, whereupon to his utter disappointment found four half-done images. The carpenter had disappeared when the king proposed to open the doors before the stipulated period. The king repented for his imprudent act and was advised by a voice from the air to enshrine those half done images and worship them. Thereupon, he built a temple and went to heaven to invite Brahma, the god of the triad, to sanctify the temple. After his departure the temple was buried under a heap of sand and forgotten. Later, while a *Raja*, named Galamadhava, was passing over the sand on horse back, the animal tumbled down and the *Raja* after dismounting the heap of sand found that its hoof had struck against the wheel on the top of a buried temple. He caused the sand to be removed and claimed this temple as his own. He installed an image of Madhava and worshipped it.[23]

Indradyumna returned with Brahma after hundreds of years and found the temple in possession of Galamadhava. When he put his claim to the temple, Galamadhava wanted evidence in his (Indradyumna's) favour. Thereupon, a *Kaka* or crow named Bhushanda, who lived a long age on account of the practice of *Yoga*, made statements in favour Indradyumna's claim and Galamadhava gave up the possession of the temple. Then Brahma sanctified it and installed the half-done images in it. Subsequently, Indradyumna appointed sons, born to Vidyapati and the *Savari* girl, as priests of the temple who were known as *Daitapati.*

In the *Skanda-purana* an exhaustive account of Jagannath is given and the outline of this account tallies with above folk-tale. It represents Indradyumna as the king of Avanti in the Malava country and assigns his date to the golden age. It relates that, while Indradyumna went to heaven to invite Brahma, a *Raja*, named Galamadhava, enshrined an image of Madhava in the temple, built by Indradyumna. The story of restoration of the temple, revealed by the local tradition appears in this *purana* in a slightly altered form.[24]

The Story of Ta-Poi:

But the most interesting of all these Folk-tales is the pathetic story of *Ta'pai,* advocating Sakti-worship. Due to its immense popularity in all the households of *Odisha,* the original prose tale has long been replaced by a simple narrative poem. But the characters, situation and the denominational worship, all indicate a very remote origin of this highly interesting story.

A merchant prince on the sea coast or Odisha had seven sons and seven daughters-in-law and only one daughter, *Taa-poi,* the youngest in the family. The merchant's affairs were highly prosperous. This had always excited burning jealousy in a Brahmin widow of the neighborhood. One day she found Taa-poi playing in the street with bamboo baskets along with other boys and girls of her age. The Brahmin lady told her, 'Ah, *Taa-poi,* you should be playing with a golden moon and silver baskets. What a shame for a rich man's daughter like you to play like these common children!' *Taa-poi* immediately demanded a golden moon and silver baskets from her parents. The old merchant felt such abuse of wealth preposterous. But the innocent girl was adamant in her demand. The fond parents yielded. But by the time the making of this golden moon and the silver baskets was only half-done the parents died. The sons there after took up their father's oversea business and made arrangements for going abroad. Before starting on their long and uncertain journey they definitely told their wives to see that *Taa-poi,* their darling sister, was looked after just as she had been by their late parents and that every little wish of her should be satisfied.

The wives were acting in accordance with their husbands' request till the Brahmin widow came on the scene again. She told the young ladies, "You are indeed fools to be busy all day to keep this girl in such comfort! It is she, when the brothers return, who will poison their ears against you and make your life hot. Beware of your sister-in-law, you silly women, She is your potential enemy!"

The picture changed immediately. *Taa-poi,* the darling daughter of the merchant-prince, was now told to look after the family goats. Soon she was in rags, and turned black with wandering in the jungles with a herd of goats, without food and drink. Only her youngest sister-in-law, was kind to her and stealthily gave her food with which she sustained her frail body. One day in the month of Aswina, when the rivers were in flood, a male goat, the favorites of the eldest sister-in-law who was the mistress of the house, got lost in the jungle. When *Taa-poi* brought the flock home that evening without the favourite animal, she was severely beaten by the eldest sister-in-law and sent back hungry and footsore into the jungle, to fetch it back. It was a dark night outside and raining. *Taa-poi,* poor girl, called the animal loudly and wandered about in the darkness. During that blind journey she stumbled upon the village goddess Mangala and kneeling down before her. She offered her the handful of rawrice bran *(khuda)* which the youngest sister-in-law had secretly tied in her apron when she was cruelly driven out of the house. There she worshipped and wept, bewailing her lot, not being conscious of the passage of time. About midnight a man approached her, attracted by the sound of her pathetic crying. After a few enquiries it was revealed that the visitor was no other then *Taa-poi's* youngest brother, who, along with her other brothers, had arrived at the port. Their ships were at anchor at the river-side, not far off from there. *Taa-poi* was taken to the ship, given a bath and clothes and jewellery. A message was sent to the wives to come and perform the ceremony of *Boita-Bandana* or the 'welcome to boats'. They came in the morning, and when questioned, replied that *Taa-poi* was lying ill at home. They, except the wife of the youngest brother, were directed to go to the stern of the ship where there was a goddess to be worshipped. She was no other then *Taa-poi* herself in her new dress and jewellery. She sat with a sharp knife in her hand, and, as directed by her brothers, cut off the nose of each woman, one after another, as they approached her to worship her. They all fled in shame to the nearby jungle and were devoured by tigers. The brothers returned home with the wife of the youngest brother and *Taa-poi,* and got new wives and settled down in happiness.

Because of the *khuda* (rice bran) offered by *Taa-poi* to the goddess Mangalla, this votive festival is known also in Odisha as *Khudurukuni Upabas* or the 'fast of rice-bran'. It is generally observed by unmarried girls in the villages in emulation of *Taa-poi,* to obtain the sympathy of brother.[25]

But, Kunja Bihari Dash describes the same folk-tale in the following form.

Once upen a time, there was a rich merchant known as Tanayabanta Sadhava who had seven sons and a daughter named Ta-poi. She was brought up very affectionately and tenderly. After the death of her parents, the seven brothers went on maritime trade to far-off islands and left the dear sister in charge of their wives. After their departure, the sister- in -laws of Ta-poi gave her no food to it, no bed to sleep and made her watch the goats in the forest. Only the wife of the youngest brother treated her well.

Once a goat named *Gharamani* was lost. The oppression now crossed its limits. Taa-poi worshipped Mangala-the Goddess of welfare and got back her goat. But, it brought no change in her miserable condition. In despair she left home, climbed up a tree in the forest and wept bitterly. The brothers now coming back after ten months could know the voice of their sister. They became very sad over this miserable state of affairs and chattered their teeth for revenge. They gave her a knife to chop up the noses of those who oppressed her. She did it. All of them except the wife of the youngest brother (whose nose was not cut off) fled away and was devoured up by tigers.The story is very popular in whole of Odisha.[26]

The story of a Barren Cow:

Gangadhar, a rich man of Kanchi had a cow named Subarni which remained barren for twelve years. His wife once suggested that the look of a barren cow is inauspicious and better she should be disposed of. Next day Gangadhara made a gift of the cow to a poor Brahmin who, finding her issueless sold her off to two butchers. Subarni divined her fate and fled away for the sake of her life followed by butchers. As she ran for days without food and water, she became exhausted and fell down senseless at the door of a rich merchant named Kubera. Hungry and tired, the two butchers reached there, but could not pluck of strength enough to tie the cow. So they approached Kubera who entertained them properly. Then they caught hold of the cow and killed it. Thus, Kubera was made indirectly responsible for killing of the cow and had to pay very dearly for it. He has totally ruined. His ships sank in the seas. He lost all his property and family. Impoverished Kubera had to beg from door to door. As his sufferings knew no limit, god appeared to him in vision and advised him never to help any sinner. He was rescued and got back his lost property and family.[27]

Kanchi-Kaveri Tradition:

According to an excellent legend signifying the renunciation of all earthly pride before Lord Jagannath, the kings of Odisha have been sweeping the cars of Jagannath, Balabhadra and *Devi* Subhadra with a golden broom before the deities start on their journey during the car festival of every year. On one occasion king of Kanchi with his family came to Puri to see the car festival. There young Purushottam Deva, the king of Odisha being infatuated by the peerless beauty of Princess of Kanchi wanted to marry her.[27 (a)]

But the king of Kanchi refused to give his daughter in marriage to a king who used to do the sweeper's work. Purushottama Deva took it to be an insult to both Lord Jagannath and himself led a military expedition against the king of Kanchi. It is stated that Lord Jagannath and His elder brother Lord Balabhadra proceeded ahead to Kanchi in the guise of two horse-man in advance of the Odishan army. The two divine brothers in their long ride under the scorching sun felt thirsty and asked for curds from the young milkmaid, *Manika Gauduni*, carrying the pot on her head. She readily served it and they drank to their heart's content. *Manika* then asked for the price. The divine brothers did not have any money with them. However, they gave her a diamond ring. The cowherd lady did not know what to do with this dazzling thing. Lord Jagannath asked her to show it to the king's men following in their heel and assured her that they would take the ring and pay the price of the curds.[28]

Manika waited with patience. At last, the king and his army reached the place. The ring was brought to the notice of the king who immediately recognized it as belonging to Lord Jagannath. He was then sure and happy that the great Lord had actually led his army. *Mainka* was considered a great devotee who was able to quench the thirst of the Lord of the universe. The king presented her with a village to be named after her, *manika patna*, famous for curds in Odisha.

Divinely assisted, king Purushottam conquered the kingdom of Kanchi and carried Padmabati away as booty. To avenge the insult hurled at Lord Jagannath he was determined to make her marry a real sweeper as a final blow to the vanity of the defeated king. But, his clever minister saved the situation by presenting her to him when he was doing the duty of a sweeper at the time of the Car Festival at Puri, who accepted her overwhelmed with joy.[29]

As a result, the Kanchi Princess became the Empress of Odisha. King Prataparudra Deva was the issue of this romantic love and marriage.[30]

This Kanchi-Kaveri tradition is very much living in the memory of the people of Odisha. This tradition constitute the main theme of the art, literature, painting and sculpture of the period. The sculptural representations of Lord Jagannath and his brother Balabhadra in the guise of horsemen proceeding to Kanchi are to be found on the wall of *Jagamohan* of the Jagannath Temple at Puri.

Bewail of the She-Dove

Once upen a time, a sea dove sent her son and daughter to husk paddy. After thrashing, the daughter kept rice on the husk and the son kept husk upon the rice in two separate baskets. They carried them home to their mother. She was pleased with the daughter, for the basket appeared to be filled with rice only and got angry with the son, for she saw the basket filled with husk only. She beat and killed him without any consideration. When she poured down the son's basket, she saw rice under the husk. She repented much for her hasty action. But, the son never came back to life again. Henceforth, she has been mournfully arousing her dead son saying, *"Serak Purila Manak Purila, Utha-re-puta-Utha"* the meaning of which is, the measure is full, O my son, arise. She goes on bewailing through ages in this melancholy tone.

The same story in different version is current in Ceylon. The cooing of the dove is interpreted in Punjab in different way. The Sea-Dove handed over some paddy to the son and same to the daughter for husking purposes. The daughter brought husk with rice over it and the mother was pleased. But the son brought rice with husk over it. The mother wanting in patience as she was smashed his head in indignation in the hole of the husking paddle.

She poured down the quota of the son on the grind she discovered to her amazement rice under husk. Out of sorrow she went on shedding bitter tears. Nobody is able to restore life to the dead son. She goes on bewailing through ages in a melancholy tone.[31]

The Folk-tales of south Odisha may be divided into the following categories:

(a) Tales of gods, giants, ghosts and witches,

(b) tales of birds, beasts, reptiles and fishes,

(c) tales of adventure,

(d) tales of typical questions and answers,

(e) tales raising problems and solving them,

(f) morals translated into one's life,

(g) tales of humour and satire and

(h) tales of sea voyages reminding us of the golden maritime days when Odisha had an overseas empire and trade with great nations of the world.

Here are some of the examples of the Folk-tales.

Story of Burning of a *Sati*:

The story of burning of a *sati* is a ballad which establishes the prevalence of *sati* in Odisha. In the present story, however, there is no mention of the application of force. On the other hand, all persuasions on the part of the dear son, daughter-in-law and the neighbours to desist her, had no effect. The women walked joyfully into the fire and met her end.

Story of two Brahmins:

According to the story, one of the Brahmins put of in a prostitute's house and the other lived in a place of pilgrims. The former was uplifted spiritually by reciting the name of God in his last hours and went to heaven. The latter a morally soundman throughout his life thought of a prostitute on the death bed, was disgraced and thrown to the hell.[32]

Story of the Squirrel:

This small reptile in a helpful mood drenched its body, rolled on dust and scattered the same on the bridge being built over the sea to Lanka by Lord Ramachandra to kill the demon Ravana and rescue Sita. Ramachandra appreciated the work of this small reptile squirrel and his meaningful efforts and moved his fingers gently on its back. The marks still exist as symbol of Ram's compassion.

We find the same motif in a little different way in the Assamese folk-tale. When Rama was making a bridge across the sea, the squirrel had nothing to offer but two bamboo leaves. But this pious act pleased Rama and he caressed the squirrel so that the print of his fingers remained on its back.

Virtuous Swans:

It is said that, two virtuous Swans lived pure lives subsisting on pearls and worshipped the pious *Vaishnavas.* A king of western India who lost eyesight from leprosy was advised by a physician to take the flesh of swan that lived on pearls only. The king sent hunters to all direction in search of such fowls. One of them went to the Manasa Lake in the form of a *Vaishnava,* decoyed and captured them. The fowls promised to restore the eye sight of the king and were taken to the royal palace. On looking at them the king got back his eye sight upon which he promised to build a golden nest for them in the royal palace, but they declined and went back flying to their old abode on the lake.

Mother's Torment during Illness of Her Child:

In spite of all her affectionate care, the child fell sick of fever. She called the village physician and administered medicine. She mortgaged the nose ring for the treatment of her child. For propitiation, she offered a pair of he-goats to Sidheswari, a piece of black cloth to Jagulai, a pair of silver rings to Hingulai, a golden betal to Paneswari and sixteen offerings to Satyapir. She was ready to stake everything for the sake of her son's life. The gods and goddesses turned deaf ears to her entreaties and the son dear to her heart died.[33]

Story of a Suicide:

The daughter-in-law resorts to course of action when she cannot bear further the oppression of her cruel husband or mother-in-law. The above ballad discloses that she in her pregnant state was mercilessly beaten and in despair she drowned herself in a pond. Her husband a village tout got over the trouble by bribing the police and there was none to shed a drop of tear on the fate of the innocent daughter-in-law.

Parting words of a Dying Mother:

Widow-hood is the greatest curse of a women's life. In the above ballad, the lady aspires to die before her husband with bangles on her hands. She is delighted to picture the scene that the drum of non-widowhood would be sounded, cowries and fried rice would be strewn, her dear husband and son would proceed to the front the husband's brother by the side of the procession of corpse.

In the last hours, she makes her son seat by the bed side and counsels him thus: You put fire to my face in the burning *ghat*, invite all my daughters and son-in-laws, purchase suitable clothes for them with rupees twelve hundred hidden underground, pay eight hundred to my eight daughters and spend the rest on my account. Do not give the slightest pain to your sorrowful father.

Story of Gandavairaba:

Gandavairaba, a mythical bird of the story of 'Two friends' brings nectar from heaven for the sake of its benefactor at the risk of its won life. The prince saved its young ones from the jaws of death.

Story of *Kuhukamandala*:

Kuhukamandala, the legendary bird appears small, but incresses its size at will and can carry a family of three members on its back to a far-off land at great speed over hills, dales, rivers and oceans. Its meat cures the diseases of leprosy. Its feathers help hunters in procuring their prey easily.

Story of Prophetic Vulture:

The mother vulture which could foretell the future consoled her young ones saying that, 1200 craftsmen would be beheaded next day and enough food be available to them. The young ones asked the mother is there any way of escape from death? She said that the building of a magic boat could save their lives and it would be possible to build the boat with the wood of the tree on which they themselves were living. The old craftsman who lay under the tree and could follow the language of birds immediately cut down the tree with the help of his friends and built the magic boat.[34]

Story of Omniscient Bird:

Whoever tried to procure this bird was turned to stone. The omniscient bird had its nest in a cave of the golden mountain. The man approaching the cave heard a terrific sound and was turned to stone. In the story of *Sarbajana Chadhei*, the princess with the grace of Goddess procured this bird, turned thousands of statues to men with the touch of a magic hand. The bird acted as one of the wisest ministers of the king.

A Mediator Bird:

Kuhukamandala like the golden swan of the king Nala of puranic fame, acted as a negotiator for the merchant's youngest son and brought for him the most charming princess from a far off Island.

Story of *Tulamuhan Kanka*:

Pretending to be sinless and sacred, a stock used to drink water with a little cotton at its beak to avoid killing of worms and insects. The credulous aquatic animals believed in its honesty and integrity and were devoured up by the socalled monk.

The Flying Elephant:

Lord Indra's *Airabata* carried a family from the earth to the heaven. The guardian of the family who had the unique experience of seeing the celestial region once, guided them all. He caught hold of the elephant's tail while other family members held each other's legs. In course of their aerial journey, the guardian narrated the fine taste and demonstrated the size of celestial cakes with his two hands. Thus, made him fall down and die with the family.[35]

The Tiger monk of the basil grove:

An old tiger unable to hunt, left its forest abode and lived in a grove of basil plants. Its saintly behaviour impressed a monkey of the neighbouring tree. The devotee fell at the feet of the tiger which caught hold of him with all its strength like a prey. The monkey somehow slipped from its clutches and displayed to the world the inner motive of the so called monk.

The Flying Horse:

Flying horse solves the problem of communication in the folk-tale world. It flies thousands of miles in the twinkling of an eye.[36]

According to J.G. Frazer "Magic is compulsion, religion is propitiation. The combination of the two exists side by side since neither method proves successful."[37] Thus, magic plays an important part in wonder tales of Odisha. In them wc find magic used mainly in the following four ways: for transformation of man or woman to a beast or bird, creeper, flower or fruit, for satisfaction of desires, for defence against formidable enemy and for impregnation.

Transformation of Man to a Domestic Beast:

In the story of 'Son of poison', the gardener's wife named Jnanadei turned Abhimanyu, the hero to a ram in the day time and gave him his original human shape at night for the sake of satisfying her sexual lust.

External Soul in Birds, Beasts, Reptiles and Insects:

In most of the *Odia* Folk-tales we find that, the life of a giant or giantess is concealed in an unexpected quarter and strict secrecy is maintained in regard to this fact. The giant or giantess depopulates a kingdom, eats up whole family of the king except the princess who is brought up as an adopted daughter. In his or her absence, the princess falls in love with an adventurer, usually a prince or a minister's son. He likes to know the mystery of his or her life. The princess pretends to weep bitter tears which the giant or giantess is foolish enough to believe as genuine and sympathetically asks her the cause. The princess seems to be worried of future after his or her death. At this, the giant or giantess proudly declares that, he or she is invincible, immortal. Neither fire can burn nor sword can kill. Nobody knows the secret of his or her life. After a great deal of coaxing the mystery of life is revealed on condition that it will never be divulged to anybody.

The princess who is full of revenge for the foster father or mother betrays it in no time. Then the life token animal is destroyed, the giant or giantess is killed and the princess is rescued.[38] The main features of the folktales of Odisha are as follows.

In *Odia* Folk-tales, in most cases, a giant or giantess can be said to possess a life token. There is only a single example of life token of a man in the 'Pomegranate boy' which is borrowed from Sanskrit. Raghaba, a legendary sea fish has a garland of pomegranate inside a round box in its belly. This garland is said to be the life-token of the boy.

We find illustrations of the life index motif in the *Odia Mahabharat* of Sarala Das of the 15th century. Indra being afraid of the curses of a powerful monk named Kusankura, deposited five of his souls at five different places: one in *Dharma*, the other in the wind, the third in the sky, the fourth in Aswini and the fifth in his own son.

In the story 'who wins the world in intelligence', the minister's son reached the mountain named 'Olasuni', killed the big blind sanke in its cave, tore its belly and caught hold of the black bee; tore it; took out a red fruit; broke the red fruit and took out a worm. As the worm was killed, the giantess died.

Passive Index of the Soul

If any harm is done to the hero or heroine the passive index is affected. A hero on his journey to a distant land might keep something with himself or with his dear wife which would indicate his or her condition by changing its own nature.

In the story of 'Two friends', the cow gave a cup of milk to the calf saying that if the cup of milk would look red like blood, then it should know that she was not in the land of the living.

In the story of *Bole hunti*, the merchant planted a plantain tree and said, "If you belong to the age of truth, you will live till I return in case of safety of my wife. If my wife be kidnapped by the prince, you will die".

The plantain tree died when Lila, merchant's wife was kidnapped. This disappointed the merchant returning from trade. He committed suicide before his kidnapped wife who also followed him along with his kidnapper, the prince.

The external symbol is always indicative of danger. In the story of Omniscient bird, the younger brother goes on an adventure, the sister plants a basil plant. If it grows well the brother in the foreign land is said to be well. If it withers or grows pale, the brother is considered to be put to grave danger or is dying. In the story of Golden Deer, the hero had a ring with two diamonds, if they turned blue, that would indicate danger to his brother.[39]

A legend is more attached to every place of pilgrimage, to almost every God. We can find our old world still living within us. These legend collected and published will give us a picture of our past though not historically authentic and will make an interesting study.

The kings as depicted in the Folk-tales seem to be rulers of small kingdoms. Their chief pastime was hunting; chief interest lay in marriage of more than one princess. They enjoyed life at the cost of their discontented subjects. They lacked in martial spirit though their sons went on adventurous, fought against giants and achieved great success. They were accomplished riders of horses.

These rulers were never trustworthy. Their order was law. The dearest queen, the obedient prince or the most faithful minister was ordered to leave the kingdom within twenty-four hours or was killed instantly on the spot. The richest man of the country might be turned to a beggar in the street for the slightest offence. There was practically no justice. Minister's advice or wise men's counsels did not count. They were only afraid of sage's curses.

Any crime was punishable with death. Mutilation of limbs was sometimes practised. If the king desired to punish the faithless queens, he would order digging a big pit in the courtyard and would call them with an artificial smile to guess the amount of paddy which that would contain. When they stood by the pit guessing they were pushed down unaware; then thorny plants and baskets of soil were poured down to make a quick end of their lives. Sometimes, pregnant queens were thrown into the pit for the king's misconception of their character. After they gave birth to their children they were forced to satisfy their great appetite with the flesh of their dead bodies.

Mostly the king was cheated by the officer and shows its blood instead to the angry king who would foolishly believe the culprit to be dead. The officer would do this intentionally, knowing fully well that the so-called culprit was really innocent. The king's whimsical and idiotic character was well known to him. The victim, however, was advised to leave the country at once, for his stay in the country might make the officer's position precarious.

The minister was intelligent and shrewd and tried to mitigate the suffering of the people by all means at his command. But the king was the final authority of the state.

Tie of friendship was strong. Friends sacrificed their wealth, happiness and even lives for the sake of friends. The Minister's son who secretly heard from a prophet vulture, the dangers that would befall the prince caused the lion's gate of the prince to be broken, advised him to discard the rice offered by the step-mother. The advice though unpalatable was accepted in consideration of his faithfulness. Once the minister's son killed a python which was going to swallow up the prince and princess in their private apartment. A drop of blood fell on the cheek of the princess which was immediately rubbed out by the minister's son. This awakened the prince who angrily said that his treacherous friend was making an attempt on the prince's life in order to marry the princess. When no explanation convinced the prince, the minister's son confessed the truth which he was forbidden to do and was faced the truth which he was forbidden to do and was turned into a slab of stone. The prince now mourning over the loss of his dear friend sacrificed all his pleasure, moved here and there with the slab on his head for twelve years, brought him back to life with the nectar stolen from heaven by *Gandabhairaba*, a fictitious bird.[40]

Malyani (a gardener's wife) who made garlands, played important part in the Odia folk-tales. Shrewd and cunning, she was an expert in the art of magic. She acted as a faithful intermediary between lovers. The prince coming from a distant land takes shelter in her house and approaches the princess in the guise of her daughter, carries on correspondence with her, concealing the letters in the garland wreathed by him. She sometimes proves very harmful, transforms the prince to a ram in the day time and turns him into a man at night to serve her whims.

In beast tales, the actors are animals which speak and act like human beings. Beasts are intelligent, considerate and noble and they never play treachery with man. The lives of tiger cubs were saved from forest fire by a benevolent prince. The grateful tiger and tigress rewarded him with one of them and were ready to serve him at any time. But the tiger would deal roughly with man if he is misbehaved. *Tuanya* and *Tuanyi* brought faggots from his forest kingdom and promised to give him cakes. But they gave him cakes out of cowdung and stone which broke the tiger's tooth and made him very angry with them.[41]

The animals were sympathetic towards each other and cooperated against the common enemy. The elephant played great part in the coronation ceremony. He poured down sacred water form a golden pitcher, which he carried, on the head of a prince or any other fortunate man, to make him the new king of a kingdom. This was practiced when the king of a country died without leaving behind a heir to succeed him.

The vulture was a prophet who knew the future of man, *Gandabhairaba* was fictitious bird. Grateful to the benefactor, he brought nectar from heaven against enormous odds. The crow is faithful and benevolent. But man sometimes acts treacherously towards him.

A crow once wished to eat a ripe *Kalara* (-a bitter fruit eaten by man). The man said, "Wash your beak and come". It went to a well and said, "Well I wish to wash my beak with your water".

The well said, "Bring a pitcher from the potter, draw water and wash your beak". The crow asked the potter to supply him with one pitcher to which he said, "Bring soil from the field". When he approached the field, it said, Borrow the horn to which it said "Bring me some milk from the black cow. I shall drink it and then lend you my horn". When it asked the cow for some milk, she said "Bring me some soft grass, I shall eat it and give you milk". Ultimately he asked a blacksmith to supply him with a sickle. The wicked blacksmith gave him a red –hot sickle. As soon as the innocent crow held it in its beak, it dropped, down dead.

Kuhukmandal is also a fictitious bird. It increases or decreases its size when necessary. It can carry a family on its back to hundreds of miles.

The giantess used her legs as fire wood for cooking. At the sight of her terrible figure, the prey sometimes escaped on fast-going horses. She at once tied a packet of mustard to the tail of the horse. The mustard was strewn on the way as the horse ran; then they grew into plants and put on flowers. That all this happened within a moment. The sons of the giantess returned and could trace the way through the lines of mustard plants. When they almost touched their victim, the prince or the minister's son uttered some incantations which covered up their path with a dense mist. The giants pursued with great difficulty. Then the path was covered with thorns which they tore up with their sharp teeth, with spat and put out, with floods of water which they swam across and pursued him unabated. Finding no other means of escape, he entered into the trunk of a tree. If the giants tried to uproot the tree from the age of truth, it at once blossomed; there grew a mango, became ripe, fell down into a pond to be swallowed up by some fish. When the fish was caught, the prince or the minister's son was rescued.[42]

The giant or giantess cannot be easily killed. His or her life was hidden in a small wooden pot in form of a black bee under the deep water of the sea or it was a black ram kept secretly in a solitary room under the earth. The secret of death was out through an adopted daughter- a stolen princess who was now in a mourned of a stranger prince. The princess knew *Kaka Charitra* which enabled her to do impossible things, turned the prince into a fly in presence of giantess and restored to him a human form when the giantess went out. If the ram or the bee was killed, the giantess died immediately.

Iswara and *Parvati* were of great help to men or women in danger. They sprinkled sacred water on the dead man and made him alive. Many surprising things were conceived by the story-teller. Flying horse, magic boat, magic jewel, etc. could work wonders. Ambujajmani built one palace, dug out a tank, planted a full-fledged garden within one night. Flying horse or magic horse could carry the rider to any palace he liked, within the twinkle of an eye. Putting on a pair of magic sandals, one could fly over great distances within a moment. A magic can gave birth to an army of men; a magic bag could produce delicious food for thousand people; a magic mango could make jewels when a man smiled. A flying tree could carry a man to his destination.[43]

Besides these stories from ancient anthologies like *Katha Sarita-Sagar, Panchatantra, Sua-Sari Kahani, Batrish Simhasana* and stories of legendary kings like Vikramaditya, Bhoja and the stories of great kings, ministers, generals who ruled over this part of country, and those of the saints, sacred places like hills, temples and rivers are the treasures handed down from generation to generation by word of mouth.

Thus, a folk-tale is half dreamy, half realistic. It depicts the simple faith, varied taste, social customs, and breadth of outlook and flight of imagination of the people in the most living language.

Riddles

Riddles also form an important part of oral literature. They appeal to intelligence and wisdom of rural-folk, rather than to sentiment. Each riddle carries a piece of wisdom, coated in humorous and intelligent language. While appealing to common sense and intelligence, it is not devoid of literary form either.[44]

Riddles indicate in a subtle and often humorous manner certain aspects of the life of the people in a question-answer manner. Through the riddles one can make out many salient facts regarding the social customs, manners and inhibitions of the people.[45]

Riddles are broadly divided into two kinds-literary riddles and folk riddles. Folk riddles are the basis of literary riddles. Sometimes the folk character can be observed in literary riddles also.

Like all other branches of oral literature riddles also are the creation of rural people. Asking and solving riddles (questions) is still one of the ideal forms of mental recreation for the rural-folk, young and old.[46] There are riddles about some of the foodstuffs and drinks as well.

Maize or Indian corn is cultivated throughout south Odisha during the rainy season and forms one of the main *Bhodoi* or rainy season crops. When very tender, it is roasted and eaten with relish. When fully mature, the grains are parched and eaten or they are grind into flour which is needed, with water into dough and eaten raw. This is known as *Jau* which is very popular among the rural folk of south Odisha.

The objects around which the riddles are woven are the most common ones in our daily life. This is the case with riddles of each and every country. Therefore, we find a common set of objects almost throughout the world. They are things both living and dead which form a part of our daily life-men and women, birds and beasts, insects and birds, household articles, objects of nature, social and personal behaviour and, food and drink. There is also a class of riddles which is asked through a short story instead of through a couplet or a short sentence. Some are also based on mathematical calculations and, therefore, are known as mathematical riddles.[47]

Use of riddles in religious practices were very common in south Odisha. In order to enhance the mystic character of the incantations, they are often expressed through riddles instead of direct language. Thus, we find a very wide application of riddles in our thought and practice. But the riddles, though they originate from the same tendency, are secular in character.

But there is a class of riddles which is still used for ritual purposes in Odisha. In some tribal areas of south Odisha there is still a social custom in which riddles are asked ceremonially by a father-in-law to his newly wedded son-in-law when he comes to his father-in-law's house for the first time after marriage. The answers to the riddles are traditional. Yet the son-in-law must reply to them before he is permitted to wash his feet and take his seat in his father-in-law's house.[48]

Even today, among the *Bauri* community of south *Odisha,* there is a set of riddles which is asked before a bridegroom's party that enter the area of the village of the bride. It is only conventional and the answers to the riddles are also traditional. But, it is apparent that there was a time when the riddles were asked as a method of intelligence test of the bridegroom and the members of his party.[49]

In south Odisha there is a belief that the author of all the folk-riddles is one and the same person and he is the great Indian poet Kalidasa.Therefore, the riddles are also known in general as the riddles of Kalidasa. Sometimes, the name of Kalidasa describing him as the author is also added to each riddle itself Kalidasa symbolizes here an intelligent man. In the opinion of the rural-folk, it is only the intelligent that can ask and solve riddles.

A riddle song is designed to test the hearer's ingenuity. It has two meanings. The outer meaning is not taken into account. The inner sense only counts. The answer is shorter in one word only in comparison with the question. Strong common sense succeeds where depth of learning fails. Like the mental arithmetic of pedagogues or the un-intelligible Sanskrit *Sloka* of a *Pandit,* riddle is a weapon of the villager used to test one's cleverness. Below is some of the examples of riddles prevalent in south Odisha.

"A boy fell down from the sky. He had a turban on his head." (Palm fruit).

"It is strange fruit, soft when unripe, when ripens, it becomes hard." (Earthen Pot).

"The old bullock died on this side of the river, but the scent went to the other side"(Jack-fruit).

The princess is dead, but nobody weeps. (The setting moon) It is red-red, if you water, the plant is dead. (Fire) Many flowers bloom, nobody plucks them. (Sky)[50]

Proverbs and *Dakbachans:*

Proverbs are another form of folk literature of the rural mass. Proverbs are not only found immensely in *Odia* literature but also form a special part of all the literatures of the whole world. The word "proverb" is derived from the latin word "proverbium" which means used by the folk.[51] The scope of proverbs are very large. According to Kunjabihari Das, "Proverbs, Sayings, Similies and Maxims are just like the grand road (*Badadanda)* of Puri".[52] These are not only useful in the day to day life but also very fascinating. In the opinion of Syamasundara Rajaguru, "the proverbs have been derived from Prakriti and Sanskrit language. Proverbs throw a flood of light on the daily life of the people."[53] Proverbs are the shortest expressions of the longest experiences of life. The proverbs deal with the fundamental behaviour of people. Therefore, as long as a particular way of life continues to exist, the same set of proverbs continue to use in a particular social group.[54]

Every village has, to its credit, a number of intelligent men and women. Proverb or *Dakbachan* is their creation. It is neither philosophy, nor poetry nor any moral propaganda though its educative value is immense and profound. It was created in some particular situation in connection with a particular person. But it was so remarkable that people remembered it and used it in connection with any man in the same situation. It carried the wisdom of its creator for ages, passed through hundreds and thousands of lips, but never lost its freshness and beauty. Proverb displays sharp intelligence, broad outlook, and strong common sense, power of generalization and the intimate knowledge of life and the living world.[55]

It is not possible to say when the proverb was created or who created it. But what belonged to one man or woman became the sacred property of the whole village or district and then of all men of all times. It won great popularity, for it was the mirror of real feelings and experiences and not imagination. It is well thought and well expressed. It is the crisp and handsome expression of experiences of day to day life. Ordinary day labourer, who never thinks, accepted it as a saying of the oracle, used it to strengthen his opinion on a certain subject. It became the ornament of the speech of the man; it decorates the lips of a lady as jewels and gems enhance her beauty. She is remarkably fond of spicing her talk with all sorts of broken verses called *dhaga, dhamali* and *chhata.*

The poets and writers adopt them to make their language forceful and rooted to the soil. Sometimes great writer's wise sayings are used by the people as proverbs. Thus, the illiterate and the intelligential carry on the exchange of each other's culture.[56]

A set of wonderful proverbs revolve round the particular seasons or periods in relations to the stars. They also reveal the duration of the particular processes of agriculture. The proverbs indicate when paddy has to be planted, transplanted, reaped and stored. They show how *banana* or *papaya* plants will have to be put in and what the depth of the pits and their distances will be. In this way the proverbs give the average unlettered agriculturist a kind of knowledge which helps him engage in successful agriculture.[57]

Some proverbs are so humorous that they make a man burst into a loud laughter. Others are so satirical and sarcastic that they almost break his heart, insult him, anger him and provoke him to a quarrel. Man is not God. He has his limitations. He is weak, narrow-minded, and envious and violent. One should not attack him at his vital with this ready weapon and wound him mortally.

He must exercise thorough control over his tongue and use them in proper place.[58]

A nation's real character is known through its proverbs. Its struggle for existence, its humour and mockery, its taste for beauty, its art and learning, its peculiarities may, to a great extent, be known from proverbs. It is the very foundation of any great language. When it is neglected, the foundation is shaken to its root. But, when literature becomes rich and prosperous and the national outlook becomes progressive, the use of proverbs diminishes. There is a saying in *Odia*, "wise men make proverbs and fools use them."[59]

In the rural areas of Odisha there is still a set of proverbs related to agricultural work. They are commonly known as *Khana's Vachan* or the sayings of *Khana*, a legendary female character having a reputation for her astrological prognostication.

There is also another set of proverbs which is related to weather forecast and elementary astronomy. They are known as *Dak's Vachan* or saying of *Dak*, a legendary male character. But by *Dak* is meant a wise man in Tibetan. Therefore, the saying of *Dak* probably mean sayings of a wise man.[60]

As already stated, the proverbs are the expressions of practical experiences of life. But, it has its limitations. In south Odisha it concerns mainly the life of women in general and the behaviour of the daughter-in-law in particular. Sometimes, it is a criticism of the behaviour of the daughter-in-law by the mother-in-law, while occasionally it is also the other way round. The proverbs are generally composed and applied in life by the womenfolk only. Women's dialect has a special feature in Odisha as elsewhere. In the proverbs women's behaviour is described in women's dialect. Such proverbs are always critical of other's character and therefore are expressed in most cases metaphorically or ironically.[61]

Besides the characters of the daughter-in-law and the mother-in-law, other members of a family are also covered by these proverbs. But the attitudes towards them are different. For example, the mother is accorded the highest position in the family circle.

The world of *Odia* proverbs is generally limited to the domestic life of its people. Besides women members of the family, almost all the household articles come within its scope. Here is one example on the husking machine called *Dhenki* in south Odisha.

"Dhenki Swargaku Gale Madhya Dhana Kutiba".Which means-

"Husking machine husks paddy
Even when it goes to heaven"

Moreover, the unorthodox behavior of Brahmins of the modern age has also been sharply criticized in *Odia* proverbs. Their greediness, illiteracy, and poverty have also come under severe criticism. Little or no faith is expressed in medicines and doctors, especially the traditional physicians known as *Kavirajas*. Practical experience of the common man is reflected in these proverbs.

There have been a few very good collections and compilations of proverbs in *Odia*. During the last century, European missionaries started collecting them for their own benefit i.e. to learn the native language. In the present century some *Odia* scholars like Kunja Bihari Dash and Natabar Samantaray came forward and have already published some valuable collections with detailed commentaries. About three thousand *Odia* proverbs have so far been collected and published.[62] These proverbs are classified in the following manner according to their subject matter.

Dak Bachan:

The *Dak bachans* which deal with such subjects like agriculture, weather and medicine are as follows.

The rising sun smilingly disappears in the cloud,
Northern clouds pass over to the south.
Blue flies brood over the fresh cow dung,
Dak bachan says, O son, it must rain.

When a star appears in the orbit of the moon it rains incessantly.

Chhata Regarding Co-Wife:

Is my luck so bad?
That I had to deal with a nine-lipped co-wife.
If this be given to the dark-skinned first wife my beautiful second wife will get angry.
Given to the fair-coloured, the lady of black complexion will be provoked.
Let this be with me.
When the fair lady will prepare my bed for sleep.
I shall present it to her.
All the four quarters be scented.

Regarding Worthlessness and Vileness of Daughter-in-Law

Mark your naughty daughter,
She breaks scores of pots and pitchers.
The daughter-in-law is of low family,
She came only yesterday, but marks her haughtiness
File on you, don't you get a rope of one cubit to hand yourself?
That widow mother had such a worthless daughter!
Why does she not drown herself in a pit?
All members of the family have been reduced.
But the daughter-in-law who cooks food has become very fat.
You brought one torn box of cane containing one seer of turmeric,
Conch sounded and bowing down in shame,
You entered the house
Will my mother-in-law die?
Shall I be the queen of the household?
Will chance do that?[63]

Regarding Conjugal Life

The bear came down the peak of the mountain to eat the root of grass (meaningless)
Did I marry this husband (should be devoured by a ghost) only to be beaten with fists?
All right, if you beat me, you yourself go and cook.
Thank god, your moustache is burnt while blowing the hearth.
That is how you are paid back in your own coin.
A hold under the belly of the thrashing horse (meaningless)

My hand was tied to that of this golden flowered husband (a miser)
He controls rice, even water.

Regarding worthless Husband:

Husband's impotence makes the wife sleep in the jungle.
Tankei Sahoo, the effeminate is ever elbowed by his wife.
Rice without any curry is even inadequate for my meal.
Why have I married this worthless husband?
He cannot fight with a soldier,
Speaks highly of his valour before his wife.

Sarcastic Notes:

You boast so much of nothing.
No ring in the finger of you foot.
And you strike the grind so often.
Had you really a ring, you would have certainly broken it.
He goes to the Jatra putting on borrowed clothes.
If you ask him the price, he will repeatedly nod his head.
Where great men have miserably failed, brainless idiots have come.
Fool, why do you make a show your prestige?
Your father was selling dry fish and your mother dry leaves for fuel.
He cannot oil his own machine but gives counsels to others.
He fasts for show but constantly thinks of food.
His father-is a labourer.
But o! The son, displays golden bangles.
The patient is thirsting for cool water.
The bad physician prescribed cold rice gruel!
A ripe plantain is not liked by a pig.
Nor dies a blind man appreciate a jewelled ring.
A golden cage never pleases an owl who bitterly weeps for its nest in the hollowed tree trunk.
Fie, Fie on you-a rotten green coconut.
You were bringing swept away in the flood current.
I sent you my helping hands and saved you.
When rooted to the soil, you fling a reply at me.
Shameless, to wash your feet.
You are drawing water from the dry well.
I tried to hold wind in my palm
Can I retain it? No

Try as much as you like, but no use.
The persons having no blood relation cannot be yours.
The unchaste lady enjoys the softest bed on the sofa.
The queen of the house is treated as a maid servant.
Milk remains unsold after strenuous drive in the street.
While liquor is sold without any advertisement.
Will the second wife be able to know the heart of her husband?
Will the leaf of yam or catchu be a betel leaf?
Grandson dies while the grand-father lives,
It presumes destruction of the family.
Who is the owner of this black cow?
Who blinds her there?
Why does this fool weep for it?
She has eaten up the god and the worshipper.
She may devour the very seat of God.
But she pretends to know nothing.
The broken drum is sounded.
The singer is a mute,
A prostitute, blind of one eye, is dancing
The whimsical ruler with worthless ministers is doing whatever he likes.
He is a rich and famous man outside but a great miser at home.
I shall do your job and mine
Your words-a garland of flowers.
But when crisis comes I must do mine and forget yours.
As a line drawn on the surface of water is not marked.
This lady is husbandless.
But look at her fashion.
They have made a secret pact of mutual sympathy and co-operation at home, but make a show of quarrel outside.
Never was this stranger seen in danger or difficulty. But to-day he poses himself to be the most trustworthy.
The shameless went to commit suicide.
And three friends accompanied him to guard![64]

Regarding Cultivation:

Plant early for luxuriant growth
If you delay, paddy field will be a pasture land.
You yourself are to cultivate your lands.

And your son can only be placed in charge of trade.
If you cultivate, hope for a full product,
If you depend on others, half of it is wasted.
The farmer supports the world.
Family can be supported if you take a few acres for cultivation.
If you cultivate many acres, you will invite destruction.
Do the work yourself and engage others
Or you will weep in the paddy field.[65]

Maxims:

House at one end of the village is for thieves.
Ultimately cultivation can serve no other purpose but the payment of tax.
Taking curd at night invites fever.
Marriage in old age is meant to be enjoyed by others.
A wicked son or a widowed daughter burns the house without fire.
Take a bitter thing if it suits your taste or not.
Read Bhagbat gita, if you follow it or not.
Too much affection makes the son indolent.
Too much affection makes the daughter characterless.
Do not keep a bad company.
It is fraught with dangers.
A son-in-law in the father-in-law's house is a dog.
A brother in the sister's house is another dog.
One, whose wife is quarrelsome, whose bullock is very lazy, natural death is no calamity to him, because he dies a death every day:
Let a man be ruined.
But his self-respect must be retained at any cost.
Because once lost, it can never be revived.[66]

Miscellaneous:

A thief dislikes the moonlit night.
A son is an eye-sore to the prostitute,
Cows and goats are troublesome to a gardener.
A daughter means a burden to the poor man.
When an unfortunate man approaches,
God Siva flies away.
Do not believe a woman, a goldsmith.

Do not believe an unchaste lady.
Do not believe a pick-pocket.
Do not believe a cut-throat.
Do not believe a weaver.
He gets his dues but steals thread.
No regard is paid to a son-in-law after the death of the daughter.
What can a mother do when her breast gets dry?
The boat becomes helpless when flood subsides.
Steal, but be caught by a noble man.
A lightening is worth a lac where there is a drought.
Does the pan know the taste of curry?
Does the belly know the pain of the back?
Damn the slavery of service, troublesome at every step.
Rather be satisfied with cold rice and '*sag*' at home.
Scorching sun of the month of *Bhadrab*,
A wicked servant, a discarded prostitute,
A widow of the up-rooted family.
Pride of these four is intolerable.
Sir, beat the first wife, no harm.
To the second wife, oh, my lord!
You have no religious urge in the mind
What is the use of this external worship?
As the country, so is the fashion.
As the teacher, so is the pupil.
Drum receives hard beatings.
But the drums-man takes money.
If you want pure milk, keep a cow.
If you wish to fight, you must have a brother to help you.
What could not be done in childhood, can never be done in old age.
If you do not do your own work, nobody, not even your father will do it for you.
There is no answer to the great men, no staircase to the sky.
If a woman has not virtue, what is the use of her beauty?
The son of a hero is a hero.
The labourer daily works for his belly, if he is detained one day by accident, he starves.
Try for me as much as you can, I cannot be anything but a half

burnt piece of wood. (Black will take no other hue).

If you paint a piece of iron again and again, it will serve you not purpose, it can never be turned into a piece of gold.

Fortune is a piece of rope,
Man is a cow tied tightly to it;
He follows to whatever direction he is drawn by the fortune.

Miscllaneous Proverbs, Sayings and Similies

1) Like the rest-post bellowing while the cow and calf are silent.
2) The family name is musk, but the family smells filthy.
3) The dog but limps wherever you might strike it.
4) While the bull pulls towards the sun, the buffalo pulls into the shade.
5) Like hiding behind a horse, fearing that the bull might kick.
6) Like dogs barking at an elephant.
7) Dead or alive, the elephant has a high value.
8) An elephant must come to lift up an elephant fallen.
9) The frog gets angry if the serpent is permitted to bite, and the serpent gets angry if it is asked not to.
10) If the times are bad, even a stick springs to life and bites like a serpent.
11) A trip to Kasi does not turn a dog into a cow.
12) If you seat a dog even on a throne, it rushes out if a piece of bone is thrown at it.
13) A dip in the Ganges does not change a crow into a swan.
14) If you feed a dog to make it grow to the size of a horse, you have to do the barking yourself.
15) Even if the horse were blind, it does not eat any the less.
16) The sheep trusts the butcher and not the *sanyasi.*
17) Everyone would grow heroic if it is heroism to beat a dead serpent.
18) Do stones wear out if ants crawl on them?
(19) The wolf offered to look after the sheep for no payment.

From the above discussion it can be concluded that the folk-tales are quite different from the modern short stories. The names of authors are mentioned in the short stories. But the Folk-tales has no authors. It is the public wealth of a particular region. The hero of the folk-tale is not a mythological or historical personality. He is an unknown and unnoticed person or a prince. Folk-tales do not belong to any particular sect or religion. These are identified only in the name of nation and language such as Odia, Telugu, Gujarati, Tamil, Japanese or Chinese. They are an important part of literature. Folk-tales are as entertaining as they are instructive.

Similarly, the proverbs, idioms, sayings, similies and maxims constitute a very interesting and fascinating chapter in the history of the folk or oral literature. Truly speaking, this is the social *Veda* of *Odia* literature which not only gives us much information about the historical facts, social and economic condition of the *Odia* people during the period under study but also provides entertainment and checks corruption in criticizing the corrupt people.

References

1. H.Yagnik, *Folklore of Gujarat*, New Delhi, 2002, p. 7.
2. K.M.Panikkar, *Folklore of Kerala*, New Delhi, 1991, p. 98.
3. A.Bhattacharya, *Folklore of Bengal*, New Delhi, 1978, p. 109.
4. *Ibid.*
5. *Ibid.*
6. H.Yagnik, *op.cit.*,p. 103.
7. K.B.Dash, *Folklore of Odisha,* Bhubaneswar, 1991, p.7.
8. K.B.Dash, & L.K.Mahapatra, *Folklore of Odisha,* New Delhi, 1979, pp.49-50.
9. *Ibid.* p.9.
10. K.B.Dash, & L.K.Mahapatra, *op.cit.*,pp.50-51.
11. *Ibid.* p.51.
12. K.B.Dash, p.11.
13. K.B.Dash, & L.K.Mahapatra, *op.cit.*,pp. 51-52.
14. K.B.Dash, p.12.
15. K.B.Dash, p.128.
16. K.B.Dash & L.K.Mahapatra, *op.cit.*,p.46.
17. K.B.Dash, *op.cit.*,pp.145-46.
18. K.B.Dash, *op.cit.*,p.124.
19. N.Datta, *Folk-tales of Odisha,* Calcutta, 1923, p.
20. P.K.Misira, *Odia Jatira Itihasa O Sanskruti*, vol.II, Cuttack, 2008, p.100.

21. Sahu, B.,
22. S.N.Dash, *Jagannath Mandira O Jagannath Tatwa*, Cuttack, 1966, p.151.
23. *Ibid.*
24. K.B.Dash, p.13.
25. M.Mansinha, A History of *Odia* Literature, New Delhi, 2005, pp.35-36.
26. K.B.Dash, *op.cit.*, pp.147-48.
27. *Ibid.*
27(a).P.Mukharji, *History of Jagannath Temple in the 19th Century*, Calcutta, 1977, p.
28. Bhagabana, Sahu, , *Cultural History of Odisha,* New Delhi, 1997, pp.151-52.
29. K.B.Dash, & L.K.Mahapatra, *op.cit.*,p.163.
30. M.Mansingh, *The Saga of the Land of Lord Jagannath*, Cuttack, pp.105-106.
31. K.B.Dash, *Folklore of Odisha,* pp.100-101.
32. P.K.Mishra, *Odia Jatira Itisash O Sanskruti*, vol.II, Cuttack, 2008, pp.183-84.
33. K.B.Dash, *Folklore of Odisha,* pp.206-21.
34. *Ibid.*
35. Ibid, p.209.
36. U.N.Dattagupta, *Folk-tales of Odisha,* Calcutta, 1923, pp.10-12.
37. J.G.Frazer, *The Golden Baugh*,London, 1963, p.31.
38. John, Beams, *Folktales of Odisha,* p.
39. K.B.Dash, *op.cit.*,p.230.
40. *Ibid*, p.205.
41. K.C.Pradhan, *Odia Loka Sahitya O Loka Sanskruti*, Cuttack, 1995, p.138.
42. K.B.Dash, *Lokagalpa Sanchayan, Odissa Sahitya Akademi*, Bhubaneswar, 977, p.79.
43. Odissa Cultural Forum, *Odisara Lokasanskruti*, Cuttack, 1978, P94.
44. A.Bhattacharya, *Folklore of Bengal*, New Delhi, 1978, p.
45. P.C.Roy Choudhury, Folklore of Bihar, New Delhi, 1976, p.81.
46. A.Bhattacharya, *op.cit.*,p.126.

47. *Ibid*, pp.126-27.
48. *Ibid.*
49. Field Study & Personal Observation by the Author.
50. K.B.Dash, & L.K.Mahapatra, p.148.
51. K.C.Pradhan, *op.cit.*,p.252.
52. K.B.Dash, *Lokabani Sanchayana (Odia Dhaga-dhamali-Eka Adhyana)*, p.1.
53. S.S.Rajguru, *Prabandhavali (Odia)* Odisha Sahitya Akademi, Bhubaneswar, p.5.
54. A.Bhattacharya, *op.cit.*,p.128.
55. K.B.Dash, p.31.
56. Gopal Chandra, Praharaja, *Utkala Kahani (Odia)*, vol.I, Cuttack, 1906, p.
57. P.C. Roy Choudhury, *Folklore of Bihar*, p.88.
58. K.B.Dash, p.52.
59. Nilamani, Bidyaratna, *Proverbs and Slokas*, Cuttack, 1903, p.17.
60. A.Bhattacharya, p.128.
61. *Ibid.*
62. Natabara, Samantara, *Odia Palli Sahitya (Odia)*, Cuttack, 1968, p.83.
63. K.B.Dash, pp.33-34.
64. Aparna, Panda, *Dhagamalika Sangraha O Tatwabodhini*, Paralakhemundi, 1923, p.22.
65. K.C.Pradhan, p.269.
66. Harimohan , Panda, *Janabachan (Odia)*, New Delhi, 2008, p.34.

3

Folk Songs

South Odisha has been the cradle of many folk dance and songs. It is said that, "In Odisha the trees and creepers sing." This is true to a great extent.[1] The daily life of the average *Odia* from birth to death finds an expression in the folk songs. The people of this region in general are emotional in nature and creative in spirit. They sing a variety of folk songs which can captivate the minds of all the art loving people of the world.[2] This chapter gives a vivid account of the nature, significance, values and impact of the folk songs of south Odisha.

Folk song is the traditional heritage of those people who have an unsophisticated way of life in a particular society and who usually give a free expression of their sentiments through their songs. It is through folk songs and folk music that we come to know the inner life, the culture, the social and an environmental set up of a community, whether living in far off jungles of in highly industrialized towns.[3]

The traditional songs and music born of the village civilization is known as folk songs and music; and the songs born of the city civilization is known as classical music or *Marga Sangita* which is again divided into the *Hindustani* and *Karnatic.* The folk song is known as *Desi Sangit* which expresses ideas of various aspects of life. Folk composition differ from sophisticated literature in many respects. They do not possess any poetic ambition for earning fame or acquiring wealth and immortality. They sing for the joy of singing, recite for the delight of recitation. The folk songs are preserved by generation of folk singers or reciters for the delight they take in singing and reciting, through love of literature.[4]

South Odisha mostly comprise of villages. Villagers lead busy lives. They do not compose to sing in their leisure hours. They sing when they plough fields, harvest crops, row boats and drive carts. They sing to break the monotony of hard work or of a long journey on foot.[5]

Folk song is a spontaneous overflow of the people that live in a more or less primitive condition outside the sphere of sophisticated influences. The term "Folksong" implies that there is an element of spontaneity as well as simplicity in it. It springs from the common man's natural desire to give spontaneous expression to his feeling and emotions in so far as these can be expressed through musical forms. It would therefore, be improper to expect a high degree of polish or finesse either in the composition or in the melodious quality of such songs.[6] It is the earliest poetry of any people, unpremeditated and unwritten, fresh and simple, genuine and natural. It is popular because it alludes to incidents connected with people's lives. It carries the voice and vocabulary of the masses.[7]

All items of folklore bear the region's stamp and therefore, the folk music is always influenced by the geographical surroundings and natural environment of a given region. The folklore and folk songs of south Odisha too possess this regional, geographical and environmental stamp.[8]

In the rural society, the boys herd buffaloes, sits on the back of a buffalo and sings on a high pitch. The cartman sings while driving a cart, the beggar sings while begging. The maidens sing on the swing and the children do so while playing. There are songs to tease someone. Women sing songs while spinning, husking corn, or grinding wheat and ragi. Lullabies are of course there. Humorous, teasing and mocking songs, ballads, romantic and lyrical songs are sometimes sung for mere entertainment. Sometimes, they play an important part in the turning point of life, viz. birth, marriage, when the daughter leaves her father's house for the mother-in-law's house or death. Songs are sung to teach the child to walk, to dance, to drink milk, to eat food, to play. To learn counting to be industrious and good-natured a child receives home education through folk songs which are unforgettable and everlasting. The songful atmosphere at home and in the village helps him, even indirectly, to become a musician, an artist, or a litterateur.[9]

The spirit of the singing is the source of folk poetry and music is its very soul. The intensity of emotion which the oral repetition imparts to the folk song is the heart-beat. A folk poem unsung is obliterated or, if collected becomes a dead museum material. A folk song is inherited and perpetuated by oral tradition from one generation to another.

The singer knows nothing about the poet or how the song changes in its course through history or how it branches out into different tunes and melodies. He simply listens to it from his forefathers and learns to love it and sings it usually for his own entertainment.[10]

Regarding the folk songs, Grim has said that, "the folk-song composes itself". Its music comes straight from the heart of the people and its idioms reveal their daily habits of speech. Furthermore, the individual author is so unimportant that it usually loses sight of the author's importance altogether.

Of course, the poet does not aspire after any reputation and does not care to put his name at the end of the poem like the ancient professional poets to go through ages. His main concern is to sing, to sing about his love and separation, his hopes and ambitions, his joys and sufferings. A folk-song is orally transmitted from person to person, from generation to generation, as inherited property. It is like a Vedic hymn orally transmitted from age to age. This pleasant self-educating process goes on for centuries. In such a process it is not possible to preserve the antiquity of a song intact because it is changed in course of time according to the dialectal changes. This is proved by the different versions of the same song.[11]

The editor of "*The Express New York*" writes in stating the reason of the creation of folk-songs: "A life of isolation without books or newspapers, telephone or radio, breeds songs and ballads. The gamut of human experience has been portrayed through this unrecorded literature of the people. These people had no literary conventions to uphold. But they were lonely, sad or glad and they sought diversions."[12]

Life in the village is, indeed, dull and dry in the modern sense, but to the villagers it is not so. They have a busy life; they plough fields, harvest crops, water plants, drive carts, row boats and sing on ceremonial occasions, in religious festivals and sing when they feel like singing. It is just a natural process (rather than a diversion) although they sometimes resort to singing to break the tedium of a long journey and drudgery of hard work.[13]

The village people are less imaginative and more realistic in their temperament. They struggle against hard realities for their very existence and have little leisure to exercise their imaginations. Their composition keeps direct contact with their life and is out with any imagination, ornamentation and ostentation. Civilizations come and go. One government is succeeded by another. But life in the village goes on undisturbed without being influenced by the progressive movement of the city life. That is why a true unadulterated prototype of typical national life is to be sought in the village and not in the town which constantly tries to transform itself to the model of administration.[14]

The folk songs of south Odisha are broadly divided into four classes, viz.

(a) those sung by women exclusively,
(b) those sung by men exclusively,
(c) those sung by men and women jointly,
(d) and those sung by boys and girls.

The first category may again be divided into-songs of husking, tattoo songs, songs of tears, play songs (*puchi geeta*), swing songs and lullabies. They charm as with their naturalness and deep poetic emotion. The second category includes-ploughman's songs, boatman's songs, cartman's songs, herdsman's songs, snake charmer's songs, songs of *Yogi* (*Chakuliya Panda,Natha yogi* etc.), battle songs (*Ranapa gita*). The third category covers- *Baunsarani* songs, love songs. The last category includes children's songs, love songs, etc.[15] But Brundaban Chandra Acharya classified the folk songs into three classes such as Social, Educational, and Religious.[16] Still there are few who classified them into Vocal and Instrumental. In Odisha as well as in some other parts of the country folk musics are both vocal and instrumental. Work songs, game songs, grind songs, swing songs, spinning songs, teasing songs, songs of fasts and festivals are vocal. But the following are the instrumental. Beggars or *Yogis* who sing mostly ballads sometimes come in twos. When one sings a line, his companion repeats it. A *dhuduki,* flute, *lyre, dungdunga, khanjani, kendara* etc. accompany their singing. The begging monk may play on lire or *ektara,* the snake charmers play on *nageswara.*

Basing on the subject matter the folk songs of south Odisha may be divided into the following categories:

(a) Work songs,
(b) Pastoral songs,
(c) Swing songs,
(d) Love songs,
(e) Ballad or Narrative songs,
(f) Songs of Tears,
(g) Children's songs,
(h) Juvenile songs.[17]

(A) Work-Songs

The songs which are sung in doing some kind of work or labour are known as work songs. These songs are sung while performing some kind of manual work. Sometimes one set of songs is earmarked for a particular piece of work only and it is never sung for any other type of manual work. In south Odisha there are songs for husking paddy with the help of *Dhenki.* Husking of paddy by rural women in the traditional way is continued for the whole night. Therefore, in order to keep themselves awake, the women sing long narrative songs. Traditional husking machines are being rapidly replaced by rice mills and as a result husking songs are seldom heard in the rural areas now-a-days.

There are weaving songs or songs sung by weavers during their weaving of cloth on the handlooms in the traditional manner. The women sing songs while planting paddy plants. Monotony of work and dullness of its character are overcome by such songs.[18]

(i) The Songs of the Snake-Charmers:

Odisha a land of high hills and dense forests, is infested with gigantic snakes like *Ahiraj* (King of snakes), pythons, *Sankhachuda,* and poisonous snakes like *Cobra, Tampa, Chiti,* and *Boda.* After the harvesting season is over, snake charmers (*sapua kela*) of this region loaded with two tightly closed baskets tied with ropes, move from village to village to show their game. They keep long hair, a moustache and put on silver bangles and golden earrings. Their song is called *Padmatola* (plucking lotuses). It deals with Krishna's plucking of golden lotuses from the lake *kalindi. Kaliya* a seven- hooded giant snake was the sole monarch of that lake. It made the water so poisonous that any animal drinking it, perished. *Kansa* ordered Nanda to supply him immediately with a hundred load of golden lotuses only found blooming in that poisonous water of the lake. His purpose was to kill Krishna, his inveterate enemy. Krishna boldly enters the water, plucked flowers and created a great disturbance in the kingdom of *Kaliya.* Messengers sent by the king, were killed one by one. At last the king of snakes angrily stung Krishna. Krishna fell senseless in the water. Baladeb brought Krishna to dry land and sprinkled nectar brought by Garuda from heaven. Krishna now revived, captured the king of snakes and danced on his seven hoods mercilessly till he got fully exhausted and submitted to him.[19]

The snake-charmer, a devotee of Lord Krishna captures snakes in his name. As soon as he sings *Padmatola*, enchanted by the music, the cobra comes out of the hole, dances moving its broad hood with the sandal mark of Krishna. The charmer captures it with the help of a stick and breaks its poisonous tooth. If it stings him by accident, his friends applies *Jalamahura* (an antidote to poison) to his wound and administers to him a little antipoisonous medicine called *Gada*. The snake charmer gets up fully cured within fifteen minutes.

The other sight of interest in the play is *Govinda musa* (a trained rat named Govinda). The rat plays to the tune of the charmer's songs. It acts almost a drama of the *Odia* family life. It acts the part of a daughter-in-law, pretends to draw the hanging rope with the little hands quickly as if drawing water, being afraid of mother-in-law, displays the tragic effects in its tearful eyes when it pretends to break the pitcher by accident. Next it searches for the earrings lost in haste. It sometimes draws water a little and seems to watch *Dedhasura* (husband's elder brother) a little. For the custom is that she should conceal herself at his sight. Then, it places a small stick on its shoulders and seems to carry a heavy load to a distance place. It dances like an actress, carries on exercises like a hero and begs like a beggar. The charmer plays on *Nageswara*- a folk musical instrument, sings songs and talks interestingly throughout the show.[20]

(ii) Songs of the *Chitakuta Keluni*:

Chitakuta Keluni is a female artist of the lower class who moves from door to door, singing charming love songs to attract young women – virgins or brides. She marks the body of the village ladies with beautiful artistic designs by puncturing and rubbing in pigment. This is done with the help of a needle, which is very painful. The *Keluni* charms the maidens with sweet love songs and thus makes them forget their terrible pain. She paints blossoming mango trees with cuckoo cooing on the arms, a garland of *Bakul* flowers on the breast, five flower arrows of cupid on the forehead, a bower of creepers with the design of running deer on the thigh. She sings "Oh diamond among ladies, your body will be decorated with flowery bowers, flying birds and butterflies, shining moons and stars. After being painted with attractive designs, go and bow down to your dear husband. He should first appreciate the art which enhances the beauty of young adies and then pay me the cost of painting afterwards."[21]

Tattooing is now going out of fashion as the sophisticated ladies considers it as a symbol of unrefined taste.

Sometimes male devotees paint their bodies with figures of Radha and Krishna, Rama and Sita, quotations of prayer songs and names of gods and goddesses believing that these would please them and keep free of sins.[22]

(iii) Cartman's Songs:

Songs of cartmen are very enjoyable and fascinating. When there were no bus, no moter car, the carts known as *sagada* was the most popular means of transport and communication. This was dragged by means of two pack bullocks drived by a cartman. He resort to singing to break the tedium of a long journey and to get rid of the monotony of life. Sometimes, he sing sweet songs and sometimes melancholy event is described by his song very pathetically.[23]

(iv) Ploughman's Songs:

The ploughmen constitute the major portion of the mass who sell their labour for two square meals a day. They work hard from dawn to dust. All the doors of culture are closed to them. They have no learning, no leisure; Rajasekhara's conception of a poetic life is all absent there.[24] No artificial waterfall decorated with rainbows, no solitary house in the beautiful garden on the bank of a lake in which swans swim or lotuses bloom. A cultivator's life is one of hard toil, stern realities and no dreams. His songs form a part of his daily work. They are not the compositions of idle hours. Work and song-song and work; one enthuses the other and are interlinked in a tie of friendship. Their work sings and their songs work. They move hand to hand. So there is no time to see whether the lines rhyme properly or not, whether he has been able to create a new meter or not, or the idea expressed is original or borrowed. Mostly the songs are very short-cut, three or four lines each, all composed in one or two meters. The line can be extended to the length of a full breath; that does not hamper in tuning.[25]

The cultivator respectfully avoids the songs of great poets, for; they neglected him and his village for ages. He sings his own songs, becomes the hero of his own poetry. He is the actor of his own life's drama. In practical feelings he is not poor like a poet. His own life is his greatest inspiration. Why should he fly to the land of dreams or imaginations in presence of rich experiences of life and nature.

> "The cultivator puts on a hat of bamboo on the head,
> goes on leveling the ground in the month of Ashar;
> scorching sun or copious rainfall never disturbs him".

The bullocks are considered to be the members of his family. They take poor food but work very hard for him. He has all sympathy for them. He believes that fate is responsible for all sufferings. That only makes the poor bullocks work so hard.

> "Move on my dear bullocks, you will eat green grass
> and drink cold water with husk. Do not delay my
> good brothers. This suffering is due to your ill luck."

The ploughman goes to cultivate his land long before sunrise, has no time to take his breakfast. When he feels very hungry he sings.

> "Kamala, your brother is dying of hunger. How to
> you stay at home, without any anxiety?"

Sometimes hunger makes him lose all his sense of propriety. He picks up a quarrel with his wife and beats her. When his hunger is appeased, he realises his folly and repents of his violence. The cultivator poet sings of such unhappy incidents after the names of a god and a goddess.[26]

They never waste their valuable hours in idle sitting in dark temples, eating, sleeping, making merriment and lending their ears to idle prayers. Ploughman's God and Goddesses are hard working and painstaking beings. They plough and level the ground, plant and weed out the fields like the common people for their livelihood. They live in cottages, take poor food and sleep on the ground without any bed.

> "Rama and Lakshmana are two brothers. One is
> ploughing and the other is levelling the ground.
> Both of them are scattering rice plants in the field,
> Sita is planting".[27]

The ploughman's songs lack in variety and grandeur in expression. But, some of them are really beautiful not from the outward structure but for the inner value. The deep pathos, the realistic tone, the naturalness expressed within the briefest possible lines are really marvelous.

(B) Songs of Tears:

The songs of tears or the *Kandana Geeta* are most pathetic and heart touching. The daughter weeps when after marriage she has to leave her affectionate parents. This weeping is partly due to parting from her parents, friends and neighbours and leaving the congenial atmosphere of home life, and partly due to fear to traditional oppression by the mother-in-law.[28] This separation from near and dear ones is really pathetic. With little worldly experience she does not know how to cope with the new situation. She weeps helplessly. Similarly, the mother's weep at the sad demise of his young son is really sorrowful.[29]

(C) Songs of *Yogi*:

A *yogi* in the village means a beggar. He has no relation with *yoga* or meditation. What he understands very well, is his sacred profession, begging. He paints his body with various designs of sandal paste, hangs a bag in the left shoulder, and holds a hollowed gourd in his left hand, a *Khanjani* or *Kendara* in his right hand or a crooked staff with eyes and ears marked. He puts a garland of beads of the wood of the basil plant showing that he is a devotee and deserves all sympathy. He arouses pity in the hearts of the religious-minded woman of the village with his pathetic songs dealing with great puranic sacrifice and charity.[30]

In the words of Mayadhara Mansingha "For centuries these *Nathas* or *Natha-Yogis*, as they are generally called in Odisha, have been the unofficial moral preceptors of rural Odisha. They generally move about from village to village and beg alms, singing ballads and *bhajanas* rich with moral and spiritual lore, to the tune of the one-stringed *Kendra*, their own simple musical instrument. The visit of a *Natha-Yogi* to a village with his quaint music and ancient ballads is an unforgettable event and leaves a deep nostalgic impression in the psychology of all *Odia* adults who find themselves wrenched away from the rural environs of their childhood days".[31]

The *Yogis* are also known as *Chakulia Panda* who appears in the village only on days of fasts and festivals like the new moon, full moon, *Ekadashi* days. The Panda does not beg door to door like other beggars but sings along the streets. He is taken to be a very sacred person and is given alms without his asking. He carries song, "Give and persuade others to give; whatever you give will be returned to you in much larger quantity."[32]

The contents of some of the songs of these *yogis* are, how the tiger's heart was melted with the sight of *Baula* cow and his calf; Karna sacrificed his own son Bishikesana to please his distinguished guest; Harishchandra gave away all his wealth, power and everything else to Vishwamitra; Sibi sacrificed flesh from his body to save the life of a dove from the attack of a hungry hawk who was Indra in disguise; and Govinda Chandra, a king of Bengal became a monk. The beggars have one utilitarian value. They attract the minds of the worldly people towards *Dharma* and make the silenced atmosphere of the village resound with music.

Though this religious sect (*Nath Yogi and Chakulia panda*) is gradually dying out, yet even today, there is hardly any village in south Odisha where one does not come across at least a single beggar, begging with a *kendara* and his song.

(D) Prayer songs

Prayer songs occupy a considerable space in higher as well as popular literature. The village devotees sing them to propitiate hundreds of gods and goddesses whose favour they seek for all their welfare. Their prayer is nothing but earnest request to fulfill their desires. Some of them are very similar to Vedic hymns in tone. In the *Rig Veda* the *Rishis* pray to *Indra.*

> "May Indra be pleased to grant us cows, horses and boundless imperishable wealth?
> May Indra be pleased to grant us wealth, rice, heroism and intellect"?

The Odia village lady prays to the Goddess of wealth;

> "O Lakshmi, be pleased to give me golden bangles for arms,
> Selected cows to adorn the cowshed.
> Ganga-Jamuna store houses for corn,
> children like the songs of Nanda,
> May my husband be hale and sound,
> May I not beg but give clothes-
> To the wretched all the year round".[33]

(E) Songs of Love:

Love is the most prominent sentiment that inspires young men and women to sing. The aborigines like *Kandh*, Sabara, Bhunya, Paraja, Gabada, Santal, Bonda, Koya and Aryans in the respective localities under the spell of their influence, assemble in some particular place and enjoy the spring festival, dancing and singing songs of love. They shake off all their sorrows and sufferings of the past year and feel inspired to begin life anew. In these days, people bloom like flowers and talk like inspired poets. Desire for marriage, sorrow of separation and satires are expressed in these songs. *Dalkhai, Rasarkeli, Baga-baguli,* and *Sajani* songs dealing with love are very popular in south Odisha .[34]

(F) Swing Songs:

The *raja parva* is one of the most popular festival of Odisha. In this festival the unmarried girls play *puchi* and *doli* with charming songs which are echoed and re-echoed in the entire rural environment of Odisha. The swing decorated with garlands of flowers, is tied to the branch of a Banyan or Mango tree. The virgins of the village gather there on some festive occasion like *Dola, Raja* or the full moon day of *Aswin.* One of them is selected as *Dolirani,* queen of the swing. When the queen takes her seat on the cushion of the swing, the virgins move her forward and backward with a chorus of charming songs. They are full of pleasant humor, and breathe jolly spirits of girlhood days. They refer to glorious future, happy, love and marriage with suitable husbands.[35]

(G) Pastoral Songs:

Cowherd and shepherd boys who move in fields, forests, hills and dales with their flocks fill their dry hours with beautiful songs accompanied with flutes. They come back home in twilight and enjoy sound sleep, rest and peace. But those with herds of buffaloes or pigs spend their long nights in open space under palm leaf umbrella sing pathetic songs. In rainy season they sleep on scanty bed on the damp ground surrounded by buffaloes in nauseating smell of dung, biting of wild mosquitoes, cold wind and heavy showers do not allow them to enjoy sound sleep and rest. These victims of nature's wrath spend their sleepless nights playing on their pet musical instrument called *Dhuduka* and go on singing their lip compositions. The songs and the melodious and melancholy sounds of *Dhuduka* along with murmuring of wind and rainfall fill the heart of villagers at the dead of night with strange feelings. The songs refer to their hard life under the palm-leaf umbrella, their dry days and monotonous movements with the herd with no ray of hope or sign of happiness.[36]

Puranic Influences on Folk Songs:

South Odisha is famous for its puranic traditions. The recitation of *Puranas* is a regular feature in almost all the villages of south Odisha. *Puranas* specially *Ramayana* of Balaram Dasa, *Mahabharata* of Sarala Dasa, Krishna Sinha's *Mahabharata,* and *Odia Bhagabat* of Jagannath Dasa exert great influence on the mass minds of Odisha. The old cultivators after hard toil in the field gather in the evening at the door of *Bhagabat Tungi* to hear *Puranas* from the *Puranas* Panda. These *Puranas* to them are the store-house of all knowledge, their law books, ethics and literature. They control their conscience and judgment at every step, assure them peace and happiness in this life and salvation after death. This knowledge of *Puranas* is exploited for lip composition of songs. One great event of *Purana* which occupies many pages in the work of great poet is sung with a masterly skill within few lines.[37] Thus, the *Puranas* had profound impact and influence on the folk songs.

The incremental repetition of the lines is a speciality of the orally-transmitted folk songs and this aspect is felt especially when such songs are sung in an occupational situation like the harvest. The tedium of physical labour can be lightened when work is done to the accompaniment of a repetitive rhythm. When one person sings and others repeat in chorus, such repetition tends to create a collective sense of purpose.[38]

Historical Influences on Folk Songs:

History indirectly influences the ploughman, the cartman, the *yogi* and make them sing of the contemporary or past events. The invasion of Odisha by Kalapahar and dethronement of Mukund Deb, the last independent king of Odisha in 1568, are recorded in the folk poetry of the time.

> "Aila Kalapahada, bhangila luhara bada
> Piela Mahanadi pani, Subarna thalire,
> hira parasile, mukunda debanka rani"

Which means:

"Kalapahar came, broke the iron fence, and drank the water of the Mahanadi; the queen of Mukund Deb served him diamond on a golden plate."[39] Similarly the contribution and sacrifice of the great freedom fighter Lakshman Naika is reflected in the folk songs of south Odisha in the following manner.

> 'Lakshman Naika *he* Lakshman Naika,
> Desh Lagi Phashi Khunte Jhulaila Beka,
> *Rakhigala, Odishara Teka*'[40]

Verbal Puzzles:

Riddles or Verbal Puzzles also form an important part of folk songs. They appeal to intelligence and wisdom of rural-folk, rather than to sentiment. Each riddle carries a piece of wisdom, coated in humorous and intelligent language.[41] A riddle is designed to test the hearer's ingenuity. It has two meanings. The outer meaning is not taken into account. The inner sense only counts. The answer is shorter (in one word only) in comparison with the question. Strong common sense succeeds where depth of learning fails. Like the mental arithmetic of pedagogues or the un-intelligible Sanskrit *sloka* of a *Pandit*, riddle is a weapon of the villager used to test one's cleverness.[42]

Riddles indicate in a subtle and often humorous manner certain aspects of the life of the folk people. Through the riddles bantered to and fro among the young and the old one can make out many salient facts regarding the social customs, manners and inhibitions of the people.[43]

Here are some of the examples of *Odia* riddles:

> "A boy fell down from the sky. He had a turban on his head." *(Palm fruit).*
> "It is strange fruit, soft when unripe, when ripens, it becomes hard." *(Earthen Pot).*
> "The old bullock died on this side of the river, but the scent went to the other side"-(Jack-fruit).

Satire:

Satire also play an important part in the folk songs. They not only criticized corrected the exploiters and wrong doers, but also created humour among the rural folk. The farmers are simple but not foolish. They are not learned so far as book-learning is concerned. But, their study of human character is un-paralleled. On the occasion of reaping or harvesting, when they assemble in the field or on the farm they portray the character of their land-lord who was a miser or an exploiter satirically in songs like the following:

> "Our master is very generous. His wife boils tamarind, gruel and water together. When the cultivator in great hunger and exhaustion asks for food, she serves him with that only".[44]

A few specimen of the folksongs of south Odisha are given in the annexure.

Musical Instruments:

Music is an integral part of the socio-cultural life of the people of south Odisha. There is no festive occasion, social or religious, where music is not considered an essential part of the celebrations. Folk instruments are closely connected with the folk music everywhere and similar is the case with *Odia* folk music. Without the accompaniment of these instruments folk music becomes dull and at times even lifeless. It is also a noteworthy feature that many of these folk instruments are hardly used in classical music.

For the *kandhas,* music is predominantly a matter of tradition, of rituals and of physical or spiritual well being. Music played an important part in village life. It is associated not only with the dance and songs proper, but also with the rituals associated with the spring, wedding and other ceremonies.

The musical instruments of south Odisha are

(1) *Dhol* and *Mrudanga* (a two sided drum),
(2) *Changu* (one sided flat drum),
(3) *Nishan* (one sided deep drum),
(4) *Mahuri* (the *Odishan Sahari*),
(5) *Pleka* (a three-stringed instrument),
(6) *Hurudi* (flute or read instrument),
(7) *Khanjani,*
(8) *Remokathi,*
(9) *Ghagudi* (a chain of brass bells),
(10) *Ghoonguras* (a chain of small brass bells),
(11) '*Gini*' and *Tala,*
(12) *Jhanja,*
(13) Flute,

(14) *Dhuduki,*
(15) *Kendara* and
(16) *Sarangi.*

These instruments are kept in the *Akhada Ghar* or *Dhangada Ghar* and every youngman learnt to play them under the guidance of seniors.

The *Dhola* and *Mrudanga* which are two sided drums forms the principal musical instrument. Out of all these folk instruments the *Dholak* is the most popular in this region.[45] The body of it is made of the larger hollowed trunk of a *sago* palm or earthen vassels. These drums are played with wooden sticks with tipped cloth.

The flat drum or kettle drum (one sided) are called *Tamka.* The body of the small variety is made of iron and that of the larger of hollowed trunk of a sago palm or soft wood. These drums are played with dried leather thongs.

Plake was a three-stringed instrument, made of two guards fixed to a round piece of wood about 12 inches long. This instrument was used to accompany the love songs of the young men. The bamboo flute was called *Hurudi. Ramakathi* was a musical instrument made of two pieces of polished wood with little cymbals fitted to them. During the *Dhap* dance the women dancers play the *Ramakathi. Ghagudi* and *Ghoonguras* are the versatile musical instruments used by the ladies during *Dhangada-Dhangadi, Ghumura and Dalkhai* dance only. *Mahuri, Khanjani, Gini* and *Tala* are not tribal musical instruments. They seemed to be of recent introductions from the plains.

The above discussion infer us to believe that, south Odisha has rich and glorious tradition of folk songs which form a major part of oral literature of our country. It is the traditional heritage of those people who have an unsophisticated way of life in a particular society and who usually give a free expression to their sentiments through their songs, legends, riddles and satires. The folk songs may not soar high in their imaginative flights. They may not have the ostentation of classical music with its flourish and elaboration. But deep in their heart, there is a melody of pure joy. Further, the songs and ballads not only reflect the cultural and economic conditions of the people but also portray the social and religious condition of the rural people as a whole. The ceremonial folksongs, in particular, depict this aspect of the social life wherein the complete cycle of man's life from birth to death is described vividly. Some of these folksongs also have a philosophical outlook towards life. Folk-music is a permanent source of happiness and entertainment even in the day-to-day life of the people in modern times. Folk-music or songs should not be taken as a mere expression of the illiterate and culturally backward masses. It is a primary source of delight and encouragement of the people at large.

But the pity is that folk music is fast disappearing from this region mainly due to the increasing impact of urban modes of living on the rural life of village. The fast growing industrial development and new means of entertainment like the cinema, television, etc. are making considerable changes in the styles of folk-singing. This change of attitude and life in general has made the task of recording and collecting the authentic folk music an immediate necessity. There is danger that the fountain source of our past traditions and cultural heritage may soon dry up. We may gather reassurance however from the fact that, folk music has certain rare aspects which can never pass into oblivion. It is the freshness and vigour of this music which will always inspire the folk poet and the folk composer. Many renowned poets of literature also base their compositions on the patterns of folk music and even folk-tunes and folk meters. Folk music will, therefore, play an important role even in future.[46]

References

1. K.B.Dash & L.K.Mahapatra, *Folklore of Odisha*, New Delhi, 1979, p.34.
2. Indu Bhusan.Kar, *Folklore of Odisha* (see Preface), Cuttack, 1991, p.1.
3. Hemango. Biswas, (ed.), *Folkmusic and Folklore: An Anthology*, vol.I, Calcutta, 1967, p.16.
4. K.B.Dash, *Folklore of Odisha*, Cuttack, 1991, p.157.

5. K.B.Das, & L.K.Mahapatra, *Folklore of Odisha*, New Delhi, 1979, p.35.
6. S.K. Bose, "Baul Songs of Bengal", in: *Folkmusic and Folklore: An Anthology*, vol.I, Calcutta, 1967, p.46.
7. K.B.Dash, *op.cit.*,p.1.
8. Trilochan.Pande, "Bhojpuri Folklore and Folkmusic", in: *Folkmusic and Folklore: An Anthology*, vol.I, Calcutta, p.16.
9. K.B.Das, & L.K.Mahapatra, *Folklore of Odisha*, New Delhi, 1979, p.120.
10. *Ibid.*, p.121.
11. K.B.Das, *op.cit.*, p.2.
12. *Ibid.*
13. K.B.Dash, *op.cit.*,p.2.
14. *Ibid.*
15. K.B.Das, & L.K.Mahapatra, *Folklore of Odisha*, New Delhi, 1979, p.38.
16. B.C.Acharya, *Odia Sahityara Samkshipta Itihasa* (Odia), p.57
17. K.C.Pradhan, *Odia Loka Sahitya O Loka Samskruti* (Odia), Cuttack, 1995, p.23.
18. *Ibid.*
19. K.B.Dash, *op.cit.*,pp.123-24.
20. *Ibid.*
21. K.B.Das, & L.K.Mahapatra, *Folklore of Odisha*, New Delhi, 1979, p.41.
22. K.B.Dash, *op.cit.*,p.125.
23. K.C.Pradhan, *Odia Loka Sahitya O Loka Samskruti* (Odia), Cuttack, 1995, p.27.
24. Debendra Satyarthi, *Meet my people*, Cuttack, 1903, p.41.
25. Dash, K.B., *op.cit.*,pp.25-26.
26. Chakradhar.Mahapatra, *Utkal Gaounli Gita* (Odia), Cuttack, 1959, pp.54-56.
27. K.C.Pradhan, *op.cit.*, p.25.
28. K.B.Das, & L.K.Mahapatra, *Folklore of Odisha*, New Delhi, 1979, p.47.
29. K.C.Pradhan, *op.cit.*,p.25.
30. K.B.Dash, *op.cit.*,p.127-28.
31. M.Mansingh, *A History of Odia Literature*, New Delhi, 1962, p.29.
32. K.B.Das, & L.K.Mahapatra, *Folklore of Odisha*, New Delhi, 1979, p.42.
33. K.B.Dash, *op.cit.*,p.130.
34. K.B.Das, & L.K.Mahapatra, *Folklore of Odisha*, New Delhi, 1979, p.43-44.

35. K.C.Pradhan, *op.cit.*,p.33.
36. K.C.Dash, *op.cit.*,p.133.
37. *Ibid.*, p.28.
38. K.N.Panikar, *Folk of Kerala*, New Delhi, 1991, p.99.
39. K.B.Dash, *op.cit.*,pp.28-29.
40. Dasarathi.Nanda, *Saheed Lakshman Nayak* (Odia), Berhampur, 1981, p.3.
41. A.Bhattacharya, *Folklore of Bengal*, New Delhi, 1978, p.126.
42. K.B.Dash, *op.cit.*,p.29-30.
43. P.C.Ray Chaudhury, *Folklore of Bihar*, New Delhi, 1976, p.81.
44. K.B.Dash, *op.cit.*,p.30.
45. Trilochana.Pande, "Bhojpuri Folklore and Folkmusic" *in: Folklore and Folkmusic: An Anthology*, vol.I, Calcutta, 1967, p.23.
46. Ibid.

4

Folk Dances

Situated on the south-eastern coast of Indian subcontinent south Odisha occupies a prominent place in the history of folk dances of India. It is the cradle of many folk-dances of Odisha. The geographical location, the topographic feature, the religious and literary background, patronage of the *Rajas* and Zamindars of the region, the beauty and bounty of the nature, all have contributed significantly to the growth and development of a number of folk dances in south Odisha.

Dances of India are broadly divided into two categories viz, Folk dance and Classical dance. Folk dances are nearer to the patterns of primitive dances. But, the Classical dances are designed by the elite and sophisticated dance teachers and codified in manuals.

Bharat Muni's *Natyasastra*, a famous work on Indian theatre recognises regional dance styles and folk dances. *In "The Dance in India", Faubion Bowers says:* "... there are the ubiquitous folk dances of the village and countryside which are of two types, social and aboriginal. Social dances are the festival dances which are still performed for amusement on special occasions in the streets and the homes. The aboriginal types of folk dances are generally vestigial ceremonial dances confined, for the most part, to the numerous aborigines, hill tribes, gypsies and depressed classes in the remotest areas of the Indian interior. All these comprise the real dance of India".[1]

In the folk dances, there are the naturalness, spontaneity and plastic movements of the limbs. A free and unrestricted flow of thoughts seems to pervade the physical movements. All feelings in the gamut from joy to sorrow are manifest. Though there seems to be some conscious effort, it is overcome by unforced naturalness. For the spectator it seems to be an art form, but to the dancer it is a ritual, performed with devotion. It took them sometime to develop into professional dances and singers. The present folk dancers and minstrels are the practitioners of vestigial dance art.

The folk dances of south Odisha are special in some respect. The Dravidian culture or the Karnataki styles are discernible in some of the folk dances of this region. The folk dances of south Odisha are so lively and colourful that they can captivate the minds of all the art loving people. These folk dances are not only simple in its form and composition, but carries the deep message of human values. The origin, growth, popularity problems and prospects of the folk dances of south Odisha are discussed below.

Danda Nata

Danda nata is the most ancient and indigenous of all the folk dances Odisha. It is one of the major theatrical forms associated with the Saiva cult. It is some what an ensemble of folk dances entwined with a plethora of songs and having a variety of characters. Dantanata has always been a part of the mass religious culture of Odisha. A series of complex rituals are connected with it and its occasion is the *Chaitra* Festival. Ritualistic in nature, the *danda* (Penance) elucidates the Rudrakali myth narrating the activities of Siva and Kali. In the month of *Chaitra* (April) the Danda nata troupes stage their performance lasting for 13 to 21 days and the period terminates on the *Mahavisuva Sankranti* which normally falls in the mid of April.

Origin of the Dance:

Its origin is traced back to the age of Tantrism i.e. 8th and 9th century A.D. (after the decadence of Buddhism in Odisha). Regarding the origin of *Danda Nata*, Prof. Kunja Bihari Dash an authority on folklores says, "The kings of Kesari dynasty who ruled over Odisha from tenth century to eleventh century A.D.were worshippers of Lord Siva. There existed great animosity among the Saivites and Buddhists. Buddhism was no longer an ideal religion to be patronised by the king or loved by the people. It degraded and exposed all its weaknesses and thus dug its own grave-yard. Saivism became the predominant religion. Buddhists degraded into down-todden untouchables hated by the upperclass Hindus. They had no other option but to worship the Hindu god Siva for their salvation. But, they were debarred from entering into the Hindu temples. So they worshipped Siva once a year in a festival called *Danda Nata*".[2] Thus, *Danda Nata* came into existance.

According to another tradition, Odisha was a great seat of Tantric learning and was known as Uddiyana *Pitha* in ancient days. The founder of Pasupata sect of Saivism held a Laguda (staff) for which he was known as Lagudisa or Lakulisa. In a number of Saivite temples in Odisha Lakulisa appears holding a staff in his hands. At one time, a sect of Saivite mendicants were also known as Dandi as they were holding a *Danda* or staff as a symbol of religious authority. Here, *Danda* or staff represents Siva. In a *Danda Nata* performance two cane-staffs are planted on the ground perpendicularly. They represent Siva and Gouri whom the dancers propitiate, but peculiarly enough, the staffs are named after Gouri only as *Gouri Beta.*[3]

Some are of the opinion that, the word *Danda* does not apply here to the staff representing the deities. They opine that, the meaning of *Danda* is the control of speech *(Bak Danda)*, mind *(Mano Danda)* and body *(Kaya Danda)* as the devotees practice such controls during the observance of the rituals. There is still another theory of origin of the *Danda Nata.* It rallies round a tribal story about how a man while hunting in the forest was caught and bitten by a deadly snake, fell unconscious on the ground. His wife deeply perturbed at the pitiable condition of her husband, starts instantly praying and worshipping God Siva and Goddess Kalika invoking their divine blessings for bringing her husband back to life. And at the end, both God and Goddess being pleased at the prayer of the women blessed her and the husband finally comes back to life.[4] Since then *danda nata* was continued to perform in order to get some miraculous happenings and blessings.

These who participate in *Danda Nata* are called *Bhakta* (*Bhakta* or Devotee) or *Dandua*. Others who observe the religious vow (*Danda Vrata*) but do not dance are also called *Bhakta*. They are first initiated to Siva *Gotra* or Siva's clan. All of them wear sacred threads and *dhotis* coloured with red-clay or turmeric and carry a cane-staff all the time. During the period of observance which may continue for 13 or 21days, they keep themselves out of their homes.[5] They live in a house generally the village club-house or the temple precinct built at a distance of the village which they name as *Kamana Ghara* (the house of desire). There, a lamp is kept burning for all the days' observance. They take a meal of rice, only once in a day. While taking meal in the afternoon, drums are beaten loudly as they are not to hear human voice during the time. If by chance they hear, they relinquish their meals for this is considered inauspicious. Those who observe *Danda nata* give up non-vegeterian food, onion and garlic. The main devotee is called *Pata Bhakta* or *Pata Dandua*.

Danda nata is derived from "*Danda*" (pole) and "*Nata*" a dance which is usually performed in a religious fair called *Danda yatra*. In this fair Lord Siva and his consort, Gouri are propitiated. The artists of this *Danda Nata* are called *Bhaktas* (devotees). *Danda Nata* troops consist of 13 *bhaktas*. They dance and sing songs for the entertainment of village community. "*Abhinava Chandrika*", a literary work of 1568, mentions about the prevalence of "*Danda yatra*". It signifies that folk-theatre was very much popular in medieval Odisha .[6] The folk song :

> "*Aiela Kalapahada, bhangila luharabada, piela Mahanadi,*
> *pani subarna thalire, hira parasile, Mukunda devanka rani.*"

Signifies that, the *Danda nata* was originated to check the rise and growth of Islam religion in *Odisha*, after the defeat and death of Gajapati Mukundadeva the last Hindu king of Odisha in 1568 A.D.

In *Danda nata,* five musical instruments namely *Dhola, Mahuri, Tamak, Kara and Kartal* are used.

Different Stages of *Danda Nata:*

The *Danda Nata* is held in four phases such as, *Dhuli Danda, Pani Danda, Bana Danda* and *Agni Danda.* These are as follows:

Dhuli Danda

Dhuli Danda starts at mid-day. The *bhaktas* roll on the hot sand in the mid-day sun of the summer, dance and sing without any sign of suffering in their faces. They bear all pains to draw the kind attention of Siva towards the devotees. The subject matter concerning agriculture like preparation of field, cultivating the land, sowing of the seeds and transplantation etc. are the main attraction in *Dhuli Danda.* Four dancers portray the scene of a corn field by inter-connecting their heads and legs in a particular manner and play the role of oxen to cultivate the land and one play the part of *Halia* (Plough-man). These are performed in a beautiful and comic style. By doing such painful physical exercises the *Danduas* believe that they are doing a penance for their sins by their prayer to God Siva and Goddess Kalika to bestow blessings on them and as well as on the sponsor *Bhakta.*[7]

Pani Danda

The second phase begins in the afternoon after the completion of *Dhuli Danda.* It begins with the dipping of the *Danduas* deep in the water of an allotted tank or river for about an hour called *"Jala Danda"* (meaning-receiving punishment or physical torture in the water). The *bhaktas* take their bath and pray to Lord Siva for fulfilling the devotee's wishes. *Pani Danda* reflects the social life of the common people based on agriculture.

In the evening the worshippers perform *alati* gathering in the premises of Siva temple or in the open sky. Flame is kept enlightened which signifies the idea that life is full of ups and downs. But one should not despair under any circumstances and keep the light of hope always burning in the heart.

Bana Danda

The staying or the rest of the *Bhaktas* during the evening time in a mango grove or in a peaceful place quite away from the village is known as *Bana danda.* In that place they arrange a separate pit to cook their dinner. After the evening *Alati* they cook their food by the help of the straw *Dihudi* applying *Jhuna* (wax) without using the match box. One of the most peculiar aspects of their food preparation is that they never use any knife or native blade (*Paniki*) for cutting the vegetables. They eat only vegetarian foods without using onion or spices during this period.

Agni Danda

Agni Danda or *Danda Nritya* begins in the mid-night. A veteran artist known as *Pata Bhakta* takes part and perform the dance with different postures of his limbs in tune with the *Dhola* and other musical instruments. The *Dholia* (*dhola* players) really play an important role. The physical feats of the dancer are beautiful and enchanting. Sometimes, the dancer holds the holy lamp. One of the dancers scatter resins on the burning lamp held by him who dances spiritedly and shout intermittently "*Kala Rudramani ho jaya*" i.e. victory to the black God Siva.

Apart from entertaining village-folk with varieties of dance and songs, the main objective of the folk-theatre is to impart moral teachings in order to remove superstitions and blind faiths in the society.

In south Odisha there are professional groups of *Danda Nata* patronized by rich villagers. Inspite of being professional they have not deviated from the rituals and the period of performance traditionally fixed. Beyond the prescribed days, the performance of *Danda Nata* is impossibility. Besides the devotees, the rich house holders belonging to upper caste Hindu society also keep religious vows to conduct *Danda Nata* performances in front of their houses if desires are fulfilled. But, such vows are not kept by the poor as it entails expenditure beyond their capacity. Therefore, these people observe the *Vrata* or religious vows by enrolling themselves as *Bhaktas.* The rich or upper class, who perhaps consider it socially derogatory to be on a par with low-caste Hindus in observing the festivals as a participant or *Bhakta,* only take pleasure and pride in having a performance in their midst. They invite the professional groups. The troupe move to the village during the day time and take rest in the village temple or a lonely place far from the madding crowd. After purificatory bath in a tank or river they finish their dinner in the evening. At about midnight accompanied by drummers they proceed to the house of the host where the performance takes place. All their expenses including charges for the performance are borne by the hosting party.[8] The expenditure comes around to thousands of rupees.

Danda Nata has a rich and varied repertory of its own. It includes different items like *Gouri Beta Bandana, Jhuna Khela, Patara Saura, Chadaya Chadayani, Siva Parvati, Fakira Fakirani, Sapua Sapuani, Kela Keluni, Binakara, Karuani, Baidhana* etc. Though deeply religious in intent, all these dances accompanied by characteristic songs present a vivid picture of the rural society. Through songs, they not only bring out stories or events from mythologies or legends, but also from many happenings concerning to the family and social life.

Gouri *Beta Bandana*

Customarily, the *Danda Nata* performance begins with *Gouri Beta Bandana,* an invocatory piece of song accompanied by mild dancing. It has been mentioned earlier that, two cane staffs are planted on the grind of performance representing *Siva* and *Gouri* (Parvati). The dancers pay their obeisance to the deities incarnate through songs and dances. The songs are all in praise of *Kali, Rudrani, Bhabani, Drakshyayani* etc. the terrific aspects of Gouri (Bhairavi). The village-folk irrespective of caste and creed sit surrounded with great enthusiasm and devotion to enjoy the dance. *Hula Huli* sound (a shrill sound of women by wagging their tongues inside the mouth) reverberates, charging the atmosphere with a magical charm. The songs are sung intermittently in the dance and *Dhola* (country drum) and *Mahuri* (wind instrument) provide the rhythm and music.[9] This item lasts for about ten to twenty minutes during which the audience settle down for the night's performance.

Patara Saura

The real performance of *Danda Nata* begins with *Patara Saura* (Panna Savara) and *Patara Souruni* (*Panna Savari*) the main characters representing the earliest human couple. In the dance, the *Saura* or *Savara* goes out hunting and dies of snake-bite, *Souruni* or *Savaruni* laments (in the jungle) over the sad demise of her husband. Then, she prays Lord Siva and by his grace the *Savara* comes to life. On this occasion, there happens to be brief dance of *Siva* and *Parvati* accompanied by songs delineating their geneology, power and characteristics through the characters by themselves. After their departure from the scene, the *Savara* and *Savaruni*, rejoysing in their happy re-union sing songs in praise of *Siva* and then dance intermittently. The songs are casted in the form of dialogues, the theme of which mostly relate to legends, love, humour and various other matters and usually of light hearted type.[10]

The dance of the *Patara Saura* is the most vigorous, difficult and exhausting item in the *Danda Nata*. In the beginning he enters the stage with bow and arrow in hands and salutes the *Gouri Beta* by falling prostrate on the ground. This is accompanied by a series of acrobatic feats. Then he pretends to enter into the forest and dances imitating all the traits of ferocious animals of the jungle while going for hunt. There, he acts to die in snake-bite. Then, comes *Patara Sauruni* in search of her husband. Finding her husband dead, she laments in songs. Being moved by her sorrowful songs, *Siva* and *Parvati* who were supposed to be sailing through the heaven descend to the earth. By their grace the *Patara Saura* comes to life. Their re-union provides a happy occasion for a dance with songs of love.[11]

Chadhaya Chadhayani

Unlike the *Sabara* couple, another couple of a clan known as *Chadaya-Chadayani* forms an interesting item of *Danda Nata.* "*Chadhaya*" means a bird hunter and "*Chadhayani*", his wife. This form varies from district to district in content and technique of the dance. In the beginning *Chadaya* enters and introduces himself to the audience through songs. He also dances intermittently. Then comes *Chadayani* with whom he indulges in a combat of knowledge through songs from which people learn many things. In order to prove individual supremacy they ask questions to each other and answer accordingly. At the end, both of them sing of love and fun, dance for a while and then leave the arena.[12]

Other Characters in *Danda Nata*

Other characters in *Danda Nata* are *Dhoba Dhobani'* (Washerman couple), '*Fakira Fakirani'* (wandering Mendicant couple), '*Sapua Sapuani'* (Snake charmer couple), *Binakarini (Binakara* Couple) and *Baidhana.* Except *Parabha (Prabha)* and *Baidhana* all other characters appear in couple. The *Binakara* which literally means, one who plays a *Veena* does not actually hold a *Veena,* but a bow fitted with jingling bells which he moves with occasional jerks to mark the timebeats. The songs set to different tunes are peculiar to each character. The *Beenakara* and *Baidhana* recite theological riddles in the closing scenes of *Danda Nata.* Sometimes, there occurs rhythmic word combats and song-duels cast in form of questions and answers lasting for several consecutive nights. They appear quite interesting to the village people who watch them enthusiastically reacting off and on with loud appreciative cheers. This variety of dramatization raises the pitch and the tempo, and in the process both sentiments and artistic skills are clearly brought out.

Throughout in all the items of *Danda Nata* the rhythm is provided by *Dhola* and music by *Mahuri* (wind instrument). During singing, *Mahuri* remains silent; the drum only maintains beats in lower ebb. *Mahuri* always provides the dance-music. The first few lines of the songs are sung in narrative style when an instrument remains silent and the refrains are always musical and accompanied by dance.[13]

Similiarity of *Danta Nata* with the *Chhou* Dance

Scholars are of the opinion that, the famous *Chhou* Dance of Sareikela, Mayurbhanj and other adjoining tracts ows its origin to *Danta Nata.* They advocate certain relevant arguments in support of their view which cannot be cast aside as baseless; rather they appear most sound and plausible.

The first and the foremost argument is that both *Danda Nata* and *Chhou* Dance are the ritual dance of the same festival as "*Chaitra Parva*" in which *Siva* and *Parvati* are propitiated. Rituals remaining the same, as the dancer devotees are called *Patua* or *Bhakta* in both the dances. The presiding deity in the *Chhou* Dance of Sareikela is *Paudi,* a local name for *Bhairavi,* the terrific aspect of *Parvati.* In Mayurbhanj the presiding deity is *Bhairava,* the terrific aspect of *Siva.* Both the deities represent the Tantric divinity as in *Danda Nata.* The ritual commonness in both the dances is quite plausible and therefore there appears the argument in support of the theory of common origin.[14]

Prahallad Nataka

The *Prahallad Nataka* is a majestic form of folk play which requires a specially built stage and a variety of decorating materials. It was the most popular folk dance of south Odisha. It is considered as royal among the folk plays as it adds a significant dimension to the festive spirit during the religious ceremonies.[15] The theme of the play centres round the deep devotion of *Prahallad* to Hari (Visnu) in the face of stiff resistance of his father Hiranya Kasyapu who tried his utmost to dissuade *Prahallad* from uttering the name of Visnu. The theme of the *nataka* has been derived from the *Nrusimha Purana* and *Visnukesari Purana,* which were composed in *Odia* during 17th and 18th centuries.[16]

The story depicts *Lord Vishnu* annihilating *Hiranya Kasyapu* and protecting the righteous *Prahallad* in course of His fourth incarnation (Nrusingha) in fulfillment of the promises made in the *Bhagabat Gita.* The play reiterates the message of *Gita:*

> "Yada yadahi dharmasya glanirbhavati Bharata
> Abhutthanamadharmasya tadatmanam srujmuaham"

Which means – "at the critical junctures, when the social order is imperiled, the evil, forces flung their perilous pangs; I shall take a birth on Earth to save the righteous by destroying the evil and to restore the land to order".[17]

The text of the play was composed by Sri Gopinatha Parichha of Paralakhemundi and dedicated to Rama Krishna Chhotaraya- the *Raja* of Jalantara and the text is limited to one hundred thirty three songs and thirty *ragas.* Therefore, the authorship of the play is generally assigned to Rama Krishna Chhotaraya (1857-1905) the Raja Saheb of Jalantara- a small principality now in the Srikakulam district of Andhra Pradesh. But, according to Prof. *Prahallad* Panda, and Kamakhi Prasad Sarma, the real author of *Prahallad Nataka* was Birabara Samanta, the Raja of Tarala. Birabara Samanta's version of *Prahallad Nataka* was prevalent in Tarala, Dharakote and Humma zamindari estates.[18] A Telugu version of this play is also quite popular in Srikakulam District of Andhra Pradesh.

Although most of the songs incorporated in this *Nataka* have been dedicated to Rama *Krishna* Chhotaraya of Jalanatra, Birabara Samanta of Tarala is known as the real author of the *Nataka.* Shyam Sundar Rajguru, the noted critic of *Odia* literature and the first graduate of Ganjam wrote another '*Prahallad Nataka*' which was staged in the Padmanabha Rangalaya of Paralakhemundi.[19] Within a few years of its birth, Prahalad Natak became so popular that several Rajas of the zamindari estates like, Padmanava Dev of Paralakhemundi, Kishore Chandra Harichandan of Surangi and Rama Chandra Sur Deo of Tarala were inspired to write other versions of the play.

Characters of the *Nataka*

In spite of large variations in the structure and the play, it is confined to five major characters like *Hiranya Kasyapu, Prahallada,*

Lilavati, Mantri and Nrusimha and six minor characters like *Ganesa, Sarasvati, Mallavira* (wrestlers), *Chandamarkas* (chamber lions), *Sapua* (Snake Charmers) and *Vijaya Chandi* (the Goddess of Victory). *Hiranya,* the demon king of Amarari, the capital of Nahur is a major character in the play. *Prahallad,* the son of the demon king, is the hero and Lilavati the queen, is the only female character.[20] *Hiranya* and *Prahallad* together dominate the play and sustain it till the end of the play. The characters dance and sing to chorus simultaneously for long hours which is quite hazardous.

Nrusingha (Fourth incarnation of Lord Visnu) is the focal point of the play. He draws the climax at the end. He appears with a wild divinity (in the form of a ferocious Nara-Singha i.e. (half man and half lion) to punish the cursed demon Hiranya bearing a huge mask .He emerges from a pillar with Nrusingha incarnation to tear open the bowel of Hiranya when he challenges His (Nrusingha's) presence and strikes the pillar with his mace in front of *Prahallad.*[21] The sixth character, *Mantri,* the minister of the king, acts as the adviser in the play.

Ganesa and *Saraswati,* though minor characters, play a major role as the deities of invocations who appear on the stage at the beginning of the play to remove all obstacles and to ensure successful enactment. The other subsidiary characters such as *Chandamarkas, Mallaviras, Vijayachandi* and *Sapua* etc. also appear on the stage in the different sequences as filler which could even be reduced on demand of time. But Nrusimha (the fourth incarnation of Visnu) appears on the stage at the end and arouses the religious fervour of the audience.[22]

Chandamarka plays the role of *Prahallad's* teacher in the play. *Mallaviras,* who function as the bodyguards of the king, are also engaged to entice *Prahallad. Vijayachandi,* the presiding deity of *Hiranyakasyapu,* appears on the stage carrying a painted mask. *Krutika Chandi,* the Goddess emerges from the fire and is sent to devour *Prahallad.* This character also carries a painted mask and also wears donned black garment.[23]

Stage of the *Nataka*

Prahallada-Nataka is performed in the open air and normally staged on a big wooden platform known as *mancha* (wooden altar) which is about eight feet high. The altar is portable and can easily be packed up and shifted. The typical platform is divided into seven segments with a neatly executed stepping arrangement leading from the base up to the top. A majestic wooden chair adorns the upper-most part of the stage.[24]

An area of about thirty square feet is used as the *mandala* (acting arena). A hallow pillar like structure made of bamboo, mat or cloth mount is placed in front of the altar at a distance which Hiranya kasyapu strikes at the end of the play and from where Nrusingha emerges. Nrusingha wears painted mask of lion, made of wood.[25] The play can be performed inside the temple yards, in front of the village *Kothaghara* (community hall) or in the middle of the street, lasting for about twenty hours continuously. The *gurus* act as directors and sometimes they also appear in the role of *Hiranya kasyapu* during the play.

Costumes and Instruments

The costumes used in *Prahallada Nataka* are very much different from those of the other folk dances and classical dance forms. The principles of designing the costumes are done according to the presentation of the characters.[25] The costumes of *Prahallada Nataka* seem somewhat similar to those of *Kathakali* dance. *Prahallada Nataka* has drawn influence to some extent from *Yakha Raga*. But *Prahallada Nataka* has its own individual stature in dance, presentation and performance.

The costumes as per the principles of the *Nataka* are all crafted and well designed. For example the *Ghagara* used by Hiranya has seven flaps arranged in pyramidal order. Each flap has its own meanings symbolizing *Swarga* (heaven), *Martya* (earth), *Patala* (Netherlands), *Tala* (still lower the Netherlands), *Atala* (still lower), *Sutala* (qualifying the above region) and *Talatala* (Supreme most regions deep below the earth). Hiranya wears the *Ghagara* to symbolize that he is the sole ruler of these seven countries.[26]

The robes designed for *Hiranya Kasyapu*, the demon king and *Prahallad* are quite different. These include trousers, socks and *Ghagaras* (a waist-band having seven colours). Hiranya Kasyapu wears big moustache and beard in typical Muslim style. The man acting as *Narasingha* (i.e. Nrusingha) wears mask of lion and white *dhoti* in *Bharat Natyam* style.[27] The female characters in *Prahallad Nataka* are launched in typical *Odia* outfit with indigenous ornaments comprising *Bahuti* (band for upper-arms), *mathamani* (head ornament), *khadu* (Bangles), *kanaphula* (ear ornament), *mudi* (rings), *notha* (nose ornament), etc.[28]

The music concert, led by the principal singer- the *Gahana*, takes the right side of the stage. The *Gahana* is accompanied by two artists playing on *'mardala'* and *'Pakhauj*, and 8 to 10 supporting persons with '*Gini*' (Cymbals).[29]

The orchestra is led by *Sutradhara* (chief singer). It usually comprises four instruments, a harmonium, a *mardala, gini* and *mukhavina*. The characters usually appear with oil mixed face and body make-ups during the performance.The musical instrument played, the pattern of decoration of Hiranya, the main character, and the *ragas* followed in the *Nataka* are essentially *karnataki* in style.[30]

At first *Prahallad Nataka* was only performed in the *Darabars* (i.e. courts) of *Rajas* and Zamindars of south Odisha. But slowly the play has spread among the common people of villages.[31]

This popular folk dance is predominantly a musical melodrama written both in prose and poetry captivating the imagination of people beyond the barriers of age, sex and social position. In the words of Dhirendra Pattanaik, "*Prahallad Nataka*" is essentially operatic. There are 120 songs in the play; each set a particular *raga* and *tala*. Although music dominates the play, the song, dialogue and the interlinked prose dialogues are equally important".[32] Dialogues (in prose), poetry and dance are blended through exquisite artistry to cast a lasting spell on the audience.

Prahallad Nataka is rich in its own norms and unique styles. This uniqueness puts it in a distinct order among other performing art forms of folk plays such as *Deshya Nata, Danda Nata* etc. Though *Prahallad Nataka* is a folk form but it embraces the classical approach to a much-matured extent. It has its own individual structure, characters and costumes.

Prahallad Nataka has a remarkable effect on the rural mass and bears enormous ethical and social relevance. The triumph of Truth over Evil, the cardinal maxim of the story is presented in a lucid and imperative manner, which has profound impact on the rural mass. There are about 180 groups of *Prahallad Natakas* in south Odisha. Among them some of the troops have already had the opportunities to travel outside the state and even outside India to entertain the audience with their magnificent performance.[33]

But, the pity is that, the *Prahallada Natak* is gradually declining and disappearing from the society due to the lack of government patronage, the proverty of the artists and the *gurus,* and the impact of the television. In order to retain this century-old popular folk-dance, steps may be taken to encourage the artists at the government and the public levels.

Dasa-Kathia

Ganjam is famous for *Dasakathia* which is the most indigenous form of ballad singing in Odisha. It is the most inexpensive but popular form of both folk dance and play that has received international recognition. The etymological meaning of *Dasa* is devotee or *Bhakta* and *Kathi* means *Kathatali* (wooden pieces played in tune with the players).[34]

It is performed by a team of two persons. Learned *pundits* with extensive knowledge in *puranas, sastras* and old literature perform this dance art by narrating different mythological themes with touches of satire and modern taste to entertain the audience.[35] In this dance, a ballad is sung by two persons viz. *Gayakas* or *Guru* and the *Palia* or disciple. *Gayakas* is the main singer and *Palia* is the assistant singer or repeater who sings with the help of the *Gayakas*. The refrain of each couplet is repeated by the *Palia*. He assumes equal importance for his witty and humours to make the singing lively.

In this dance, the singers sing with a pair of castanets of wooden clappers. These clappers are not hollows but solid and resonant, fitted with a bunch of tiny ankle bells. The *Gayakas* play with the two pair of clappers simultaneously in both the hands and prove his skill and dexterity. But, the *Palia* held the clappers in the left hand with four fingers in between to keep them apart and played by the right hand with the thump pressing the upper one with a jerk to strike below. In this folk play the *Gayakas's* instrument is called *Ramatala and Palia's* is known as *Laxmantala.*[36]

These two persons stage the whole drama. The main topics covered by the *Daskathia* team are *Subhadra Harana, Nilendri Harana, Usha Harana, Surekha Harana, Sobhavati Harana, Sachala Harana* and *Chandrakala Haran, Chandrabati-harana, Sita-harana, Tripuramohini-harana, Chitraketu-Sarana, Chitrasena-Sarana, Dandiraja-Sarana Kansa-Marana, Karna-Marana* etc. They act all the parts, change their tone hour after hour and introduce humorous stories to break the monotony. They utilize their good knowledge of *Puranas* for attracting mass minds. They are *patuas* in singing ordinary and Puranic songs; *palawallas* in dress and tone; and *Gotipuas* in their dance and action.[37]

At intervals during the singing of the ballad, the *Palia* puts questions in simple prose-dialogue and the singer (*Gayakas*) answers through the songs. By this, the musical narration becomes more explanatory to the common village audience. Intermittently, the *Palia* also sings doggerels and banters to provide enough comic relief. Both the singer and the *Palia* not only sing, they enliven the performance with unsophisticated dramatic actions and mild dancing.[38]

Dasa-Kathia is said to have been originated in the 15th century in the village *Pitala* of Ganjam district.[39] According to a reaserch scholar of folk theatre, Bayamanu Charchi, Agadhu Sahu of Khandara near Hinjilicut was the pioneer artist who popularized this Folk Dance. Thereafter, their eldest son *Krishna* Chandra *Gayakas*ratna and Binayak Sabat devoted their energy to the enrichment of this folk play. The theme of the play is taken from the great episodes of *Ramayana, Mahabharata* and other *Puranas.* The compositions are mostly chosen from that of medieval poets who flourished between fourteenth to eighteenth centuries. These folk-plays are titled as *Subhadra harana, Karnabaddha* and *Jambhubati harana* etc. *Dasa-Kathia* is composed with *Chhanda, Chautisa and Chaupadi.* Poems of Kabi Samrat Upendra Bhanja, Kabi Surya Baladev Rath, and Gopal *Krishna* are profusely used to enthrall the peoples' mind. *Dasa-Kathia* is usually performed in the open sky in the middle of the village street or in somebody's courtyard or in the precincts.[40]

The *Dasa kathia* singers mostly belong to Ganjam, the southern most district of Odisha where most of the well-known *Odia* poets of medieval period flourished. Generally, the traditional singers (*Gayakas* and *Palia*) come from the community of lower Brahmins who plough the land and are debarred from taking part in the traditional ritual services. Now a days there are singers from other communities also. They move throughout the length and breadth of south Odisha during the fair weather days to perform their plays. Their performances are usually held in the mid-street or in somebody's courtyard or in temple precincts depending on the nature of patronage.[41]

Of all the singers of the *Dasa kathia, Gayakas*aratna Baidyanath Sharma and his disciple Bhimasena Satapathi were most popular. For their unique style of presentation they have won many laurels in and outside the country .He has greatly influenced the present group of singers. There are about 150 *Dasa-Kathia* troupes only in Ganjam district. The list of villages having *Dasakathia* troops is given in the appendix-iv.

Dasa-Kathia has close resemblance with *Hari Katha* and *Burakatha* of Andhra Pradesh and *Baul* or *Kabigana* of West Bengal.[42] Though Agadhu Sahu of village Khandra is said to be the originator of this folk-form, *Krishna* Chandra *Gayakas* Ratna of same village gave real shape to this folk dance. *Gayakas* and *Palia* are dressed with colorful robes, turban, *Ramanandi Chita,* and *Ghungur* now-a-days.

In recent times, the credit of popularizing *Dasa-Kathia* beyond national frontiers goes to late Baidyanath *Gayakas*aratna and Bhimsen Satapathy. The *Dasa-Kathia* has been used during election campaigns since it is a powerful means of mass communication. No other creative medium is used so extensively and is so popular in Odisha in the recent past as *Dasa-Kathia* has been. It is being used by Government organisations to propagate developmental activities in the rural areas.[43] Before the advent of Television, All India Radio and Government media used it to bring the message of family planning to the rural masses. Even now, the State Government has taken up this popular milieu to propagate their different programmes for social awareness.

Bharat Leela (Subhadra Parinaya or *Duari Nata)*:

Bharata Leela also occupies a special place among the folk-dances of south Odisha. It has its origin in Ganjam district. It's creator was Dinabandhu Das of Kalyanapur near Ganjam town. His creation of *Subhadra Harana Suanga* became familiar as *Bharata Leela.*[44] But, his composition was not accepted and termed as *Leela* by the-then society and it was called as *Huguli Bharata.* But, later on, Bhima Panda of Magura near Aska improved this to a great extent and gave the touch of a folk-theatre to it. In course of time, Shyam Sundar Sabat of village *Kandh* Kharida near Hinjilicut collected the palm leaf manuscript of Dinabandhu Das, corrected it and gave it the touch of a *Leela.* He himself played the role of a *Duari* and named it '*Duari Nata*'. Thus, the origin of the *Bharata Leela* can be traced back to 1840 A.D. At present Nabaghana Parida of Kabisurya Nagar (Boirani) is the most popular director or *guru* of *Bharat-Leela.*[45] It is heartening to note that, this *Leela* was staged and became very popular Folk Dance in Rengoon (Burma) where nearly fifty thousand Odias were serving.

Bharat Leela is relatively shorter in the length of performance and has only six characters such as Arjun, Subhadra, *Duari*, Satyabhama, *Hadi* and *Hadiani*. Arjuna the third Pandava and the King of Hastinapura is counted as a major character and Duari, Arjuna's gatekeeper acts as the hero. The course of conversation and ultimately the marriage between Arjuna and Subhadra (an important part of the *Mahabharat* story) is presented in this *Leela* in a dramatic style with humorous dialogues. The role played by the Duari in establishing contact between the other two characters through the series of queries is of great interest to the rural audience. The '*Bharat Leela* is also known as '*Duari Nacha*' as the *Duari* (gate keeper) plays a prominent role as a mediator in *Subhadra Haran*.[46]

All over the world, the folk plays draw their plots from mythologies, epics, tales, ballads or romantic legends. The rural audience is familiar with these tales; hence the emphasis is laid on characterization and intricacy. *Duari Nata* or *Bharat Leela* prevalent in the district of Ganjam in Odisha is such a play which draws its plot from the epic tales of *Visnu Purana* and *Mahabharata*. It is therefore called *Bharat Leela*. But it is more popular by the name of '*Duari Leela*' as *Duari* or the sentry remains the most important, indispensable and pivotal character of the play.

As it is told, in the verse-play, Subhadra the cousin sister of Sri Krishna madly falls in love with Arjuna, the most handsome and heroic brother of the Pandavas. When Subhadra offers her love, Arjuna bluntly refuses, as she would be like a sister to him. When argued, he takes various pretexts and all his pretexts are counteracted by *Duari*, who supports Subhadra for her unflinching love and devotion to Arjuna. At last Arjuna yields to the true love and agrees to marry Subhadra.[47]

In course of arguments and counter arguments between the characters, smaller episodes from *Puranas* and other religious texts are also told as corollary to the main episode. For instance Arjuna argues that he being a *Kshatriya* by caste and she belonging to the mild-maid community the marriage is not possible. Then *Duari* brings out an episode from some texts and narrates musically about how and when a *Kshatriya* married a mild-maid. When it is argued by Arjuna that Subhadra is not a woman of elegant features, the *Duari* narrates the characteristics of all types of women quoting authorities to prove Subhadra to be the best type. The altercation between the two proceeds till the end of the play which is punctuated with several songs of variety, moral fables, witty remarks and verses of wisdom in support of their contention. On the other hand the play in crux is a battle of wits between Arjuna and *Duari*. Therefore the repartee is simply an exposition of the knowledge of the *Sastras*. Chapter from books and verses are also quoted in support of their arguments from the religious texts. To this extent, this is a secular form, for much of its humour are contemporary.[48]

Duari Leela is held throughout the night and even it runs for consecutive nights. In order to arrest the attention of the audience, the *Duari* improvises subplots, which may use local reference or satirical comment on the current socio-political secene. These sub-plots employ music unrelated to the main theme.

Though, Arjuna, *Duari*, Subhadra and Satyabhama are the basic characters of this play, the teen-aged boys act in *Bharataleela* as both male and female characters. They play the role of Subhadra and Satyabhama and also the dancing girls. The dialogues of Arjuna and Subhadra are casted in *Odia* prose. The *Duari* speaks in colloquial local language and he is free to improvise. All the prose dialogue is introductory to particular situations of events and often serves as interludes to song dialogues. The songs strictly set to traditional tunes are meant for Arjuna and Subhadra. Though songs of *Duari* may include traditional tunes, he freely imbibes from the prevalent folk songs and dances.[49]

Bharata Leela is staged under the open sky. No stage is required for the performance of this *Leela*. Only a *mandala* is prepared limited to eigth to ten feet diameter. To prepare the *mandala,* the *bharataleela* performers mainly use the *tarpaulins* or the mats. The patromax lights or electric bulbs are also used to illuminate the *mandala* in the night performances. A *katha kurchi* (wooden chair) is the only property of the *mandala.* Arjuna, the hero of the play use it as his throne, bed, dancing area and it is used as the shrine of the deity in different episodes and scenes of the play. Arjuna performs his action carrying a *khanda* in his right hand and a handkerchief in the left. The *deepalis* (ghee lamps), *mayura pinchha* (peacock's tail) *Khajurichanchuni* (date leaf broom), *tokei* (basket) and *madakancha* (wine bottle) could be taken as the stage articles used by *sakhis, Hadiani* and *Hadi respectively.*[50]

Duari the gate keeper wears a *chedi* (half pant), an *angi* (half shirt) and a *kaba* (waist coat). For makeup, *Duari* uses pink colour paints and draws a U-shape insignia on his forehead. He wears a knotted wig, locally called *ganthibabuli.* It covers his head and upper parts of the shoulder as well as the neck. The front side of the wig is chipped with the petal like aluminium *balachhappa* (hair clips) as well *tahia* (*atiara*). The *tahia* always rests on a *padaka* (golden pandant) and it is pinned up in the wig on the forehead. On the left side of the chest he pins round *padaka* (pendants) and triangular and conical *chhappas* also to signify himself as the servant of a king.[51]

Arjuna is dressed like a warrier with a long velvet coat embroided with *zari* and tinsel. He wears silken trousers and on his back an *uttarana* hangs. He wears nylon stockings like a horse rider and his wrist bands are adorned with plastic *manibandha.* He uses pink colour paints and draws a *suryachita* sun mark on his forehead.

The subject matter of Bharata *Leela* has been derived from *Odia Mahabharata* (*Madhyaparva*) of Sarala Das. The base is the immortal love story between Subhadra & Arjuna. The main characters of this *Leela* are *Duari*, Subhadra, Arjuna and Satyabhama and *Chaukia SriKrishna, Asta Patta Bansi, Balarama, Nand Raj, Purohit, Dagara, Gayakas, Hadi and Hadiani are its* side characters. *Duari* is the central figure of this *Leela.* The success of the *Leela* predominantly depends upon him. He creates sense of humour and carries the audience with him.[52]

It is a mine of artistic excellence. We find amalgamation of different *rasas* like *Bira Rasa, Karuna Rasa and Sringara Rasa in Bharata Leela.* Dance place no less a part in making this *Leela* a grand success. It is the field to express one's artistic hidden potentialities. More than one hundred *Bharata Leela* teams are there in Ganjam district alone (see Apendix-2). Among them the countable fews are *Kandh* Kharida, Tiapentha, Duanpalli, Arakhapur, Badapada, Khalingi, Kumuruda, Kainchapur, Lochapada, Nuagada, Kuruli, Kabisuryanagar, Kalasandhapur, Nabaratnapur, Mamudhiya, Gunthapada, Goudagaon, Puhundi, Choudhury Tikarapada, Vijay Laxminarayanpur, Khariaguda, Sarabadi, Hadichira, Solaghara, Polosara, Mangalpur, Dharakote, Sheragad, Gangapur Sasan, Banthapalli, Pratapur are important.

Those who are established as outstanding *Duari*, the names of Dinabandhu Das, Shyamasundar Sabat, Ramachandra Reddy, Bhima Panda, Satyabadi Sabat, Trinath Pattnayak, Dambaru Sahu (Duanpalli), Dukhishyam Behera (Mahuritihar Pentha), Ananta Parta (Arakhapur), Juria Gouda of Kharida, Kantaru Behera, Ulla Dalai of Kankorada, Bajia Sahu of Sundarpur, Lachhana Reddy of Satapandia, Sibaram Sahu of B. Karada Badi, Kasinath Behera of Dadarakhola, Bharata Samantara of Gudiapalli, Kirtana Gouda, Rankanidhi Gouda, Dandapani Dalua of Kendubadi, Kasinath Das of Dadara Khola, Chakrapani Badatya of Nabaratnapur, Chandamani Sahu, Chandra Sekhar Nayak, Bipracharan Nayak, Durjyodhana Naik, Kampa Gouda of Tinkachai, Sadananda Swain, Nabaghana Parida of KabiSurya Nagar, Dandapani Behera of Kulagada, Sanyasi Behera of Sundarpalli, Haribandhu Mohanty of Kalasandhapur, Satrughna Swain of Mundamarai, Santosh Kumar Padhi of Patapur may be mentioned here.[53]

Truely speaking, *Bharat Leela* is the index of all the Folk Dances of south Odisha. *Duari*, the director demonstrates the role of *Chhadheya, Dasakathia, Ghudhuki, Pala, Dandanata, Prahllad nataka* etc. in different tunes and styles through this dance. It not only entertains the villagers who work from dawn to dusk in their field, but also enlightens them a lot.

Radhaprema Leela (Sakhi Nacha):

Radha Prema Leela is another folk-dance of south Odisha in general and the Ganjam district in particular. With enchanting songs it enjoys a respectable place and can be considered as the queen of the *Leelas.*[54] Depicting the eternal love story between Radha and Krishna it has the unique capacity to appeal the persons of all ages.

It had its origin in the royal palace of Chikiti. This *Leela* saw the light of the day in Chikiti royal family, which was once famous for their patronage of art and literature in south Odisha. There are different opinions as to its creation. Sitaram Mahapatro, a leading scholar has said, "Realising the wordly indifference and contemplative turn of mind of son Kishore Chandra, Biswambhar Rajendra, the *Raja* of Chikiti directed the then scholars to compose this literature so as to bring him to the path of enjoyment and earthly pleasure. After its composition and performance, Kishore Chandra led a happy married life."[55] According to the artist and musician Tarini Charana Patro, "Due to certain unavoidable circumstances there was misunderstanding between Kishore Chandra and his life partner. Kishore Chandra did not visit his wife's palace. But, when this *Radha Prema Leela* was exhibited, their life became happier and they led a nice conjugal life".[56]

Another celebrated scholar and the critic of folk-literature Hemant Kumar Das has admitted that Raghunath Rajguru was the original creator of *Radha Prema Leela.* Further, he has justified the inclusion of the melodious songs composed by the great scholar Kabichandra Hanuman Royguru.[57] From this we can come to a conclusion that there was a joint venture between Biswambar Rajendra Deo and Raghunath Rajguru to stage a show as far as the composition of this *Leela* was concerned.

This folk-dance form is based on the divine and sacred love between Sri Radha and Sri Krishna. In the original scripture, we find hundred eighty songs in different rhythms. In palm-leaf literature, we notice hundred eighty-four songs and the invocation of goddess of music. With lucid dialogues and pleasing music, it requires a small wooden pendal specially built for the performance for the selective characters like *Radha, Dutika, Visakha, Sudama, Balarama, Nauria, Sunari, Kachara,* and various shapes of Lord Krishna.[58] Kishore Chandra Deb, the ruler of Chikiti is said to be the creator of this *Leela* It was recognized as an important form of folk-play by the middle of the 19th century.

The origin of this *Leela* may be traced back to the year 1868.[59] *Radha Prema Leela* is staged under the open sky. There are nice decorations and stage arrangements for it. Lord Krishna makes his appearance in different characters and tries to allure the sweet heart of Sri Radha. The language of the *Leela* is simple and the style is lucid but description is spontaneous. Sri Radha's companions and friends dance in joy amidst Sri Radha and Sri Krishna.

The divine love of Sri Radha and Sri Krishna is a rare phenomenon to witness in this *Leela.* The dance, the music, the dress, colourful decoration, characterization, dramatization, soul steering dialogue, coordination and the poetic dictation have brought *Radha Prema Leela* nearer to any celebrated drama of any literature.

The *Radha Prema Leela* stage is quite decorative compared to all other folk theatres. The stage looks like a *kunja* and resembles a *pidha* structured temple. Tarpaulin and mats are spread around the *mandala.* The *kunja* symbolizes a *tamalavana (passiflora* garden*) brundavan* or *kadamba brukshya* (*Kadamba* tree). Radha always remains in *kunja* accompanied by her *sakshis.*

The musicians play their musical instruments *mrudanga, mardala, dholiki gini, jhanja* and *ghagudi.* The *kunja* is studded with painted wooden toys and *jhaliri* (coloured papers cut in geometrical designs) of different sizes. The performers use *mathia* (earthern pots) *kundhei* (painted toys), horse cutout, *danga* (boat), *jaupedhi* (lacquer boxes), *kathasua* (wooden parrots), *baunsabadi* (bamboo sticks) and *kathamundula* (wooden ball). In special scenes, painted *Kurma* (tortoise), *Matsya* (fish) and other masks are also used by the characters. The characters enter the stage carrying their prescribed properties or sometimes such things can be brought up by one of the members of the group.[60]

This *Leela* has been much influenced by the original creations of *Jagannnath Ballava Natak* by Roy Ramananda, *Jugal Rasamruta Lahari* by Sadananda Kabisurya Brahma and *Gita Govinda* by Jayadev, *Sri Brundaban Chandra Bihar* by Gajapati Jagannath Narayana Deva, *Gopinath Ballava Natak* by Raghunath Parichha of Paralakhemundi.[61] The performance based on personal relations is immensely enjoyed by the spectators. The love play between Radha and *Krishna* here has been personalized on the lives of the prince and princess of the royal family of Chikiti. On the other-hand mortal love longing of the prince has been given a divine faith in the basic intension of this performing play.

Rama Leela

The *Rama-Leela* based on the life story of Lord Ram is being performed throughout the south-East Asia since the ancient period. It has its deep impact on Indian culture and Indian way of life. The great seer Valmiki is the creator of this Holy Scripture. Indians, more or less, are deeply attached to Sri Rama consciousness. It is needless to say that the subject-matter and the inner spirit of *Valmiki Ramayana* have become a part and percel of the people of Odisha which led to the composition many *puranas, epics, theatres and leelas* on the life and deeds of Lord Ram. The performance of *Rama Leela* are ceremonially connected with the worship of Rama starting from the day of *Rama Navami* in the month of April and is deeply rooted in the mass religious culture of the people.[62]

But, in Odisha it was staged from 16th century after the composition of *Jagamohana Ramayan* by Balaram Das. The *Bichitra Ramayana* by its author Biswanath Khuntia is accepted as the first written form of *Odia Leela* literature as claimed by the eminent scholar Nilamani Mishra. Mrutunjaya Rath, another critic, goes a step forward, he came to a conclusion that, *Bichitra Ramayana* was staged on the eve of *Rama Nabami* festival at Puri. The *Rama Leela* performance presents the episodes from the *Ramayana.* The story begins with Rama's boyhood activities and terminates with the killing of Ravana by Rama.[63]

A number of *Rama Leela*s were composed by different authors. Krushana Chandra Rajendra (1770-1790), the *Raja* of Chikiti wrote the first *Rama Leela* known as *Chikiti Rama Leela* which contains more musical verses and less prose dialogues. Raghunath Singh, the ruler of Dharakote wrote *Dharakote Rama Leela.* The Baisya Sadasiva of Huma region in Ganjam district, Raghunath Parichha of Paralakhemundi, Keshava Patnaik of Madhusudanpur near Palur, Kalpataru Das of Balipadar, Khanshama Lochan Pattnaik of Buguda, Bipra Janardan of Ghumusar, Biprakunja Judhistir Sahu of Hinjili, Magati Sahu of Bethuara near Dharakote have composed *Rama Leela*s. But, Bimbadhara Sanasamanta of Huma is said to have composed the real *Rama Leela* in 1905-06, which had commanding appeal to the elderly sections of the society.[64]

It is learnt that most of the *Rama Leelas* have been composed by the poets of Ganjam district. It is heartening to note that uninterrupted flow of devotion towards Rama by the people of Ganjam district as pointed out by Kedarnath Mohapatra is the speciality of Ganjam *Ram Leela.*[65]

It is quite relevant to record here the sincere observations of great critics in the context of *Rama Leela* of Ganjam district. Regarding *Rama Leela* of Vaisya Sadasiva, Priya Ranjan Sen speaks, "Only in *Rama Leela* of certain districts do we come across the name of an author called Sadasiva".[66] Kedarnath Mohapatra has written, "*Sri Rama Leela* of Vaisya Sadasiva extends its spheres even to western Odisha . There was huge gathering to witness Sri Rama Nabami festival. People spend many sleepless nights in observing the *Rama Leela* in *Odia* language. This *Rama Leela* was very popular".[67] The great poet and critic Mayadhar Mansingh writes,

"Among the *Odia Rama Leelas* Keshab's *Rama Leela* tops the list". Keeping the enactment of *Rama Leela* during his childhood he observes, "this *Rama Leela* earned an undying reputation near Palur. Its beauty lies in its sublime presentation. Once you get into the theatre, it is very difficult to come out of it. Such is the tremendous impact of *Rama Leela* carried over the mind of the audience".[68] Palli Kabi Nanda Kishore has thrown light on Keshava's *Rama Leela* in the following words, "The *Rama Leela* is presented in such an ornate way that the more we read or hear the more interest it creates; the urge and thirst for that *Rama Leela* increases a lot".[69] On *Krishna* Chandra Rajendra's *Rama Leela*, Kedarnath Mohapatra's view is significant. He says, "This *Leela* was very popular in the areas of Ganjam, Kalahandi and Jaypore. The eminent scholar Binayak Mishra was full of praise for its noble presentation, its sweet language and its lucid style. We find similar thoughts so far as the artist of *Rama Leela* of Ganjam is concerned".[70]

One can well imagine the creativity, quality, quantity and the well-presentation of *Rama Leela* in Ganjam district. Ganjam district has gained prominence in this field.

The names of the first *Gayakasas* of *Rama Leela* in Ganjam district are Jagannath Padhy of Krishna Chandra Rajendra's *Rama Leela*, Agadha Kahalia of Dharkote, Jagannatha Badatya of Kalpatra Das, Udayanath patnaik of Kamal Lochan Pattnaik, Baidyanath Maharana of Bipra Janardan, E.Khali Patro of Raghunath Singh, Kandiya Gouda of Kunja Bhanja, Bachha Padhy of Judhistir *Rama Leela*, Duryodhan Barada of Magati Sahu. The noted *Gayakasas* are *Gayakas Ratna* Natabara Sahu of Debabhumi, Ghanashyam Panigrahi of Balipadar, and Bidyadhar Sabat of Jahada and Trinath Pollai of Khandeduali etc.[71]

The number of *Leelas* in *Ramayana* varies from author to author. Generally *Rama Leela* is divided into seven *Kandas* like "the *Ramayana's Saptakanda*". There is no difference in its story. This *Leela* is staged under the sky. In the earlier days wooden toys were placed in place of main characters. A lamp was lit. The actors displayed their historic (dramatic) talent through different facial expressions as per the story demanded. The *Gayakasa* while singing presented his total self before the statue of Lord Rama. In the later stage, the artists put on the costumes as per the situation demanded. Two *Gayakasas* are constantly present in the *Leela*, one is *Sri Gayakasa* and another is *Padi Gayakasa. Sri Gayakasa* puts on *tilak* on his nose and brow, ear rings, *swarna khadu* in the hands, also *baju bandha, kankana,* the golden rings in thc fingers, the turban on his head. The dress of *Padi Gayakasa* is like that of *Sri Gayakasa* but he does not wear turban. Both wear *pata* of Berhampur. The *Gayakasas* of Ganjam district sing their melodious songs in the high tone. This is their speciality. One can hear their sweet melodious voice and the sweet song upto three kms. distance in the dead of night.[72] We never find such types of costumes in the other *Gayakasas* of other districts. The dress of female characters of this *Leela* is presented keeping the culture of Odisha in view.

Mrudanga and *Tala* are the chief musical instruments of this *Leela.* The musical show of this *Leela* is being managed by two *Bayakas*, more than five *Tabalas* and *Palibala*, one harmonium player. Furthermore, the chief of the *leela's* musical singer *Gayakasa* and the *Bayaka* and artists lead an austere life on the day of performance of this *leela.*

This *leela* is performed on the holy occasion of *Sri Rama Navami.* Before the commencement of this *leela*, the sacred water is sprinkled chanting the *mantras* on Lord Rama's statue placed in the chariot. The *leela* comes to an end after chanting the powerful *mantras* (*mangala charana).*

The significance of *Rama Leela* of the Ganjam district lies in its good presentation, the melodious songs of the *Gayakasas*, the musical rhythms and the dazzling devotional dances. The *Rama Leela* is confined to fifteen to twenty five characters. Of these, seven are major characters such as Rama, Sita, Laxmana, Bharat, Satrughna, Ravana and Hanumana.[73]

Rama:

The actor playing Rama must be a person of sound health, innocent and a soft voiced one. He puts on a white or raw silk *Berhampuri pata* and a velvet *sanju* (armore). Sometimes he appears on the stage with yellow *dhoti* and *odhani.* He uses ornaments like *kankana, mudrika* (finger ring) and puts on a *paita.* Generally, Rama wears a *jata* (matted wig) on his head and in different episodes he wears a *mukuta.* The *jata* is covered with flower rings and his crown and royal clothes are decorated with plastic beads with golden or silver *zari* strings. Rama always carries a bow made of bamboo or wood and a decorated wooden or straw board *tunira* (quiver) on his back. His make-up colour is light green. His forehead is marked with a 'U' shaped *tilaka.*[74]

Sita:

Sita, the heroine of the play, usually is played by a teen-aged boy who takes special make-up and costumes to distinguish from other female characters. She decorates her hair with an artificial long *Beni* putting on *rang* (red) or *baigani* (violet) i.e. violet colour *Berhampuri pata* sharee. A transparent silk *(veil)* is used as her *odhani.* The *Beni* is decorated with garlands prepared in *itala* (red tulip) and other flowers. Like the other female characters, this character also uses ready-made and well-shaped *hukuphala, saya,* raika. Sita uses a small *kirti* on her head and golden ornaments like *khadu, bala, sankha* (bangle made from coanch shell), *hasta padma* (palm links), mudi for hands, *antapatta, nagram, sevatiphula, jhara, mathamani, chandrakanti* (girdle), for ears *madhumati, jhika, jhumpi* (ear pendant) etc. and necklace like *ambakashihara* (mango-shaped pendants used for necklace), *sorisiamali, khasulu,* and for nose *dandi, guna* etc. are used.[75]

Ravana:

Ravana, the ten-headed demon king of Lanka, appears as a major character in complete make-up. His face is painted in blue and a *sivachitta* (three stepped small horizontal lines) marked on the forehead in white, which gives him the clear identity as a devotee of *Lord Siva.* Nine other painted masks are added horizontally. The eighteen painted wooden hands are also fixed on his shoulders. He puts on a red colour *pata* with a well-decorated velvet long coat, a wig, a huge crown, long and thick necklace, decorated armour, painted leather anklets, original or bold crepe made moustache and *kundalas* (ear balls). He always acts with a long aluminium sword or bow. His eyebrows are mascared with thick black crepe fixed with spirit gum, and eyelashes are marked in white.[76]

Like *Krishnaleela, Ramaleela* is also performed in a field of the village street i.e. in open air and on the ground. The musicians sit in a half circle line on a mat or tarpaulin. The musical instruments like harmonium, *mrudanga, dholiki, gini and jhanja* are played by the musicians. *Dhanu, Sara khanda, gada, bankibadi, kamandalu* (ewer), *danga* (boat), etc. are found as the major play articles used by the characters in different scenes and sequences. In special scenes the painted mountain settings and papier mache painted boulders are used. The nine headed painted Ravana mask, crowns, animal masks, wooden swords, weapons are the significant stage articles of the *Ramaleela* performers. In some areas the *Ramaleela* groups also uses the *mancha* and huge nine headed masks for Ravana, which can be taken by bullock-carts.[77]

Ramaleela groups use the decorated *chandua* (canopy) on the stage. The four corners of the *chandua* are tied-up tightly to four polls of the stage. Patromax lights are hung up on these polls to highlight the arena point prominently.

Krishna Leela:

Krishna Leela is another popular folk art form of south Odisha. It is based on the divine life of Lord Krishna. Though this *leela* comes much later then the *Rama leela*, it has become an integral part of the time honoured tradition of Sri Krishna worship. The *Geeta Govinda* of Jayadeva, the *Jagannatha Ballava Nataka* of Roy Ramananda and the *Odia Bhagabata* of Jagannath Das has laid the strong foundation of the Sri Krishna worship in

Odisha. While the story of *Krishna Leela* centers round the *Bhagabata* by Jagannath Das, the dramatic style is very much influenced by *Geeta Govinda. Krishna Leela* reached its abridgement in Odisha during 18th century, whereas in Ganjam district this could not see the light of the day till the first half of the 19th century. History bears eloquent testimony to the fact that, Babaji Dukhi Shyam Das composed the first *Krishna Leela* of Ganjam. He took the initiative to stage it in Baunsia village near Athagada. He himself had directed this *leela*. This was named as *Athagadia leela*. The exact period of composition of Dukhishyam's *Krishna Leela* is not known. However, basing on the land document of Dukhishyam Das- the poet and the different interviews with the *leela Gayakasas*, the composition period is traced to the middle of 19th century.[78] But, this *Leela* was an admixture of both Bengali and *Odia* script. An individual by name Ganapati Rana of village Dhanarasi translated this into *Odia* language and was staged. This has been familiar as *Bhanga Dukhishyam Krishna Leela*. Later on, it was staged in the village Jakara, Kelajhuri, Takarada, Gosani Nuagam, Rangipur Sasan etc. Budhi Badtya, Bhagaban Behera, Bauri Gouda, Guru Sahu, Mohan Das have established themselves as outstanding *Gayakasas*.[79]

After that, Raghunath Parichha of Paralakhemundi, Harihara Sadangi of Goutami, Raja Lakshmi Narayana Deva of Badakhemundi, and Madhusudan Panigrahi had composed the *Krishna Leelas* in *Odia* language. Madhusudan Panigrahi translated certain Sanskrit slokas and incorporated into *Krishna Leela* while other *Leela*karas followed their own pattern of composition and in their own style.[80]

During the 19th century, a large number of people from south Odisha were migrated to West Bengal for Job. Dukhishyam Das was among them, who learnt and performed *Krishna Leela* there. When he returned to Ganjam on the eve of the First World War, he spread this *Leela* in Ganjam. Most probably this *Leela* was flourished in Ganjam from 1911 A.D.[81]

Two *Bayaks*, expert in musical instruments would be constantly found in this *Leela.* One is chief *Bayak* and the other is *Padi Bayak,* who plays the *Mrudanga.* More than five to seven *Tala Bala* and *Palia* and often, the onlookers participate along with the *palias.* This *leela* was conducted with much pump and pleasure during *Janmastami* and other festivals. The *Adhikari* (Manager), the *Gayakas,* the *Bayaks,* the artists lead an austere life on this *leela* day. The *Balya Leela* (childhood plays of Lord Krishna), *Dadhi Manthana Leela* and *Kaliya Dalana Leela* are displayed in one day stage performance. In some places, like Brahmana padar, Purusottampur, Baunsia a total of forty-eight *Leelas* as depicted in *Srimad Bhagabat* of Jagannath Das basing on the life story of Lord Sri Krishna from his brith to the coronation ceremony of Ugrasena broadly classified into forty-eight parts are conducted even for one year at a stretch.[82]

But this has not become possible in different parts of Odisha so far. This shows the real development of this folk art in Ganjam district and also the love of the people for art and literature. Just like *Rama Leela,* in *Krishna Leela* also, the statue of Lord Krishna is placed in the *Dola Bimana* and *leela* is performed before him. *Krishna Leela* was staged in different villages like Baunsia, Purusottampur, Debabhumi, Nimina, Sorada, Belaguntha, Polasara, Tikarapada and more than sixty *Sri Gayakas* are found in Ganjam district alone.[83]

The familiar *Leela Gayakasas* of the period under study were Budhi Badtya of Baunsia, Bhubaneswar Mohapatro of Purusottampur, Arata Jena of Humuki, Dutikrishan Padhy of Bhetanai, Khetrabasi Swain of Jhada, Somanath Behera of Debabhumi, Purna Pradhan of Kalamba, Dandapani Behera of Sorada, Purna Chandra Tripathy of Polasara, Pandu Lenka of Gutami, Akula Padhy of Subalaya and Somanath Swain of Gobindapur.[84]

There are five major characters such as *Krishna, Balarama, Nanda, Yasoda* and *Kansa* and ten minior characters like *Rajaka (washerman), Bakasura (crane demon), Sandhasura (bull demon),*

Akrura (minister of Kansa), Bhutta (ghost), Kaliya (mythical- serpent), Putana (demoness), Sakatasura (cart demon), Dhibar (boatman) and Aghasura in the *Krishna Leela.*[85] All the roles in this play are enacted by men. Generally boys below sixteen years of age act in this play.

Krishna:

Krishna is the hero of the play. Light blue color is applied on his body while the *Vishnu tilaka* (mark symbolizes Visnu) is on the forehead. He wears a white or pink silken *panchi* (small dhoti). A *ghagudimala* (jingling bell) is tied around his waist and a *Kirti* (small crown) is found on the head decorated with *mayurachula* (peackck's feather). *Krishna* plays the aluminium flute wearing *khadu* and *kankana* (bracket). The boys who act in the play grow their hair to an enormous extent which is helpful in their performance on the stage.[86]

Balarama:

Balarama, Krishna's foster brother, paints yellow as his body make-up. He appears on the stage carrying a small *katha langala* (wooden plough) to identify himself as the god of the farmers. He also wears a yellow or white *dhoti.* The head ornaments are nicely covered with the *kirati* and wig and his neck is decorated with glass and plastic beaded necklaces. On the wrists and feet *khadu* and *gulusu* (anklets) are worn respectively.

Nanda:

Nanda is the foster father of *Krishna* and Balarama. He uses pink for his make-up using *patakachha* (silken *dhoti)* and *odhani* as his garments.

Yasoda:

The wife of Nanda, makes up her body and face with light yellow or pink colour. She wears a *jaupata* (lac dyed silken saree) and a warm colour *chhita raika* (spotted blouse), *Saya* (Petti coat) and *kanchula* (bodice) as her inner garments. Traditionally, Yasoda wears golden ornaments. She uses *mathamani, sevatiphula, nagram* etc. for her head, for nose *dandi, Tara* (star), *lavangalata* etc., for ears *madhumati* and *phasia* (ear ring), for neck *khasulu, kandulaphalia* (red garm like necklace) *sorisiamali* and *naanu* (girdle). On fingers *mudis* and on ankles *paati, paunjhulu* (silver anklets) are used. A silver *antapatia* (waist belt) is tied on her waist. But with the change of time plastics and imitations have taken their place.

Kansa:

Kansa, the King of the *Mathura* and *Krishna's* maternal uncle, is always treated as the villain of the play. To create a demonic appearance this character applies dark blue for his body and face. A white *suryachita* (sunmark) is painted on his forehead. The eyelids are painted red, eyebrows thick black and cheeks light pink, a thick moustache prepared in crepe is fixed and the palms are colored in *alata.* On his head he wears a *mukuta* (head gear). *Kansa* wears velvet a long coat with a red *panchi* (trouser). The feet are covered with *moja* (feet anklets) and *nagarajota* (pointed shoes). Kansa comes on the stage holding in one hand a colourful mace structured out of bamboo strips and covered with coloured papers and in the other hand an iron or aluminium sword.[87]

Apart from the other subsidiary characters, *Bhuta* carried a mask over his face and he wears black make-up. *Bakasura* and *Sandhasura* perform their roles with the crane and bull masks and white garments respectively.

All the male and female roles are enacted by only the male characters. A ten feet diameter arena is considered the *mandala* on which the play is performed. Like all other folk theatres, the *Krishna Leela* performance can also be enacted in the middle of the street or in front of a temple of the *kothoghara* (community hall). The musicians sit in a half circular line on a tarpaulin or a mat. The *gayaka* sings the songs loudly and the *palias* follow the lines of the song repeatedly. The musicians play *mrudanga, mardala, dholiki and gini.* The patromax lights are hang up on the polls at the four corners to illuminate the performing arena. The women sit on one side and the other spectators cover the three sides of the stage. The narrow gangway is also found in this play which connects from the stage to *bhesaghara* by which the characters enter and exit. The village temple, *matha, kothoghara* and residential house can be used the *bhesaghara.*[88]

The *Gayakasas* of *Krishna Leela* in Ganjam district decorate themselves as that of *Gayakasas* of *Rama Leela.* Here also, we find turban on their head. The *Gayakasas* bears the sacred thread known as *Paita.* He works as a co-ordinator between the characters and the incident of this *Leela.* Spiritualism but not the mere recreation, plays a vital role in this region. The observers of this *leela* while reaching the stage puts the very dust into his mouth. The cry of *Haa-* the Bangali influence on the *Krishna Leela* performance is visible.[89] More specifically on the dialogue structure, this has a link with the *Bhakti* Movement and emergence of several religious institutions dedicated to Radha and *Krishna. Krishna Leela* groups have also the connection with the *Kirtan* groups sprang up in south Odishan villages from the 16th century. Unfortunately, the tradition of recital of *Bhagavata* and the performance of *Krishna Leela* are based on two different traditions. While the *Bhagavata is* an emergence from the local need, *Krishna Leela* is an influence from the Bengali *mahantas* of south Odisha. Therefore, it can be said that, the themes of the Folk Theatres of south Odisha have been given a twist to accommodate local niches to make them more acceptable in the social milieu.[90]

Much difference is found between the *Krishna Leela* of south Odisha and north Odisha, regarding the costumes and ornaments. The costumes and the dresses are highly sophisticated in south Odisha. Since it was staged in the open air many *leela* articles were not used. But they used *Garuda* made up of wood, wooden and spring snakes and *Dadhi Bhanda.* The audience were simply carried away by the wonderful sights, sounds and the beauty of nature through the melodious songs presented by the *Gayakas.*

As described above, *Krishna Leela* was the most popular folk-drama of south Odisha presented in various styles and forms. For hundred of years it is cultivated as an amateur activity. But due to the advent of Television and Cinema this *leela* is fast declining. At present *Krishna leela* has almost disappeared from the scene and are rarely performed in south Odisha. Only a countable team of Ganjam district performs *Balya Leela, Dadhi Manthan Leela,* and *Kaliya Dalana Leela* only. But it must be admitted that *Rama Leela* and *Krishna Leela* are not meant for entertainment or for the breaking of monotony, but for the creation and spread of religious and spiritual awakening among the people.

Oshakothi:

Oshakothi or *Kothisala* is another folk dance of south Odisha which is mainly confined to the lower caste people of the society. It is based on ancient tradition of *sakti-cult* prayer to goddess *Kali, Chandi* and *Mangala.* It is said that *Oshakothi* is originated from Boirani (Kabisuryanagar) of Ganjam district.[91] Chaudhury Parida of Kabisurya Nagar had great contribution to the enrichment of Oshakothi. Dance, music and ritualistic performances are some of the salient features of this folk-dance. Goddess Mangala is worshipped in this folk-dance. The dance is performed during the month of *Aswina* (September).

Legends concerning the origin of *Osakothi:*

Although there are several legends explaining the origin of the *Oshakothi* tradition, they all have in common, the character of a low-caste woman settled among the under privileged groups who began worshipping the Goddess Mangala after a conflict with the royal house. Arakshita Bisoi, *a* priest of *Mangala Kothi* (i.e. Osakothi) of Routpeta street in Berhampur, in 2000 A.D. opined that, "Once there was *chandaluni*, an underprivileged woman named Shriya, who had seven sons. She was the sweeper in the king's palace. When she was sweeping the street near the palace, the queen who was a barren lady expressed her displeasure because it was her (untouchable) face she had seen first in that day". Equally, Shriya also replied that, "it is inauspicious to have seen the face of the queen because she was *anthukudi* (a barren woman)".

"The queen wanted to take revenge and reported the matter to the king. The king took away the five sons of Shriya and had them killed in the forest. Shriya went into the forest to search for her sons. Seeing them dead, she cried aloud. That was the time when *Siva* and Parvati wondered around in the wilderness. They heard Shriya and asked her to observe *Osakothi* by erecting a *Chhamundia.* She replied that she could only do it with all her sons alive. *Siva* ordered her to turn her head away. Then he sprinkled water on the dead bodies, and the sons came back to life. As instructed by the goddess, they joined their mother and worshipped goddess Mangala. After that, she observed Osha for twelve years. When the queen saw the seven sons of Shriya. She was told to perform *Oshakothi.* Then she herself began *puja* of the goddess and was subsequently blessed with seven sons. Since then, *Oshakothi* was performed by the people to be blessed with sons".[92]

A second legend was collected by Arabinda Patnaik from an unknown old *Harijan* informant which is as follows, "On the way to heaven, the five *Pandava* brothers rested on the verandah of a Brahmin house in the kingdom of Avanti. In that house, no one was ever blessed with the birth of a child; no child lived longer than one night. The sympathetic *Pandavas* became worried. Arjuna prepared himself to protect the household. He erected a *kothi* and a *chhamunda* with the help of arrows. Thus, *Yama* the God of Death, was barricaded out. At night, the messengers of *Yama* appeared, but had to leave unsuccessfully. Consequently, an agreement was reached with *Yama* that whoever worships this *Oshakothi* will bear sons, and all children will remain alive.[93] Everyone will become fortunate.

"The news spread fast throughout the kingdom and (the sweeper woman) Shriya *Chandaluni* heard it. When she was sweeping the streets near the palace of Avanti, the next day, the queen expressed her displeasure because it was her (untouchable) face she had seen first that day. Equally, Shriya thought it inauspicious to have seen the face of the queen because she was *anthukudi,* a barren woman".

The legend was recounted to us in 1999 in a similar fashion by Uchhava Naik. "There was a sweeper-woman named Shriya. The queen of the kingdom where Shriya lived had no sons. Shriya said: 'I will not take anything to eat, if I see the face of that barren woman (every day)'. The queen heard this and became very sad. She slept on the ground that was not even plastered with cow-dung, keeping her face downwards. When the king returned to his palace, he searched for his queen. The queen wanted the king to make a promise before she would talk to him. The king agreed. Then the queen asked him to kill all the sons of Shriya. The king sent out seven *paika* soldiers to kill them. When her sons did not return, Shriya went into the forest and cried aloud. *Siva* appeared and restored the sons to life by sprinkling water on them. As instructed by *Siva*, Shriya made a *kothi* on the *ghat*, from the cremation ground. She collected the pot and a *sieve* from the ghat and prepared a *dhanakolia* instrument. She worshipped *Siva* and *Parbati*.

"*Siva* appeared in the king's dream and asked him to go to Shriya and beg for her forgivenenss. The king acted accordingly, touched the feet of (the untouchable) Shriya, and learned the performance of *kothi* from her. Then he was blessed with sons".[94]

Period of Observance:

Osakothi is generally begins on *Aswina sukla astami*, the eighth day of the bright fortnight of the month of *Aswina* (September/ October) and lasts until *Dusserah*, the tenth day of the same fortnight. It may also extend until *Asvina Purnima*, the following full moon night. *Osakothi* is observed in the month of *Asvina* because this is the *Sakta masa*-month of the Sakti, the 'all-pervading Powers of the Goddesses. Similarly in south *Odisha*, the month of *Chaitra* is considered best for *Sakti* worship. The period of observance is not fixed to specific dates because the performing groups depend largely on:

(a) the availability of a painter,

(b) the consensus of the people observing it, and

(c) the economic viability of the performers. Nowadays, the core of the rituals generally coincides with the *Durga puja* of the urban and Brahmanical society.[95]

Although rituals connected with *Sakti* are performed throughout *Odisha, Osakothi* is peculiar only to south *Odisha,* or *khai kothi,* which is performed in Western *Odisha,* specifically in and around Sambalpur.

Thus, in all legends, the *Osakothi* tradition starts from the untouchable group, the upper castes joining only later. The propitiation of *Siva* or the Goddess was to avoid the death of sons. About five to ten artists perform this dance. The Performers of the *Osakothi* are:

(1) *Adhikari,*
(2) *Jani,*
(3) *Gayeni* (Singer),
(4) *Bayeni* (Instrumentalist),
(5) *Hadi Baja* (Drummer),
(6) The *mangala* performers,
(7) *Devata.*

They sing the episodes from *Mahabharata, Ramayana, Bhagavata* and other *Puranas* based on *Malasree Rag.* Dance music and ritualistic performances are some of the salient features of this folk play. "*Dhana kolia*" a peculiar type of instrument is used in this folk play.[96]

Because of the abudance use of Television, Cinema and modern dramas, the *Oshakothi* tradition is fast disappearing from the society. Hence, the revival of folk dances like *Oshakothi* is highly necessary as it can be utilized as an alternative platform to create peoples' consciousness in combating social evils like dowry deaths, environmental pollutions and human right violations.

Ranapa Nacha:

'*Ranapa*' was another famous folk dance of south Odisha. But, it is confined to the Chhatrapur block of Ganjam district. It is believed to have originated in Ganjam district itself. Some art lovers say that the word '*Ranapa*' is derived from the word *Rana* which literally means battle and 'Pa' which means feet. At first this dance on stilts was prevalent among the cow-herd communities of south Odisha. But, gradually it assumed the form of a folk-dance in the village Narendrapur of Ganjam district and spread to different communities and places.[97]

The peasants, who joined the battle at the time of need, invented this technique of walking with stilts to set up their speed in reaching the battle field. The stilts enabled them to hasten their pace by taking large strides and saving time. Before the dance is performed, the *Dhola, Changu* and *Turi* are played by the artists in order to arouse *Virarasa.* The young village dancers standing on the stilts dance with utmost ease to the accompaniment of *Dhola and Mahuri.* The Artists dance in such a manner that they never fell down while dancing.[98] Songs relating to the boyhood exploits of Lord Krishna, the episodes of *Karna-Arjuna yudha* and *Bhima-Dusashana yudha* are sung intermittently.

The folk legend Bhagaban Sahu who renovated the *Ranapa* dance to suit the present day tastes is credited with perfecting and popularizing this traditional indigenous dance not only within the country but also in abroad.[99]

Basically performed on a big plain ground, "*Ranapa*" began to be shown on stages and auditorium too. Bhagaban sahu, in his research article on *Ranapa* made it clear that though several improvisations and alterations had been initiated into this folk dance, due care had been taken to retain the basic traditions of the *Ranapa* dance. To quote from excerpts of Bhagaban sahu's article, one can get an idea of his research.

Nearly 12 artists thrown into two rows perform the dance with the rhythm of *Dhola* and *Mahuri.* They were simply singing songs relating to Krishna's boy hood life and dancing to the rhythm of "Bajeni", an anklet made of iron which produces a jingling sound.[100] Bhagaban Sahu of Narendrapur with his party presenting this dance has dazzled many spectators in and outside India on ceremonious occasions and made this dance immensely popular.[101]

Kandhei Nacha:

Kandhei nacha or Puppet dance was prevalent in many parts of south Odisha and was very popular among the rural folk. Ganjam has the oldest tradition of puppet dance. In Upendra Bhanja's literature a lot of stories and references are available on puppetry. Puppetry in Ganjam began and flourished as a part of family tradition supported by royal families. The art of rod puppetry requires specific and rigorous training and the use of a number of costly puppets.[102]

The peculiarity of this dance is that the dancers are puppets. The performer remains in the background and narrates mythological stories by moving the puppets in a fine string. He does it with such skill that the puppets appear to be moving and dancing on their own accord. The artist harmonises dialogues with the movements of the dolls through sheer craftsmanship and makes the dolls speak like human beings. A stage approximately 8 feet in length, 5 feet in breadth and 4 feet in height is fitted against a dark backdrop to project marvellous visual effect.[103] This form of dance is not only popular in Odisha and India but also highly acclaimed even outside the country. The Doll dance traditions are preserved and propagated in the villages like Badakodanda, Sanakonda, Buduli and Rajakunda of Ganjam district. After independence due to lack of patronization, the puppetry tradition of Ganjam has lost its glamour. Still, a few families are fond of puppetry in some villages of south Odisha in a very limited scale.[104]

Bagha Nacha (Tiger Dance):

Bagha Nacha (Tiger Dance) is an imitative dance performed as a folk dance in south Odisha . A dummy tiger and a man perform the dance. The bamboo tiger is made up of cloth, paper and colours in a traditional mask making technique only available in this area. Two dancers get inside the dummy tiger-body and position themselves inside in such a way that the dummy-body looks some what like a real tiger. The legs of the dancer positioned on the front become the two forelegs and the two legs of the dancer positioned at the back form the hind legs. The dancers wear trousers like dress which looks like legs of tiger.[105]

The dance is presented like a fight between a tiger and a hunter. With amazing synchronization, the two dancers move so artistically as per the rhythm played that movement of the tiger appears realistic. The instrument like *Dhol, Mahuri* and *Changu* are used to create the environment and rhythmic sense. Roaring, watching, jumping and running movements are displayed in this dance.[106]

In some areas of south *Odisha,* another variety of tiger dance is prevalent in which the whole body of the dancer is painted like the coat of tiger with yellow and black stripes from head to foot to give the look of a Royal Bengal Tiger. The dancer dances with various prowling movements of a tiger to the uncanny rhythm of *Changu.* Mostly, this dance is performed in the religious processions during *Thankurani Yatra* by the men of vigour and stout body. The dancer is surrounded by a group of *Changu* players who encourage him to dance.[107]

It is associated with the ritual festivals of the Mother Goddesses Durga who rides on a Tiger. The body of the dancers are painted in yellow and black in a striped pattern and also the coat of a leopard. In the *Thakurani yatra* of Berhampur it is a custom of many *Manasikadhari* to perform this dance.

Dhana Koila

Dhanakoila is a ritual dance named after the musical instrument of that name. *Dhanakoila* is an instrument consisting of an earthen pot, a flat panel prepared from bamboo piece, *kalapati, batuli* and *Patar Chumuka.* The dance is performed before the devotees for five consecutive days. During this dance, *Kalasi* (woman endowed with mystic powers) answers the questions raised by the mass.[108]

Besides the above dances, *Dasiri Nacha, Kela Nata, Dhoba Nata, Sankha Badya, Veera Badya, Ghuduki Nacha* etc. were prevalent in the south Odisha during the period under review.

There is no denying the fact that the folk-dances of south Odisha have displayed the native genius of the *Odia* people which carries deep messages of human values.

Tribal Dances:

Most of the tribal communities have retained the rich and varied heritage of colourful dance developed over centuries. Dance is the part and parcel of the life of the tribals. It is the most important source of recreation which all men and women alike are most passionately fond of. No festival or ceremony is considered complete which go without a dance performance.[109]

Although every tribe has its unique pattern of dance, there are several characteristic features which are common to all. Tribal dances are usually accompanied by songs and orchestra. Both men and women, young and old, dance but the accompanying orchestra is usually provided by the male members. Invariably the dancers sing to the accompaniment of music. To them, dance and song are group activities forming integral parts of the celebration of religious festivals, wedding and funeral and occasionally for enjoyment and relaxation. Dance and song are named after the specific ceremony with which they are associated.

Tribal dance is characterized not only by its originality and spontaneity but also for its rhythmic movement of limbs, the free expression of emotion and colourful dancing costumes and attire. The theme of the song is considerably influenced by the natural phenomena of the environment and the subject matter of folklore and legends relating to the supernatural forces current among them.[110]

Demsa Dance:

Among the *Paraja*, the most popular dance is known as 'Demsa'. Girls who put on typical short sarees and deck their heads with flowers form a long row by interlocking their arms. They move with typical swinging motion in a graceful formation. The girl who leads the dance holds a bunch of peacock feathers by which she gives direction about of their movements. The dance starts with a stylized walk in slow tempo ending in a fast moving climax. The music is provided by the male members.[111]

Dhangada-Dhangidi Dance

Dhangada Dhangidi dance also known as Kandhuni dance is one of the most important dance of the Kandhs. The grown up girls and boys of Kandh caste never sleep in their own house. All grown up girls in the village sleep in a separate common house known as *Dhangidi Idu* and youths sleep in another house called *Dhangada Idu.* The Dhangada-Dhangidi dance is performed by these unmarried grown up boys and girls with the instruction of the village mother. Whenever any guest comes to the village Dhangidi dance was celebrated to entertain the guest as a mark of love and devotion.[112] The parents generally go with such party to call their daughter from her father-in-law's house. In this dance, persons belonging to both the sexes sing beautiful folk songs in groups and dance after each stanza of the song. While dancing the girls play on *ramokathi* and make graceful movement of body, waist and hand. They (dangidies) perform the dance by moving forward and backward and sometimes sitting and circling. The Dangadas play on their instruments such as *dhol* (a two-sided drum), *changu* (one-sided flat drum), *nishan* and *mahuri.* They do not dance while singing. The dance is generally performed on the occasion of marriage and other social functions.[113] Sometimes they perform this dance in their dormitory for self entertainment.

Kandhs and Parajas have their *Pus Parab* dances and dances celebrating special occasions like festivals and marriage. The Kandhs have a dancing place in every village, surrounded by stones or wooden seats and shaded by venerable trees. The dance hall is the open arena in the village street. The performance of both sexes use to pay particular attention to their dress and to the arrangement of their hair. The Dhangadas and Dhangadis would emerge from their community homes and the village street akhra would reverberate with their songs and dances. The singing and dancing are eternal like the hills and the moonlight nights.[114]

These folk dances had a remarkable effect on the rural mass and bears enormous ethical and social relevance. The triumphs of truth over evil, the cardinal maxim are presented in a lucid and imperative manner in most of the folk dances which has profound impact on the rural mass.

Folk dances of Odisha has developed in the rural area as in other states but due to rapid industrialization, the people's culture which developed on the basis agricultural life is undergoing major changes. Even those who have not yet moved to industrial area from their rural homes feel the impact of industrial life through various agencies. While previously they enjoyed long cultural performances covering weeks, fortnights and even months, now they prefer shorter, ready-made programmes, like the cinema, radio and TV programme. The cinema and T.V. has penetrated into the remotest villages. The folk dances are fast disappearing from the society due to the lack of patronage and onslaught of radio, cinema and T.V. Thus, folk-dances are rarely played, folk-songs are rarely sung, Folk-tales are rarely told, folk-dramas, folk-ballads are rarely performed, and folk-riddles are rarely asked.

The irony of the fate is that the folk dances, folk theatres, folk songs, tales, folk art, folk festivals which provided recreation, entertainment and subsistence to thousand and thousands of the rural people and spread the ideas of morality, universally brotherlihood, truthfulness, honesty and victory of righteous over evil forces are declining fast. These folklore traditions which are the valuable wealth of our society are not given the due recognition that they deserve.

That is the reason why the society of south Odisha which enjoyed perfect peace, better harmony and understanding between the divergent communities and races during the period under review is now regarded as a cockpit of murderers, docaits and looteras. Hence, steps may be taken to preserve all these folklore traditions alive either at the Governmental level or by the NGO and Private enterprises.

References

1. F. Bower, *The Dances in India*, 1939, Calcutta, p. 73.
2. K.B.Das, *Folklore of Odisha,* Odisha Sahitya Akademi, Bhubaneswar, 1991, p. 66.
3. D.N. Patnaik *Folk Dances of Odisha,* Odisha Sangeet Nataka Akademi, Bhubaneswar, 2000, p. 2.
4. *Palm Leaf Manuscript on Dandanata* composed by Ananda Chandra Kabichandra preserved in the DandaKali Temple of village Kalasandhapur of Ganjam district. No Date, No Page.
5. N.C. Behuria (ed.), *Odisha District Gazetteer: Ganjam*, Cuttack, 1992, p. 231.
6. *Ibid.*
7. H.K. Das, *Odia Lokanatak* (in odia),Cuttack, 1983, p.168.
8. *Palm Leaf Manuscript on Dandanata* composed by Neelakantha Patnaik and preserved in Dandakali *Ghara* of village Kulagada near Aska of Ganjam District, No Date, No Page.
9. D.N. Patnaik, *op.cit,* p. 4.
10. Sanyasi Nayak, *Bruhat Kamana Danda* (oriya), Berhampur, 1984, p. 116.
11. *Ibid.*
12. *Ibid,* p. 94.
13. *Palm Leaf Manuscript on Dandanata* composed by Ananda Chandra Kabichandra, *Op.Cit.*
14. D.N. Patnaik *op.cit,* p.4.
15. Bhagabana Sahu, *Prahallad Nataka-The Popular Folk Dance of* south *Odisha,* in: *Journal of Odishan History,* vol.XXIV, Dec. 2011, p. 211.
16. Jiwan Pani, '*Prahlad Natak : A Theatre of Liberated Reality*', in: *Essays on the Theatre and Theatre Crafts of Eastern India,* Eastern Zonal Cultural Centre, Calcutta, 1989, p. 84.
17. *Odisara Loka Nataka*(in Odia), Utkal Sahitya Samaj, Cuttack, 1998, pp. 254-260.
18. Interview with Arjuna Adhikari-a veteran *guru* of *Prahallad Nataka* in the village Tentuapada of Ganjam District on 1st January 1994.
19. *Odisara Loka Nataka op.cit,* p. 256.
20. Banambara Acharya (ed.), *Natyashastra* (in *Odia*), Odisha Sahitya Akademi, Bhubaneswar, 1963, pp. 2-4.

21. A.N. Tiwari (Ed.), *Reference Odisha,* New Delhi, 1999, p. 289.
22. *The Samaj,* 1.7.89
23. A.N. Tiwari (ed.), *op.cit,* p. 288.
24. Interview with A. Adhikary, *op.cit.*
25. Personal Observation of the Author.
26. A.N. Tiwari (ed.), *op.cit,* p. 304.
27. Remesh Pany, '*Folk Dances*', in: *The Cultural Heritage of Ganjam,* Bhubaneswar, 2004, p. 324.
28. B. Charchi, The *Contributions of Ganjam District to Odia Leela Sahitya,*(unpublished) Ph.D Thesis submitted to Berhampur University in, pp. 332-341.
29. A.N. Tiwari (ed.), *op.cit,* p. 288.
30. H.C.Das.(ed.), *Traditions of Folk Theatre,* Advanced Centre for Indological Studies, Bhubaneswar, 2000, p.31.
31. *Ibid.*
32. H.C.Das, *et.al* (eds.), *Traditions of Folk Theatre,* Advanced Centre for Indological Studies, Bhubaneswar, 2000,p.31.
33. Bhagabana Sahu, *Prahallad Nataka-The Popular Folk Dance of* south *Odisha,* in: *Journal of Odishan History,* vol.XXIV, Dec. 2011, p. 211.
34. Bhagabana Sahu, *Cultural History of Odisha,* New Delhi, 1997, p.
35. R.C. Mishra, *Folk Dance, Drama and Music in the District of Ganjam: An Overview,* in: *The Quarterly Journal of the Mystic Society,* vol. 101, no.1, January-March, 2010, p.11.
36. S.K. Satpathy, *Dasakathia* (*Odia*), Berhampur, p.
37. K.C. Behera, *Odisha ra yatra o Paramparika Lokapriya Natyadhara* (*Odia*), Cuttack, 1997, p.
38. *Ibid.*
39. R.C. Misro, *op.cit.,* p.11.
40. I.B. Kar, *Glimpses of Folk-Theatres,* in: *The Cultural Heritage of Ganjam,* Bhubaneswar, 2004, p. 345.
41. N.C. Behuria (ed.), *Odisha District Gazetteer: Ganjam,* Cuttack, 1992, pp. 229-230.
42. *Ibid.*
43. P.Sumabala, *Bura Katha and the History of Andhra Pradesh,* in: *Journal of Indian History and Culture,* (Chennai), vol.xv, September 2008, p. 99.
44. H.K. Das, *Odia Lokanataka* (Odia), Cuttack, 1983, p. 122.

45. K.C. Behera, *op.cit,* p.66.
46. B. Charchi, *op.cit.,* pp. 332-341.
47. *Odisha ra Lokanataka,* Odisha Sahitya Samaja, Cuttack, 1998, pp.224-227.
48. K.C. Pradhan, *Odia Loka Sahitya O Loka Sanskruti,* Cuttack, 1995, pp. 227-235.
49. Banambara Acharya, *op.cit.,* pp. 2-4.
50. *Odisha ra Lokanataka,* Odisha Sahitya Samaja, Cuttack, 1998, p.232.
51. D.K. Tripathy, *The Role of Fine Arts in the Folk Theatres of southOdisha: An Art Historical Study,* Ph.D Thesis (unpublished), Berhampur University, 2000, pp. 63-65.
52. B.Charchi, *Bharata Leela* in *Odishara Lokanataka,* Odisha Sahitya Samaja, Cuttack, 1998, pp. 229-32.
53. Cultural Heritage of Ganjam, o*p.cit.,* p. 340.
54. B. Charchi, *op.cit.,* p. 233.
55. Alekha Pradhan, Rajakabi Radhamohan Rajendra Dev-Eka Sahitya Samikhana, unpublished Ph.D. Thesis, Berhampur University, 1983, p. 61.
56. B. Charchi, *Bharata Leela* in *Odishara Lokanataka, op.cit.,*p. 234.
57. H.K. Das, *Odia Lokanataka, op.cit.,* p. 121.
58. Interview with the *Guru* of Radha Prema *Leela* of village B.L.N.Pur near Chikiti, Dated 21.01.1999.
59. B. Charchi, *The Contributions of Ganjam District to Odia Leela Sahitya,* p. 132.
60. Interview with Director (*Guru*), Radha Prema *Leela* of village B.L.N.Pur near Chikiti, Dated 21.01.1999.
61. H.K. Das, *Odia Lokanataka, op.cit.,* p. 121.
62. D.N. Patnaik, *op.cit.,* p.1.
63. B.C.Samal, *Odia Lokanatakara Sanskruti* in: *Odishara Sanskrutika Parampara,* vol.I, Cuttack, 1989, pp. 127-128.
64. D.N. Patnaik, *op.cit.,* p. 3.
65. Kedaranath Mohapatro, *Khurudha Itihasa* (Odia), Cuttack, 1983, p 101.
66. P.R. Sen, *Modern Odia Literature,* Calcutta, 1974, p. 108.
67. Kedaranath Mohapatro, op.cit, p. 101.
68. M. Mansingh, *The Saga of the Land of Lord Jagannath,* New Delhi, 1963, p. 43.
69. *Ibid.*

70. B. Charchi, The *Contributions of Ganjam District to Odia Leela Sahitya, op.cit.*,p. 79.
71. *Ibid.*
72. Interview with the *Gayaka* (Director) of *Rama Leela* of Nandigrama of Ganjam District on 05.01.2001.
73. D.K. Tripathy, *The Role of Fine Arts in the Folk Theatres of* south *Odisha: An Art Historical Study, op.cit.*, pp. 56-57.
74. *Ibid.*
75. *Ibid.*
76. *Ibid.*
77. D.N. Patnaik, *op.cit.*, p. 10.
78. B.Charchi, The *Contributions of Ganjam District to Odia Leela Sahitya, op.cit.*, p.
79. *Ibid.*
80. H.K. Das, *Odia Loka Natak*, p. 114.
81. S.K. Satapathy, *Krushana Leela* in *Odisha ra Loka Natak*, vol. I, Utkal Sahitya Samaj, Cuttack,1998, p. 243.
82. Information collected from N. Sadangi, the *Krishna Leela Gayaka* of village Padadigi on 02.01.2002.
83. B. Charchi, *op.cit*, pp. 333-334.
84. *Ibid.*
85. D.K. Tripathy, *op.cit.*, p. 55.
86. *Ibid.*, pp. 69-70.
87. *Ibid.*
88. Jagannath Das, *Sirmad Bhagavata* (*Odia*), Cuttack, 1983, p.
89. B. Charchi, *op.cit.*, p. 334.
90. S.Nahak&A.J.Dora, *Osakothi-Folk Theatre in Cultural Heritage of Ganjam*, Bhubaneswar, 2004, pp. 301-304, 346.
91. *Cultural Scenario of Ganjam*, p.
92. Interview with Choudhury Parida of Village Kabisurya Nagar (Boirani) on 27.09.2001.
93. Sivarama Rath, *Oshakothi*, Berhampur, 2000, p. 11.
94. Dinanath Pathi, *op.cit.*, p.
95. Sivaram Rath, *op.cit.*, p.
96. *Ibid.*

97. Sujata Patnaik, *Folk Legend Bhagabana Sahu,* New Delhi, 2006, pp. 31-32.
98. *Cultural Scenario of Ganjam,* p. 17.
99. Prahallad Panda, "Folk Dances of Ganjam in *Cultural Scenario of Ganjam",* p. 36.
100. *Utkala Prasanga,* Oct. 1996, p. 23.
101. D.N. Patnaik, *op.cit.,* p. 47.
102. Sudha Mishra, *Performing Folk Arts of* southern *Odisha (Ganjam)* in *Mardaraja,* Khallikote, 2009, p. 157.
103. Ramesh Pany, "*Folk Dances"* in: *Cultural Heritage of Ganjam,* p. 326.
104. Sudha Mishra, *op.cit.,* p. 156.
105. N.C. Behuria (ed.), *Orissa District Gazetteer-Ganjam,* Cuttack, 1992, p. 234.
106. Sudha Mishra, *op.cit.,* p. 156.
107. D.N. Patnaik, *Folk Dances of Odisha,* p. 43.
108. Cornelia Mallebrein, *Living Gods on Earth,* New Delhi, 2002, p.11.
109. R.C.S.Bell, *Orissa District Gazetteers*: Koraput, 1945, p.87.
110. Sitakant Mahapatra, *The Rainbow of Rhythms,* Jagatsinghpur, 2005, pp.100-101.
111. *Ibid,* p.102.
112. S.Thiady, Phulbani: *The Khond Land,* p.35.
113. N.Senapati(ed.), *Orissa District Gazetteers,* Kalahandi, Cuttack, 1980, p.116 .Sitakant Mahapatra, *op.cit.,* p.104.

5

Folk Festivals and Beliefs

Fairs, festivals and fasts are regarded as the essence of the life of the people of the southern part of Odisha. They are more conservative and superstitious than the people of other regions of Odisha and even the neighbouring states. From the moment of birth to the funeral ceremony, his life is an eventful journey of social ceremonies, rituals and festivals. They take every element of the past dictated by the tradition as sacred trust and consider a little digression from it as sin. They observe many fairs and festivals throughout the year either out of their superstitious beliefs or religious bent of mind. There is a proverb in Odia "*Bara masaku tera yatra*" which means, in Odisha there are thirteen festivals in twelve months. However, if we take the festivals, fairs and fasts together the actual number will be much more than thirteen.[1]

Festivals are those which are usually referred to as the fairs or *yatras*. But *oshas* and *bratas* (or *vratas*) are those which are intended to regulate the private life of the people by taking recourse to *upavasa* (fast), *ujjagara* (vigil) and *upasana* (worship). The *bratas* celebrated in Odisha can be categorized into two, viz., *Sastric* (Sastriya) and *Laukika*.[2] The *bratas* performed as per the principles and rituals laid down in the *Vedas* and *Sastras* are called *Sastriya bratas*. Whereas, those *bratas* for the celebration of which no principle is being laid down in the *Sastras* and *Vedas* are called *Laukika bratas.*[3] For the performance of *Sastric bratas* the *Brahmin* priest is required to officiate. Further, *sankalpa* (volition) worship of *Ishta Devata* (one's family deity) and recitation of mythical or *Puranic* stories relating to the gods and goddesses in good tone by the Brahmin priest is essential in the *Sastric bratas.* But in *Laukika bratas* the recitation of stories are made by the women. [4]

Bratas (or *Vratas*) are performed by both by men and women. But *oshas* are performed only by women. In respect of the performance of *bratas* (*Sastric*), the presence of Brahmin priest is essential. But, in case of *oshas* the women performed the recitation of stories, offering of flowers, fruits, etc.

There are some *oshas* which are performed by *kumaris* (unmarried girls), some are by *sadhabas* (married girls) and some are by *bidhabas* (widows). There are some celebrations where the *kumaris* as well as the *sadhabas* take part.[5]

In south Odisha the term *Osha, Brata, Upavasa, Parva and Yatra* are used more or less synonymously. The Odia word *Osha* probably derives from the Sanskrit word *Upavasa* which literally means "to remain fasting i.e. to abstain from taking food/worldly activities". The fasts are undertaken by individual in fulfillment of personal vows either on one's own personal interest or in the interest of one's loved persons.[6]

For a devote Hindu, there are many days in a month on which he has to undertake a fast, requiring him to eat only at sun-down, to go without the normal rice meal, to eat only fruits, or not to drink even water. A widow, especially in *Brahmana* and high caste families, has to undergo many austerities in almost all the fasts. Needless to say, fasting is accompanied with abstinence from non-vegetarian dishes, sex and other normal pleasurable activities. Such fasting earns one religious merit with the aim of securing release from the cycle of re-births. Following are the most popular *bratas* prevalent during the period under review.

1. Somanath Brata

It is not known from how many years the *Brata kathas* (or votive tales) are universally current in Odisha. But, from linguistic evidences and the religious worship advocated in these tales, scholars have placed these in the 13th-14th century A.D. From the medieval *Vrata* literature we come to know of the celebration of *somanath Vrata* in Odisha.[7] It falls on the tenth day in the bright fortnight of the month *Aswina.*

Janaki Ballabha Mohanty in his work entitled "*Somanath Vrata Katha*" opines that this *Vrata* has come from *Syam Veda.* The women folk on the 10th day in the bright fortnight of *Aswina* worship Somanath or Siva and conduct the *Vrata.* The Brahmin priests do the worship. The place of worship is decorated in *muruj* (colourful powders). *Gua* (betel-nut), *Vratas* (white threads) etc., are used in the worship. The women after the worship break the fast with taking *Prasad* (sacrament) and wear the white thread. A mythical story in the honour of Lord Siva to glorify his prowess is recited. As per the story, Birabikramajita, the most powerful *Raja* of Patali *Nagara* of the Malaba country ridiculed the *Somanatha Vrata* when he was advised some cloth merchants to conduct the *Vrata* to achieve some good results and fulfill his desires. Parameswar or Siva when came to know of it, became angry and cursed *Raja* Birabikramajita. As a result of it, the *Raja* suffered from leprosy. The *Raja* got cured of the disease only when his queen performed the *Somanatha Vrata* with much austerity. Besides there are other stories current in Odisha relating to Somanatha *Vrata.* A poor Brahmin who was the head of a big family got huge wealth by performing this *Vrata.* A saint who refused to hear the importance of Somanatha *Vrata* suffered from leprosy and got cured of the disease with the performance of the *Vrata.* A *gouduni* (milk-maid/woman) whose curd pot fell down got back the actual price of the curd by performing *Somanatha Vrata.* The main idea behind the *Vrata* is therefore, to get wealth, to be free from disease and to be blessed with a long life.[8]

2. Sabitri *Vrata:*

Savitri *Vrata* is observed by Hindu married women on *Jyestha Amavasya* which roughly corresponds to the English month of May. Savitri is the deified virtuous woman who had brought back her husband Satyaban to life by doggedly pleading with Yama-the God of Death.[9] The observance of this *Vrata* is restricted to married women only and not for the widows and spinsters. The married woman seeks Savitri's grace for making her husband live as long as possible, thus proving herself to be virtuous and devoted. The wife presents a number of delicacies to her husband at the end of her fast.

3. Sudasa *Vrata:*

Sudasa *Vrata* is observed by woman on the 10th day (Tithi) in the bright fortnight when it falls on Thursday. Lakshmi-the Goddess of wealth is worshipped with offering of ten steamed rice cakes *(Manda)* under great austereties. With a sacred thread of ten strands, ten knots are made praying to Lakshmi in Her ten forms and names and tying together ten grains of raw rice (*arua*) and ten blades of *durva* grass in a sacred leaf, an arm band is formed and worn for religious merit, prosperity and well being. According to this myth, a king had got back his kingdom and wealth as his wife observed *Sudasa Vrata*. This *Vrata* as mentioned in the book is adopted from *Padma Puran* and observed for good luck. *Raja* Bikramaditya's queen celebrated this *Vrata* and secured all fortune for the royal family.[10]

4. Kedar *Vrata:*

The famous sage Naimisa advised Kunti the mother of Pandavas to perform the *Vrata* in order to get back her empire. In the *Satya Yuga* (age of truth), there lived a poor Brahmin who had two daughters-Bhagyabanti and Punyabanti. They put on torn rag and went to the jungle to pick up cow dung-cakes to sell them for livelihood. Once, they saw the angles celebrating the Kedara-*Vrata* in the forest. They advised the wretched girls to worship Kedara who would certainly redress their sufferings and bring wealth and welfare to the family. The two girls put off their rags on the bank, took bath and saw to their amazement, the rags had turned into costly silk. They put them on, used banian fruits as arecnuts, leaves as betels, collected twenty-one kinds of flowers and worshipped Kedar with great reverence. When they returned home, they saw the little cottage turned into a beautiful palace and all cow dung-cakes changed into solid gold. The king of the country married the eldest, and the minister married the youngest sister. The King once out of pride threw away the *Vrata* of ordinary cotton thread and presented the queen with a golden one. All his property suddenly disappeared, for God took full revenge on him. The king and the queen had to move from door to door begging. Then with the advice of the youngest sister, the queen again celebrated the *Vrata* and got back all her wealth.[11]

5. Bajramahakali *Vrata:*

A merchant had seven sons and seven daughters-in-law. The youngest daughter-in-law while washing rice for cakes to be offered to Bajramahakali, ate two grains unknowingly. *Kali* at once appeared, caught hold of her hand and threatened to inform her mother-in-law about it.

She implored her with folded hands to excuse her and promised anything if she could keep it secret. The Goddess asked the daughter-in-law to give all children born to her. Then the *puja* was performed with splendour. After some months as a son was born to the youngest daughter-in-law, *Kali* took him away through the window. Similar was the case with the second, third, fourth, fifth, and the sixth. When the seventh child was to be born, the mother-in-law drove her away at night. It rained incessantly. She suffered much but uttered the name of the Goddess. In her difficulty the Goddess appeared and took care of her and the newly born child, and accommodated them in a temple. Then she was sent back to her mother-in-law's house in a palanquin with her seven children. Hence forward the *Vrata* of Bajramahakali became very famous.[12]

6. *Rabinarayan Vrata:*

This *Vrata* is observed when '*Ekadasi*' falls on Sunday. The Sun who is worshipped that day, grants children to the childless, wealth to the poor, good husbands to the virgins.

There was a rich merchant in Saurastra whose daughter-in-law and daughter gave much wealth to a Brahmin. He blessed the daughter-in-law to enjoy life fully and cursed the daughter to suffer as it was written on her fore-head. He was asked by the merchant's wife- the cause of his two opposite wishes. The Brahmin asked her to dig the grind where the daughter was sleeping. She dug and found a broken earthen pot and a broomstick. With the advice of that Brahmin she approached a potter's wife and asked her about it. The potter's wife could not foretell the catastrophe till the marriage ceremony was over. She kept strict watch on the bridegroom and the bride in the night of marriage. The messengers of the God of death came to take away the life of the bridegroom. The potter's wife, who was at the door, did not permit them. Even, the God of death Himself was not allowed. He angrily killed her seven sons and the husband. In the morning the potter's wife saw them all alive by utterance of the name of the Sun. The bride and the bridegroom led a happy and prosperous life. These miracles could be performed by the potter's wife for she observed *Rabinarayan Vrata.*[13]

7. Rai Damodar *Vrata:*

This *Vrata* is celebrated by widows in Odisha throughout the month of *Kartika.* They lead a very sacred life, take one meal daily, and worship *Damodar* with Rai and Lakshmi. The final ceremony is held at Puri in the last five days of the religious month, called *Bagapanchak* when the cranes turn pious and abandon eating fish.

The legend behind this *vrata* is as follows. The leader of *pandas* of the temple of Jagannath gave his daughter in marriage to the Lord. Her name was Rai. She asked a boon of Lakshmi that she would be worshipped with Jagannath one month in a year. She granted the boon with certain reservations. Rai Damodar worship was thus introduced in Odisha and continued for 25 days in the month of *kartika*. But Lakshmi-Narayana is worshipped in the last five days of the month.[14]

8. *Nisa Mangalbar Vrata:*

This *Vrata* is to be observed on every Tuesday of the month of *Aswina* by married women only. There was also a story behind this *vrata*. Once the sons of a merchant went in search of a rhinoceros for the *Sradha* ceremony of their father and unfortunately killed the best cow of the king by mistake. The King sent messengers to all directions to search for the cow. They were fully exhausted in the search, and finally saw the bones of the cow scattered near the house of the merchant. The king in anger arrested all the sons and put them in the prison. The Goddess appeared before the merchant's wife and advised her to observe *Nisa Mangalbar Vrata*. She obeyed her and was able to secure release of her sons. The king as he knew this became furious and ordered to kill all of them. The merchant's wife prayed to the Goddess who made them alive again.[15]

From the above analysis of the *Vrata-Kathas*, it is revealed that the names of the authors of these *Vrata-Kathas* are not known. But, the literatures of the *Vratas* throw flood of lights on the different kinds of food items, dress and ornaments, historical geography of different towns and kingdoms, system of weights and measures, currency system, system of *grama panchayatas*, religion and cults of the people of the region during the period under review. These *Vratas* also spread the ideas of morality, virtues, good conduct and good behavior in the society.

There seems to be an undertone of morality in the *Vrata-Kathas*. Goodness of heroism is rewarded. Wealth spent for good cause seems to receive divine sanction. On the other hand vices are deplored. Selfish people are made to suffer. Life of a mischievous fellow ends in a tragic way. All his property is destroyed. Kidnappers commit suicide or are turned to lower animals. God seems to remain behind all good men and all good actions. All bad intentions are bound to fail. Property confiscated by violent means may be restored. The dead may be brought back to life. But, the story of "dead may be brought back to life", criticisers of *Vratas* be died of sudden heart attack seems to be imaginary, impossible and illusion.

Besides the above *Vratas*, the following fasts were also prevalent among the Hindu community of south Odisha during the period under review.

Fasts (*Osha*):

The rural folk of this part of Odisha observed a number of *Oshas* during the period under review. Though all these *Oshas* were observed with some blind beliefs, myths, and imaginary ideas, it had its salutary effects on the society. The fasting, the devotion, and the concentration of mind of the people on Gods, Goddesses or supernatural objects not only preached its medical value, but also spread the ideas of moral values, virtues, wisdom of truth over evil and check corruption, robbery, dacoit, murder, rape and debauchery in the society. Perhaps this was the only reason for which the social life of the people in the villages was more peaceful than the urban areas.

A slight difference exists between the *Vrata* and the *Osha* (fast). The *Vrata* was a voluntary religious observance practiced both by males and females while the fast was observed only by females. The *Vrata* was observed with some end in view i.e. for fulfillment of certain desires. The fast originally had no such aims and aspirations. The vow means a promise, a determination to undergo hardship to attract the attention of the God towards devotee. Fast means to live near God, Fire or *Guru*. In the Vedic age, the devotees lived in the house of sacrifice *(yagnya)* without any food. When the sacrifice was completed, they had to break their fast with the offering. The fast and the vow gradually spread among the people from the higher to the lower caste.[16] The difference between the two gradually disappeared. Now the local vows and fasts in Odisha are observed in the same way.

In both of them people abstain from food till the worship is over. Some do not take water. If thirst endangers their life, water is offered though ears and not through mouth. Needless to say, fasting is accompanied with abstinence from non-vegetarian dishes, sex and other normal pleasurable activities. Such fasting helps one to earn religious merit with the aim of securing release from the cycle of re-births. The stories of the local fasts, written either in Odia prose or poetry, mention clearly the aims and objectives of worship, the requirements, or depict the glory of local Gods and Goddesses as in those of the vows.

A brief account of some of the stories of local fasts is given below:

(i) ***Jahni Osha***

Janhi Osha was one of the very popular *Oshas* of south Odisha which is observed by the unmarried girls only. *Brundabati* is the presiding Goddess of this *Osha.* Some Folk-tales depict the glory of the Goddess and describe how she compels all virgins to observe the fast and punishes those who stand in their way. Jambabati's son was bitten by a snake, for she laughed at a devotee, but was made alive after due prayer and worship. Radhi, a virgin was cured of her leprosy. The five sons of Sukanti were stolen and hidden in the hollow of a tree for she was against this worship. Her five sons were restored to her after worship of *Brundabati.* The Goddess threatened a lady in a dream that if her daughter would not observe the fast, all her sons would be killed within seven days. A girl's hand rotted and fell piece by piece, because she plucked a *Janhi* a forbidden fruit for virgins in the month. She got recovered after worship. In this manner the *Osha* was originated and began to continue till today.[17]

(ii) Kharkhari Osha

This fast is observed by the virgins of south Odisha on every Sunday of *Chaitra. Kharkhari,* the Goddess of this fast is worshipped at the root of the basil plant. She is requested to grant them good husbands, for they have attained maturity and become fully fit for marriage.[18]

(iii) *Khudrukuni Osha*

The most interesting of all the votive tales of Odisha is the pathetic story of *Taapoi* which has got related to the celebration of *Khudurukuni Osha* mostly by unmarried and newly married girls on every Sunday of the month *Bhadrava.*[19] The *Taapoi* story, recited during the performance of this *Osha* reminds us the glorious maritime trade of Odisha carried out by the *Sadhabas* (merchants connected with the overseas trade) since the olden times. In it is depicted the social custom of the Odias performed during the time of departure and arrival of their trading ships as well as the procedure for the conduct of *Khudurukuni Osha.*

There was once upon a time a rich merchant named *Tanayabanta* who had seven sons and a daughter named *Taapoi.* She was brought up very tenderly. After the death of her parents, the seven brothers went on trade to far-off islands and left the dear sister in charge of their wives. After their departure, the ladies gave her no food to eat, no bed to sleep and made her watch goats in the forest. Only the wife of the youngest brother treated her well. Once a goat named *Gharmoni* was lost. The oppression now crossed its limit. *Taapoi* worshipped Mangala- the Goddess of welfare and got back her goat. But it brought no change in her miserable condition. In despair she left home, climbed up a tree in the forest and wept bitterly. The brothers now coming back after ten months, could know the voice of their sister. They became very sad over this miserable state of affairs and chattered their teeth for revenge. They gave her a knife to chop up the noses of those who oppressed her. She did it. All of them except the wife of the younger brother (whose nose was not cut off) fled away and were devoured up by tigers. This fast was observed by virgins as a precaution against the tyranny of the brother's wife.[20]

Mostly young unmarried girls and newly married girls worship Mangala, the Goddess of welfare, on every Sunday in the month of *Bhadrava.* The *Udjapana* (closing ceremony) of the *Osha* takes place on the last Sunday of the month. As part of the ceremonial observations of this particular *Osha,* the girls on these Sundays pluck different types of flowers in the morning and go to the river or pond, take bath, then construct earthen temple (a miniature of a temple) offer *naivedya* and then return home. In the house they draw sketches of sea-going vessels on the grind with a paste made of raw-rice or with coloured powders over which Goddess Mangala's symbolic statue is made to stand. Goddess Mangala is offered *khuda* (rice bran/broken rice), as She is fond of it. Because of this *khuda,* this votive festival is known as *Khudurukuni Osha*. The story which the girls recite in the evening before Mangala is a narrative on how the only daughter Taapoi in a rich *sadhaba* family with seven sons was tortured by her brother's wives when the brothers were away from home on an over-seas trade mission. Taapoi worshipped Mangala, the Goddess of Welfare, and over came all the hurdles put in her way. Through Mangala's wrath, the sisters-in-law were punished for their misdeeds and Taapoi was blessed with good fortune.

The *Khudurukuni Osha* propogates the Sakti cult in a popular manner among the common people, particularly among womenfolk without the paraphernalia of temples and priests. The lovely pathetic figures of Taapoi in this story perhaps caught the imagination of the people, particularly of women and thus made it universally accepted in Odisha.[21]

Taapoi was the apple of the eyes of her seven merchant brothers. This became an eye-sore of her seven sisters-in-law. When the brothers went to far-off islands for trade she was tortured by her sisters-in-law. Everyday she worshipped the goddess Mangala for the safe return of her btothers.They returned safely and punished their wives for their mischief towards their only sister.

Since, *Taapoi* used to offer *Khuda* (broken rice) to Mangala, which she collected by begging, Goddess Mangala was also known as *Khudurikuni*. Today this festival is celebrated only by the unmarried girls of *Vaisya* communities. They worship *Khudurkuni* on all Sundays during the month of Bhadraba. A clay image of *Khudurkuni* is installed and worshipped in the house of one of the fasting women. The image is immersed in the river after the last ritual.[22]

In the Rushikulya, Bahuda, Bansadhara river mouths, there are numerous mounds and former harbours that retain their names associating them with maritime activities, including *Boyitadiha, Boyitakuda, Kudapatna, Jahajapariya* (ship field) etc. At the later site, an image of Ramachandi still exists, the *Sadhabas* used to halt to pay homage to the deity for a safe journey.

(iv) *Sathi Osha*

Sathi is a powerful local Goddess widely respected by village mothers. She is responsible for the welfare of all children. She is the Goddess of destiny who writes the future of man on the forehead on the sixth day of the birth of the child. The following story written in old prose is narrated during this *Osha.*

The brother's wife and the niece went out to bring a basket of soil. The niece was hit by shovel and killed. The brother's wife wept bitterly over the accident. The Goddess *Sathi* appeared and made the niece alive on condition that she would give all her children to the Goddess. She did as promised, but was driven out of the house by the mother-in-law. The Goddess gave back all children who were so long brought up with her care after the performance of this *Osha.* She returned home in a palanquin accompanied by all her children. Since then this *Osha* was performed by the woman-folk.[23]

(v) Bhudei *Osha*

The Budhei osha is the favourite *Osha* of the rural woman. Buddhibaman, a local God, capable of granting eyes to the blind, children to the childless and curing leprosy and other virulent disease, is worshipped on every Wednesday of the month of *Bhadraba.*[24] The curry-stone adorned with vermillion, collyrium and flowers, represents the God.

The wife of a wine-dealer was cured of her leprosy. Her five sons were killed by the King. Life was restored to them all. The angry king could do no harm to her, for the God is much more powerful than any human being. A Brahmin lady suffering from labour pain prayed to God for easy delivery and was relieved of the same by a dose of medicine administrated by the god on condition that she would observe the fast regularly. A lady, pregnant after the worship of God, forget to fast after the birth of a child. The God kidnapped the child and only restored to the lady after promise of worship.[25]

(vi) *Bali-Trutiya Osha*

This fast occurs on the third day of the bright fortnight of *Bhadraba.* The images of Uma and Maheswar, built of sands, are worshipped by married women only with great devotion. *Padmapurana* records that Parvati observed this fast with earnestness and married Siva. Citing the example of Parvati the young girls observe this *Osha* in the hope of getting good husbands.

(vii) *Bada Osha*

It occurs on the fourteenth day of the bright fortnight of *kartika.* Thousands of people gather at Dhabaleswar a mountain island in the midst of the river Mahanadi near Cuttack and worship Siva with great devotion. On the next day boats of the skin of plantain tree well decorated with lamps, are floated in a pond or river reminding us of the time when Odia merchants were going abroad for trade.

In normal times no other public worships of the village Gods are held, but if an epidemic breaks out or there is sacricity of rain, special worships, as prescribed, are held. On such occasions the festive aspects of the celebrations are kept in abeyance, but due care is taken for observations of the rituals in their minutest details, for they are meant for propitiation of the angry deities.[26]

(viii) *Dutiya Osha*

This fast is observed on the eighth day of the black fortnight of *Aswina.* Dutibahana born of a Brahmin widow in love with the Sun is the presiding God of this fast. Sterile and childless women or women whose children are dead, abstain from food even water and observe this fast. All sorts of fruits symbolizing the success of their efforts are offered to Dutibahana who in the story of the fast is depicted to have astonished the world with great miracles.

(ix) *Dhanumanika Osha*

The Goddess of wealth is worshipped on every Thursday of *Margasira* in every Odia home. She once approached a rich merchant's wife in the guise of a poor old woman and asked her to observe the fast. She puffed up with pride, drove her out with harsh words. The merchant and his wife were reduced to poverty and begged from door to door. Their daughter who worshipped the Goddess was married to a rich man, sent jewels in a pumpkin which were turned into charcoal. After-due worship, they got back their lost property. Their seven sons returned home with seven ships loaded with jewels. The little cottage was transformed into a big palace.[27]

(x) *Nagul Chauthi Osha*

Naga or serpent worship in India goes back to the ancient time. Since the *Vedic* age to this modern age people of different religious sects worship *Naga* or snake.

We find *Naga* in the body of Lord Siva. Lord Siva is well known by the names Nageswara and Nagabhushana. Thus, *Naga* is worshipped along with Lord Siva and in all the Siva temples *Naga* (made out of metal) is placed above the *Siva Linga.*

The *Naga* images in different forms (like *Nagakanya, Nagabandha,* partly *Naga* and partly human image, Balarama image with snake etc.) are found in Odishan temples. The *Naga* images pictured in the Odishan sculpture.[28]

In the *Vrata* literature of medieval Odisha, we find the clear mention of the *Nagula Chaturthi* on the fourth day of the bright fortnight of *Kartika.* On this day *Naga* and *Naguni* (made out of metal) are worshipped. Women worship the images of *Naga* and *Naguni* on this day near a snake-hill in order to protect the family members from snake bite. The cultivaters also worship *Naga* (cobra) as it protects the crops by killing the rats. They worship snake as *Khetrapala.*[29] They are accepted as the representative of Lord Siva and his consort Parvati. In the *Vrata* literature the procedure for the *Nagul Chauthi* is nicely narrated. The main purpose for this celebration known from this *Vratakatha* (votive tale) is to be blessed with sons. A story is narrated relating to the *sadhaba-bahu* (the house-wife of a trader family), who was blessed with seven sons by performing *Nagul chauthi* Vrata. A *sadhaba-bahu,* who tasted the *bhoga* (sacrificial food) before its ceremonial sacrifice, lost her eyes. She got back her eyes only when all the family members prayed before *Naga* and *Naguni.*

The association of Brahmin priest in the performance of this *Laukika Vrata* is the most interesting thing. It is done with a view to accord a higher socio-religious recognition to the *Nagul Chauthi.*[30]

Festivals and *Yatras*

The rural folk of south Odisha observe a number of festivals and *yatras* round the year. A festival which keeps the people amused in the monotony of hard work and worries of worldly affairs, almost occurs in every year. Its advent is awaited with great eagerness. For it brings a promise of leisure and pleasure. It is always accompanied by a feast- a great diversion for people whose standard of daily living is poor. It is chiefly meant to make the people religious minded and create an atmosphere of sanctity. A festival is chiefly devised to educate the mass through amusement, to attract their minds to the Almighty who appears before them in concrete form for different means of desires. It also inspires people to visit different places and facilitates exchange of ideas with various persons.[31]

These fairs, fasts and festivals differ from caste to caste, tribe to tribe, and from region to region. Although the Bengali culture had its influence on the people of north Odisha to a great extent, the Andhra or Dravidian culture is discernible in south Odisha. This was because the Telugu speaking people constitute a good percentage of total population of the area. Besides this, the geographical situation of the area also contributes to this as the southern part of Ganjam touches Andhra Pradesh. Above all, the history of the area shows that during the British period the region was under Madras Presidency under the Chicakole *Circar.* For that reason, the region was more attached to the south than the north.[32] Obviously this had its deep impact and influence on the fairs, festivals and fasts of the region.

Fairs are usually held at inter-village or regional level with great congregations. Festivals are observed at village, inter-village or regional level. It is heartening to observe that it is not rare to find a fast and fair combined. For example the *Sivaratri* involves a fast on the Siva *Chaturdasi* day for fulfillment of certain desires, and at the same time a fair drawing people from various neighbouring villages centered round the local Siva temple for observing *Ujjagara.* Some kind of blind beliefs or superstitions are discernible in almost all the folk festivals, fasts and beliefs.

Thakurani Yatra

Thakurani Yatra is considered the most typical and famous amongst all folk festivals celebrated in south Odisha. Basically this is the outcome of most flourished Sakti cult of Odisha in this particular region. Sakti cult is so popular in this region that every village, even every individual household worships Her either as presiding deity or as the protectress.[33] That is why the *Thakuranis* of this region are popularly worshipped with devotion and faith. At many places of this region the *Thakurani yatras* are observed. The *yatra* takes place bi-yearly at Berhampur, every three years at Bhanjanagar and once in twelve years in Kabisuryanagar. Usually the *Thakurani Yatra* is observed in the month of May in the different places of a region. Among all the *Thakurani yatras* of south Odisha, Berhampur *Thakurani yatra* is most famous. It is imperative here to discuss the Berhampur *Thakurani yatra* in detail.

Thakurani Yatra of Berhampur

Budhi Thakurani is considered as the presiding deity of the Silk City Berhampur. In Hindu tradition almost every village has presiding deity called *'Grama Devati'*. But very few urban centers, cities and towns have presiding deities like Biraja of Jajpur and Samaleswari of Sambalpur. *Thakurani* of Berhampur is considered as the presiding deity of the city. The people of Berhampur have absolute confidence on *Thakurani* for their protection in perfect *Grama Devati* style. *Thakurani* was initially associated with the weaver community of Berhampur and weaver community has earned the name 'Silk City' for the city. Hence it is no wonder that *Thakurani* is the presiding deity of the city. She is regarded as Mahashakti, Ugrachandi, Sarbamangala etc. She is being worshipped by one and all irrespective of caste and socio-economic status.

The actual date of the commencement of the worship is not known but is certainly very old. Traditionally it is believed that once *Raja* Narendra Deva of Mohuri estate went on a trip to south India. During this tour he visited Rajmahendri among other places. There he somehow happened to meet the members of the Telugu Lingayat (*Dera*) weaver community. He was greatly impressed by their weaving technique. On his invitation some of them came and settled at Berhampur near Mohuri palace under royal patronage. In due course, the *Dera* community started weaving the famous Berhampuri *Patta* and earned the title of 'Silk City' for Berhampur.

The weaver community (*Dera*) brought with them their tradition of '*Ghata Yatra*'. Probably since 1767 the festival is being celebrated every two years during the month of *Chaitra* (March/April). The festival is celebrated as the home coming of the Goddess. *Thakurani* is conceived as a young woman given away in marriage who visits her father's house in every two years. And this period of her being away from the temple at her father's place is celebrated as the festival period.

When the community (*Dera*) came to Berhampur they settled in eighteen settlements. Each *Dera* settlement had a Chief who was given the title of *Senapati* by the king of Mohuri. The chief of the eighteen *Senapatis* was given the title of *Desa Behera*.

Desa Behera was the chief worshipper of the *Thakurani.* Every morning he used to worship the *Thakurani* by offering flowers among other things. Tradition holds it that on one *Chaitra* Tuesday at mid-night *Desa Behera* heared a young women crying infront of his house. She was wearing a black saree and her hair was undone. On being asked about the reason for crying, she said that she was on her way to her father's house and unable to locate. *Desa Behera* as an affectionate father offered her to spend the night in his house and that he would guide Her to Her father's place the next day. After he has said this, the women walked into the bushes in other side of the road and vanished. The old man followed her for sometime but in vain.[34]

The next day when he went to the temple to worship the *Thakurani* his worship was practically refused by the Goddess. When he placed flowers on Her head it fell down and the same was repeated quite a number of times. *Desa Behera* realized that his worship has been rejected and out of deep remorse he sat on *dharana* (*Adhia*) near the image. After sometime heavenly voice told him that his worship will not be accepted. A father cannot worship his daughter. It is true that he was Her chief devotee but, since last night he has become Her father. But the daily worship must go on. Hence, the *Thakurani* directed him to engage the person whom he would meet first, immediately after coming out of the temple, as the priest. Incidentally the man whom he met was a barber who had come to meet him. And since then the priests in this temple are barbers. However, the *Desa Behera* continues to worship the Goddess inside his own house, after all that is Her house.

When *Desa Behera* expressed great remorse for being deprived of the worship, *Thakurani* told him that she would leave the temple and visit his house once in every two years as his daughter. On being invited by the father she will go there to spend some time in the company of Her family and friends with great pump and ceremony and then come back. And since then this *Thakurani Yatra* is being organized.[35] Initially it used to be celebrated only by the people of *Dera* community under the leadership of *Desa Behera* but later on it has become a mass based and popular festival of Berhampur.

On the *Maha Sivaratri* day which generally falls during the month of *Phalguna* in the festival years, the Chiefs of the 18 *Dera* communities meet at the residence of *Desa Behera* in *Desa Behera Sahi.* When they decide to hold the festival the matter is reffered to the community (Kula Sabha) for approval. Thereafter important persons of the town discuss the matter. Hence the approval of the representative of the entire town including the *Thakurani* Herself is necessary for holding the festival each time.

When the decision is taken to hold the festival, the *Desa Behera* along with other devotees go in a procession to the temple to obtain the consent of the *Thakurani* for the purpose. They return back with her willingness in the form of a garland (*Agnya Mala*) on a bamboo basket. Then the Holy Pole (*Subha Khunti*) is placed near the temporary temple where the *Thakurani* would stay during the visit. The establishment of the pole marks the commencement of the process for the festival. A temporary thatched temple is constructed for Her stay and worship during the period.[36]

After everything is over the invitation is sent to Her for the homecoming. The *Dera* Chiefs observe fasting during the day and in the evening all of them along with *Desa Behera* and his wife go to the temple in a grand procession to invite her. After performing ceremonial worship there, they return back with garland of *Itala* (*Itamalla*) flowers in a basket. The garland is kept inside the temporary temple and worshipped as Goddess throughout the festival. From the third day the garland is kept inside a well decorated earthen pot (*Ghata*) and worshipped. Besides the main *Ghata*, eight other *Ghatas* are worshipped as the *Parsvadevatas.*

The period of the festival is the period of rejoicing and merry making for the entire locality. Not only the daughter, who is given away in marriage has come but the Goddess Herself (not the moving image or *Chalanti Pratima*) has come to their house. The devotees enjoy the occasion. The entire population comes in close personal contact with the Goddess. The Goddess also goes around meeting the friends, relatives and neighbours. Nevertheless, regular worship continues in the main temple.

From the third day the *Ghatas* move around the locality. The main *Ghata* with the garland of *Itala* flowers (*Itamalla*) brought from the temple inside, is carried by the wife of *Desa Behera* and other eight *Ghatas* are carried by the wives of other *Dera* Chiefs (*Senapatis*). The ladies who carry the *Ghatas* observe fasting during the day and in the night take the *Prasad* from the Goddess for the entire festival period. The whole area is decorated with flowers and chariots. The town is excited with cultural activity. As many as 25 chariots (*Kalakunja*) are prepared for the purpose, which are named as Ramachandra, Laxman, Nagarjuna, Narayan, Kali, Jwalamukhi, Bana Durga, etc. This gives an opportunity to one and all to welcome the Goddess at their doorsteps.

On the last day thousand of ladies from all over the towns as per their *manasika* carry *Ghatas* along with the nine ladies from *Dera* community and go round the locality. All of them observe fasting and live on *Prasad* only. The wife of *Desa Behera* worships and carries the *Sahasra Chhidra Ghata* (*Ghat* with thousand holes). After going round the town they reach the main temple where the *Ghatas* are immersed which marks the end of the festival.

There is no fixed time and rule for the period of the festival. She can stay as long as She wants like for five days, seven days, fifteen days, twenty-one days or even more.

During this period, worship is performed in the temporary temple by the same set of priests as in the regular temple. Brahmin *Sevakas* are also engaged during the period to perform some offerings like *Sahasra Kumkuma Puja*, *Raja Bhoga* and *Homa*. The *Sevakas* of the *Devi* temples from the outskirts of the city also assist the regular *sevakas* to accommodate the crowd.

Unlike the other Goddess of Odisha, there is no animal sacrifice during the festival. Rice, curd, sweets, bananas, coconuts and other items constitute the *Prasad.* The *Grama Devatis* or the presiding deities of the villages are normally in wild form for which they were worshipped outside the village in small temples or under trees. In Odisha, *Dasamahabhuja* (Durga) is worshipped at ten different places as Samalai, Mangala, Bhagabati, Sarala, Hingula, Bhattarika, Charchika, Ugratara, Biraja and Tara Tarini. In *Grama Devati* form Durga has many names and forms. *Thakurani* of Berhampur is one such presiding deity who protects the town. In Ganjam there are four such Goddesses who are considered as four sisters i.e. *Thakurani* at Berhampur, Khambeswari at Aska, Boirani at Kabisuryanagar and Rama Chandi near Purushottampur.

Gradually *Thakurani Yatra* has come to be associated with commercialism. As such the *Dera* community is known for production of high quality *patta.* They were rich and could afford a festival with pomp and gaiety. In due course, people from other business communities like the *Kumutis* associated themselves with the festival. The *Bada Bazar* area is the commercial headquarters of entire south Odisha. The *yatra* involved large scale flow of people and consequently good business. The period of the *yatra* is directly depends on the business turn over. Today, the *yatra* has become a very good medium for sales promotion. Deliberate and successful efforts have been made by the business community to make it a mass based festival in order to attract involvement of more people.

Another very important activity associated with *Thakurani yatra* is the *Besha* system. Originally those who had some sort of *Manasika* wishing the welfare for their family and children would take up various types of *Besa.* But today it has almost become a profession for many. However, so far this is restricted among the children and males only. The theme of the *Beshas* are mythological, social as well as cultural such as Krushna, Rama, Balarama, Siba, Hanuman as mythological characters and Ascetic, Tantrik, Astrologer, Police as social characters etc. *Bagha Nacha*, Tribal Dance etc. form important cultural items. People take up *Beshas* irrespective of caste and socio-economic status. If children from leading families are seen going round the streets in different *Beshas* so the children of poorest of the poor are also seen doing the same.[37] Different folk dances like Bharata *Leela, Dasakathia,* Radhaprema *Leela,* Prahallada *Natak, Kandhei Nacha,* Ranapa *Nacha, Baghanacha* and animal mask dances are performed at the different places of the town on the occasion of *Thakurani Yatra.* The *Thakurani Yatras* are also performed in the different villages and towns of south Odisha among them the *Thakurani Yatras* of Kabisuryanagar, Pitala, Ichhapur, Rayagada, Bhanjanagar, Baliguda, Karapada, Jarada, Digapahandi, Koraput, Jeypore and Aska are famous. Both Telugu and Odia communities worship *Thakurani* as a result the *Thakurani* remains a symbol of communal harmony and goodwill between two communities.[38]

Besides the *Thakurani Yatras* the rural people of this region observed a number of *yatras* like *Pana Sankranti, Sitala Sasti, Raja, Garbhana Sankranti, Prathamastami, Baruni Snana, Dasahara, Dola Jatra, Makara Sankranti, Jhami* Festival, Ram *Navami, Ratha Jatra, Sivaratri,* etc. All these festivals are celebrated to commemorate the birthday and marriage ceremony of Gods. Performance of folk dances and *natakas* was the common feature of south Odisha during these festivals and yatras. But, all these folk performances have their special significances on the special occasions. For example, in Rama *Navami Yatras,* Rama *Leela*; in Janmastami and Nanda Utsaba, Krushna *Leela*; in Pana Sankranti, *Danda Yatra*; in Nrusingha Chaturthi, Prahallad *Nataka*; in *Dasahara, Oshakothi* are performed in a grand manner in different villages of Odisha. People of this region in general are religious minded and usually gather in temples to offer their prayer to the almighty mainly during leisure hours. They get mental peace and satisfaction. They also meet at a common place where the priest recites and explains from the religious text like *Bhagabat, Mahabharat, Ramayan, Haribansa* and other *Puranas.* Singing musical instruments like *Khanjani, Gini, Mrudanga* or harmonium is also another popular form of entertainment to the rural mass.[39]

Beliefs and Superstitions:

Like the people of Northern and Western Odisha, the people of southern part of Odisha also followed a number of folk believes and superstitions. But the people of this region, especially the Kandhs, were more conservative, ignorant and superstitious than the people of the rest parts of Odisha and even the neighbouring states. They believe in the supernatural power of the *Kalisi, Patua, Bejuni, Deshari, Shamanins, Witches, fortune-tellers, Sorcerers* and fetish gods and goddesses. Owing to their blind believes and superstitions, the rural folk of south Odisha practiced a number of social evils and other hated practices. It is imperative to discuss these things in detail.

Patua:

Patua, a well-known term in Bengal and Odisha is derived from the Sanskrit word '*Pata*' meaning a cloth. Those who perform the main role in the *yatra* by wearing *pata* cloth are known as *patua.* The *patuas* who take part in this *Yatra* in both the provinces are low class people. Out-casted from the community of the Hindus and Muslims, they led a very miserable life. If a higher class people joined as *patua* for fulfilling a promise made at the time of sickness or any other difficulties, they are excommunicated by the society probably out of fear of the Goddess.[40]

An interesting account of their degradation has been gathered from an old *Patua* by name Gurusaday Dutta and discussed in his introduction to *Patua-Sangit* "We are the sons of Biswakarma. We have been driven to such a humiliating position due to our ill-luck. One of our predecessors drew a picture of Siva in a carry-creature manner without his permission which made him very angry. He cursed us that we would hence-forth be driven from both the community. We now pray like Muslims and also draw the picture of Hindu Gods".

In Odisha, *Patuas* are Hindus only in name. They are forbidden to worship the Hindu Gods in the Hindu temples.

They are hired as *palki*-bearers by the Muslims. They may be represented by an animal, a pot, an offering, a place of offering, an inspired priest or seer or the temple itself. They bestow mental faculties and miraculous powers upon the devotees. The *patuas* are of three kinds i.e. *Ghata Patua, Khand Patua, Phoda Patua.*[41]

Ghata Patua:

He derives his name from *Ghata* which he worships. He keeps in balance a *ghata* on a piece of wood placed on his head. The *ghata* is decorated with sandal paste, vermillion, coloured flags and garlands of flowers. He dances, sings and carries on physical exercise in different villages. Villagers pay him in cash or kind for the worship of Goddess. The amount thus collected is spent on a day of festival called *Jhamu-Yatra.*

Khanda-Patua:

The word *khanda* means sword. As they display their *yatra* on a *khanda*, they are known as *khanda-patua.* This *Patua* stands barefooted on the sharp edge of the sword and is borne on shoulders a small wooden temple in a procession cheered by the crowd.

Phoda-Patua:

This *Patua* drives or inserts a big needle in his tongue or a big nail on the back and astonishes the crowd with miracles. *Tantra* still continues to exert its influence on the rural folk in this *Patua Yatra.* What seems to be a superstition, looked from outside, has become a part of their religion.

Patua jatras really adds to the festivity, beauty and joy of village life. It is one of the best mediums of mass education. It popularizes our old literature, disseminates education and culture among the masses.[42]

Popular Beliefs:

Credulous people of the country inherit from their fore-fathers certain beliefs which are so deep-rooted in their minds that they cannot eradicate them even in face of progress of civilization. Their process of thought and action is never scientific or logical. It is traditional and religious. When they cannot explain the causes of flood, famine, earthquake, volcanic eruption or any virulent disease, they presume it to some outside agency. They try to propitiate the God, Goddess, Giant or Spirit supposed to be behind their suffering. The fact is that their difficulty is not removed, and hundreds die of cholera or small-pox. In spite of the progress of civilization, it does not deter them from clinging to the time-honoured superstition. They explain that the Goddess caused the disease, for she could not be propitiated properly. So they perform different types of sacrifices and believe in superstitions which are given below:

Tribal Beliefs and Superstitions:

The religion and religious beliefs of the tribals of south Odisha was somewhat different from that of the people of the plains. They had different nomenclature for their Gods and Spirits with varying degrees of their powers. Many deities of individual villages, hills and forests were also worshipped by them. All their Gods, used to be propitiated by regular sacrifices, and all the tribes observe a number of ceremonies and festivals which are closely connected with their agricultural operations. Therefore Hunter has rightly said that, "the religion of the tribes is essentially one of blood".[43] Among them, the Kandhs of Odisha were extremely conservative, ignorant and superstitious. Their socio-religious susceptibilities were deep and peculiar. They followed many irrational and inhuman practices like human sacrifice and infanticide. The human sacrifice was the very foundation of their socio-religious life.[44]

Their pantheon consisted of eighty-four deities of whom *Tari Penu* or the Earth-Goddess was supreme. She was the supreme deity of the race, the solemn symbol of the productivity of nature and Her worship united the whole kandh race by a nexus of blood into a race.[45] The Kandhs had deep reverence for this deity and had been worshipping Her since time immemorial.

Human Sacrifice or *Meriah* Sacrifice:

The human or *Meriah* sacrifice was one of the most horrid and gruesome practices that prevailed among the Kandhs of south Odisha during the period under review. Out of their blind believes and superstitions, the Kandhs sacrificed human beings before their main deity *Dharani Pennu.* Kandh country in which the human sacrifice was performed extended from the north of river Mahanadi to as far as south of the river Godavari. In Angul, Boud, Balliguda, Bissam-Kataka, China-Kimedi (Sana Khemudi), Pedda-Kimedi (Bada Khemundi), Dasapalla, Ghumusar, Jeypore, Kalahandi, Sorada and Patna, the practice was prevalent at an enormous extent.[46] Besides, the *Rajas* of Jeypore and Kalahandi did it to propitiate their presiding deity-Goddess Manikeswari.

Origin of the *Meriah* Sacrifice:

The origin of *Meriah* sacrifice among the Kandhs can be traced to their legendary accounts. The Earth Goddess was the supreme deity of the *Kandhs*. She was the solemn symbol of the productivity of nature. The Kandhs had deep reverence for this deity and had been worshipping Her since the time immemorial.

Regarding the origin of the human sacrifice, the legends of the Kandhs narrate: "Originally, the Earth was a crude and unstable mess, unfit for the comfortable habitation of man. It was not at all conducive for cultivation. Once, the Earth Goddess said "Let human blood be split before me". A child was then sacrificed. The soil became firm and productive forthwith. Then, the deity ordered, "Man should repeat the rite and live".[47] From that day the human sacrifice was started among the Kandhs. In course of time, it became the foundation of their socio-religious life, and the religion of the *Kandhs* became essentially one of blood. The Britishers called the human sacrifice as '*Meriah*'. The word was probably derived from the Kandh word '*Mervi*' or Mirivi[48] which was their famous god.

Causes of *Meriah* Sacrifice:

There were mainly four reasons behind the *Meriah* sacrifice. Firstly, the human sacrifice was offered to the Earth Goddess to ensure immunity from diseases and accidents and to increase the fertility of the soil. Secondly, the Kandhs considered human sacrifice was quite necessary for the cultivation of turmeric, their most profitable and favourite crop. They believed that the turmeric could not have a deep red colour without the shedding of human blood in the fields where it was grown. Thirdly, they wanted to propitiate the Earth-Goddess by the sacrifice of most precious victim that man could offer, so that the Goddess might grant favourable seasons and crops.[49] Fourthly, whenever famine or pestilence or epidemics broke out in the Kandh territory, public as well as private ceremonies of human sacrifice were performed.[50] By such rites, it was believed that the deities could be satisfied.

With the passage of time, this horried practice was also sanctioned by the Hindu *Rajas* who ruled over the Kandhs. In Jeypore and Kalahandi, the kings on great occasions such as going out to fight, building a fort or rebuilding an important village were in the habit of propitiating their presiding deity Manikeswari by the immolation of three human victims called *Junna.*[51]

Victims of Human Sacrifice:

Generally, the human sacrifice was performed on the full moon day of *Margasira* or *Pausa* corresponding to the month of December or January after the harvest was over. It was performed either by an individual or by a joint effort or several individuals or villages, both as periodical festivals and extraordinary occasions.[52]

The victim or *Meriah* might be of any age, sex or caste, except a Kandh or a Brahmin.[53] Generally, the victims for human sacrifice were the poor low caste Hindus, i.e. *Pans, Dams* and *Haris.* When the victim was a Kandh, he was not sacrificed by his own men or in his own village. In that case, the victim was exchanged or sold to other villagers.[54] If the victim was a girl, she was married by her purchaser. Her children became *Meriahs* and were liable to sacrifice. A *Meriah*, if grown up, was kept in chains, otherwise treated kindly.[55]

The victim or *Meriah* was acceptable to the Goddess only if he or she had been purchased, or had been a born victim, i.e., the son or daughter of a victim father or mother. The price of the *Meriah* varied from Rs.60/- to Rs.130/-. It was paid in grain or cattle, or a piece of land. Low caste people in distress often sold their children for being victims.

The agents employed to procure victims were usually low caste Hindus like *Panas* or *Haris*. These agents sometimes purchased, but more frequently kidnapped the children from the plains and sold them to the Kandhs.

Generally, grown up victims were preferred for the sacrifice. The reason was that rearing the children for the purpose was a costly affair. Despite this fact, children were purchased and reared up till they grew up to be adults. *Meriah* being regarded as a consecrated being was treated with extreme affection and was welcomed wherever he went. A *Meriah* youth on attaining maturity was generally given a wife, who was herself usually a victim and with her he received a piece of land and farm-stock. Their children were also became victims.[56] Nearly 1260 victims were sacrificed in the Kandh areas every year.[57]

Modes of Human Sacrifice:

The British officers like Russell, Campbell and Macpherson have given graphic account of the manner in which *Meriah* sacrifice was performed. When a sacrifice was decided upon, news was sent to all members of the community. Crowds of men and women assembled to witness the sacrifice. It was followed by several days of wild rivalry and gross debauchery.

Ten or twelve days before the sacrifice, the hairs of the victim were cut off. On the day before the sacrifice, the victim dressed in a new garment was allowed to wander in the village, to eat and drink anything he desired and even to have sexual connection with any of the women whom he wished. Then the victim was taken from the village in solemn procession, with music and dancing, to the *Meriah* grove, which was a clump of high forest trees standing a little away from the village.

In this grove, the victim was tied to a tree on which no birds should have built their nest. He was then anointed with oil, ghee and turmeric and adorned with flowers. A great deal of reverence was paid to him throughout the day. The crowd danced round him singing music and addressing the Earth Goddess *Dharani Penu*:

> "Oh god, we offer this sacrifice to you, give us good crops, seasons and health".[58]

On the next morning, the orgies which had been scarcely interrupted during the night were resumed and continued till noon when they ceased. Then the assembly proceeded to consummate the sacrifice.

The victim was again anointed with oil and turmeric, and each person touched the anointed part. As the victim might not make any show of resistance the bones of his arms and if necessary his legs were broken. But occasionally this precaution was rendered unnecessary by stupefying him with opium. In the place of sacrifice, the victim's head and neck was inserted into the reft of a splited bamboo. Then its ends were held tight by the sacrificers. Then the priest wounded the victim slightly with his axe whereupon the crowd rushed at the victim with their knives and cut the flesh from the bones, leaving the head and bowels untouched till the victim alive.[59]

In some places, the modus-operandi of the sacrifice was different. The living victim was dragged along with the fields. It was followed by drunken and excited Kandhs who cut the flesh from his body with their knives. They of course took care to avoid the head and intestine so as not to kill him outright.

In Chinna Kimedi region, there was yet another mode of sacrifice. The effigy of a wooden elephant was fixed on the top of a stout post and it was made to revolve. After performing the usual ceremonies, the concerned victim was fastened to the proboscis of this elephant. Then, amidst the shouts and yells of the excited multitudes of the Kandhs, the elephant was rapidly whirled round. A signal was given by the officiating priest. Then the crowd rushed in, seized the *Meriah* and cut of his flesh with their knives as long as life ebbed.[60] Campbell discovered fourteen such effigies of the elephants which were used formerly on this occasion.[61]

In Bissam Katak *Maliahs*, one peculiar mode of sacrifice prevailed. On the day of sacrifice, the *Meriah* was surrounded by the Kandhs, who beat him violently on his head with heavy metal bangles, which they specially wore on these occasions. In doing so, if he did not die, they strangulated him by putting his head inside a slit bamboo.[62]

In Patana and Kalahandi areas, the sacrifices were performed in diversified forms such as stoning to death and beating to death with bamboos and such other torturous modes. In whatever way the rite was performed, it was invariably accompanied by the most revolting cruelty.

The flesh cut off from the victim was instantly taken home by the persons who had been deputed by each village to bring it. In every village; all who stayed at home fasted rigidly until the flesh arrived. The bearers of the flesh deposited it in the place of public assembly, where it was received by the priest and the heads of the families. The priest divided it into two portions. He offered one portion to the earth Goddess by burying it in a hole in the ground. Then each man present there added a little earth to bury it and the priest pour water on it. The other portion of the flesh was divided by the priest into as many shares as there were heads of houses present. Then each head of house rolled his share of flesh in leaves and buried it in his favourite field.[63]

The human sacrifice practiced by Kandhs in their remote hill fastness continued till British government acted resolutely for suppressing it. In an era of mental stagnation, this abuse continued without affecting the conscience of thinking men. But, when the time came, society showed eagerness to abandon this pernicious and obnoxious custom.

Now the buffalo sacrifice took the place of the human sacrifice which is known as *Kedu* sacrifice or *Chaita parva* among the

Kandhs after it's suppression in the 19th century. While performing the sacrifice, the Kandhs apologized to the deity for not being able to offer a human victim in view of the prohibition imposed by Lieutenant Colonel Cambell and Captain Macpherson popularly known as Kyamal Makmel Sahib. The Kandhs still regarded human sacrifice as the proper method of propitiating their gods, and the buffalo sacrifice as a less effective substitute.[64]

Omen and Folk Beliefs:

Omen form the part and parcel of the folk beliefs and superstitions. In the society of south Odisha during the period under review a number of omens and superstitious beliefs were prevalent. It is pertinent to discuss them in detail in the following pages.

Folk beliefs in a society develop sometimes out of irrational explanations of practical experiences, and sometimes due to absolute ignorance of natural laws. For example, there is a folk belief in south Odisha that it is inauspicious for three Brahmins to travel together, though there is no orthodox corroboration for such a belief. Probably it has its origin in some tragic incident of the past.[65] Such folk beliefs are numerous in rural life. Only a few can be cited here.

The people of this part of Odisha believe in omen and dreams. They take omen from certain incidents that happened. On coming out of house if a cat crosses infront of them they turn back and relinquish the business for that day. A great number of examples show how the people of this region believe superstitiously in different gestures and science of different part of the body. Sensation in the right or left eyelid of a person has some meaning for the future.[66]

Sneezing is inauspicious while starting on a journey. Sighting a beggar woman with a begging-bowl, a washer-man, a milkman, a barber, an empty vessel, a widow, a dark-complexioned Brahmin, a beardless man, a fair complexioned *Chandal,* a Muslim without beard, a dwarf, a crow cawing while perched on a dried branch of a tree are likewise inauspicious. But it is auspicious, while starting on a journey, to see a prostitute, a cow with a calf, a woman going with an empty pitcher on her hip to fetch water, a full pitcher, and quite a number of articles like flowers, flags, etc.[67]

Liberal exceptions are also always made. For example, though sneezing is generally inauspicious at the time of starting on a journey from home, sneezing of the old, or children and of a person afflicted with cough, or sneezing intentionally, need not be taken into consideration.

Calling a person from behind at the moment of his starting is inauspicious, but if the mother calls the son at that moment it is auspicious. Therefore, in almost all the houses it is usual for a mother to follow her son at the moment of his journey from home and, after he has gone some distance, to call him back by name. This can only be done by the mother and by no one else. There are certain folk beliefs with regard to certain animal. The crow is inauspicious, but when it caws at one's house, it signifies that some relative would visit the house.[68] Otherwise, the crow is considered as the custodian of the departed souls of deceased persons. During funeral ceremonies, the food meant for the deceased is offered to crows so that it can reach the departed soul through the crow. Food to deceased fore-fathers offered on the occasion of the annual new rice ceremony or *navanna* is offered through the crows. Cawing of crows during the night is considered inauspicious.

The narrow-minded village priest is a parasite who in the name of religion also misguides the rural folk. He is responsible for continuity of many of the superstitions. If a vulture or an owl sits on the roof of the house, the house-holder is to make penance for that.[69]

The word *Sapa,* meaning snake, the name of any class of snakes, poisonous and non-poisons, such as *dhamana* (Krait), *dhanda* (water viper) etc. or any word synonymous with a snake is carefully avoided after dusk, especially by womenfolk. They prefer to use such words as creeper (*lata-patra, lata, latti*), rope (*dari)*, worm (poka), Astik Muni (the sage Astik) or the long one (*lamba-ta).* This habit of kenning is applied to other creatures also. In some areas the word *mamu,* meaning maternal uncle, is used for the elephant after dusk. In Koraput and some other places of south Odisha the word *Bada munda* (big headed) is used for the tiger during the night. There is no prejudice, however, against uttering words meaning lion, bear and even ghosts and goblins though they are also equally dreaded. The only explanation that can be given for this is that snakes, tigers, and elephants are more real in this part of Odisha than other animals and spirits.[70]

In common with the rest of India, people in Odisha believe that the serpent and the mongoose are eternal enemies. In the *Odia* idiom *Ahi-nakula samparka,* which means eternal or constant enmity, the relationship between these two animals is referred to. It is believed that if a snake gives protection from the sun to a sleeping man by spreading its hood over his head, the person will be a 'king', or a very well-to-do man like a king, one day. According to a tradition *Kapila*-a cowherd boy became Gajapati Kapilendra Deva, the king of Odisha as a snake gave protection from the sun to him while he was sleeping under a tree.[71]

It is always inauspicious to see a serpent on one's left when one is proceeding towards some place. But if seen on the right, it is auspicious. A jackal, on the other hand, indicates good luck when seen on the left and bad luck when seen on the right.

The common people believe that the earth rests on the thousand fold expanded hood of the serpent known as *Vasuki.* Becoming weary due to long holding of the heavy load on its head, it transfers the burden from one hood to another. This causes earthquakes.[72]

Serpents are believed to be the guardians of hidden treasures. The idea of associating serpents with hidden treasures must have come from the fact that both the hidden treasure and the serpent lie underground, though the serpent's relationship with wealth is also to be found in the popular belief of its possession of the head-jewel (*Naga Mani*). It is believed that the snakes are the watchers of the *Ratna-Bhandara* of the temple of Lord Jagannath at Puri.[73]

It is inauspicious to sleep in the evening. Turning the head to the North or West is to be avoided. Only dead man's head is placed in that direction. He who places his hands on the chest in sleep, dreams a lot. The Goddess of wealth forsakes a man who scatters food carelessly while taking his meals.[74]

Red papers should not be handed over to anybody: for that may make him angry. One should not take his food facing west. Only beasts do that. Rubbing nails one against the other excites men to quarrel. Two brothers should not shave on the same day. That is practiced in funeral ceremony. White spot on the nail is a good sign. If so happens, the man may hope to put on a new dress. If a man feels an itching sensation on the right-palm, he may hope gaining money. One should not beat one's uncle. That makes his hands tremble in old age. Utterance of the name of God at the time of death brings salvation.

A girl should not decorate her hair with *Kaniar* flowers. In that case the God of destiny compels her to become a second wife. She should not touch a broom stick with her feet; it means an insult to *Sathi*-the presiding Goddess; the slab of stone for powdering spices should be treated with respect; for the above Goddess resides there also.[75]

Taking *radish* in the month of *Magha* amounts to taking beef. If a woman takes twin plantains, she becomes the mother of twin children. A plantain should not be cut into three slices. Boiled paddy should not be measured. That is practiced in the funeral ceremony. If a woman combs her hairs on the day of *Sradha* ceremony, the up-rooted hair falls on the fore-father's *Pinda* (meals). Thursday is the day of the Goddess of wealth. A woman is forbidden to take bitter things and non-vegetarian foods that day. She should not wash the earthen pots; cut her nails, malish her body with oil, put on any new cloth. She should not lend money or paddy to any outsider, if she does so and disobeys, she is reduced to poverty.

An inauspicious woman possesses a high forehead, long front teeth; the little fingers of her feet never touch the ground; her eyebrows touch each other; she laughs loudly, trots like a horse.

A lamp is kindled in the birth place of the child for twenty-one days to avoid ghosts. The mother spits on her chest, on the clothes when she goes out to forbid ghost taking possession of her body. The uncle pushes fried rice and pulses with a sound by the ears of the child to prevent him from becoming deaf. Palm leaf and iron pen are kept by the child's head on the sixth day of the birth; for, Goddess *Sathi* will write his future luck on the forehead. That palm leaf is used for preparing the horoscope. The mother ties a hair of the horse's tail in the neck of the child, stains his fore head with collyrium or cowdung as a precautionary measure against evil look of witches. The name of any disease is not uttered before the child. A woman with a red cloth is not allowed to approach the birth place. He who calls the child a monkey, even out of joke, should rub his ears and strike his cheeks thrice.

A pregnant woman should not burn a brinjal in the hearth, for it creates an ulcer on the head of the child. She should not burn the shell of cocoanut for that will make her child bald.[76] She should take a large quantity of '*Sag*' (leaves used as curry). Then her child will have luxuriant growth of hair on the head. If she takes meat, the child's body will be full of hair.

Evil omens are presaged not only by men but also by beasts, birds or even by some trees. If a man's left eyelid or women's right eyelid quivers, this forebodes some evil events for the persons concerned. If a male jackal howls or a raven caws on or above a particular house it forebodes the sudden death of some member of the family. Similarly, great mishap befalls a house, if, according to the popular belief, an owl sits on the roof or hoots on a nearby tree. If a lizard falls on the right side of the man or on the left side of the woman, he or she is blessed with a son or wealth in the near future but if the opposite happens, it results in the death of some family member or loss of property. Just to give one or two examples of the beliefs concerning plants, one may cite the popular practice of celebrating a symbolic marriage with a *sahada* tree before a man marries a third wife. The coconut, it is believed, never falls on anybody's head but only on sinner's.[77]

All religious practices of the villagers are motivated by the *puranic* conception of heaven and hell. The rural folk believe that good and bad actions of men are noticed keenly by luminous eyes and noted carefully by skillful hands of God. All men are brought to judgment in the court of *Yama*- the god of death, who rewarded or punished according to the weight of their virtue and vice.

They believe heaven is the place of all beauty, sweetness and joy with golden lotuses blooming in the celestial Ganges and charming angels dancing. All pious souls live there after death. Hell is meant for all wicked people who steal, kill and do harm to others in all possible way. The culprit is thrown among poisonous snakes, scorpions, hungry tigers, crocodiles, rabid dogs, burning fire, dirty pools and beaten cruelly by *Yama's* terrible messengers.

The earthly gods in the form of idols if worshipped earnestly recommend strongly the case of a devotee for heaven and condemn the criminals for burning in the hell. Thus the life of the villager is regulated by *Dharma.*[78]

So the rape, murder, robbery, stealing and killing were very rare among the rural folk than the elite folk of the urban areas during the period under review.

Fetish Gods and Goddesses:

Most of the people of the village are ignorant of higher or metaphysical aspect of Hinduism. The Vedic Gods like Bishnu, Rudra, Varuna, Hanuman, Ganesha are mere names to the mass minds. They are symbols of aristocracy. These Gods were too great for the villagers and so inapproachable.

These people cannot rise above their daily necessities, their worldly feelings and ambitions. If they are poor, they desire to be rich. If they are childless, they long for children. If they go hunting, they wish themselves all success. Who will fulfill their desires? Who will redress their innumerable grievances? Who will help them in danger and save them from disease and degradation? Whom will they approach for consultation in a complicated situation? Who will fill their heart with hopes when they are disappointed? Who will protect them against the cruel enemy, deadly snakes and savage beasts? [79]

So they created certain Gods as off-springs of their daily necessities. Most of them have no temple, not even a shed against sun and rain. They are instituted by the roadside, on the bank of some river or Pond, under some shady tree or in the open field. Many of them are not represented by any anthropomorphic images or idols but are symbolized by little mounds of clay, by uneven blocks of stones.

The fetish gods fell far below the dignity and splendour of the Vedic and Puranic Gods. The villagers left no stone unturned to bring them to the same status. Thus, they become as powerful and virtuous as the Vedic and Puranic Gods. Hundreds and thousands of Goddesses with local names were treated to be the manifestation of Durga. She acquired new names as *Jugulei, Hengulei, Paneswari* and *Patrasuni, Kandhuni Devi* etc. in south Odisha. Thousands of goats, rams and fowls and even buffalos are sacrificed before the fetish gods in south Odisha. In a small mountain island of the lake Chilika, goats, sheep and fowls are left behind by people desiring the grace of Kalijai, the goddess. It is a pitiable sight to see these animals die of the dearth of food and water.[80]

The exact number of these Gods and Goddess are not known, which may be more than one hundred. A fetish god is a common sight in Odishan village. Approach a Banian tree, you will see its root coloured with vermillion and painted with silver eyes. Torn red rags, dry garland broken mud-horses scattered to and fro indicate the disorderliness of management and the irregularity of worship of these Gods and Goddesses.

Ranaghanta:

It is a gigantic piece of stone, coloured with vermillion. She is the Goddess of war, worshipped for self-protection and victory in the battle-field. Chakara Bisoi, the main leader of the Ghumusar rising worshipped this deity and united all the people of Khond community against the British army when they were on the verge of defeat.[81]

Sacred Man of Odisha :

Sacred man of Odisha is called *Kalasi.* He is the most feared man in the village. The God or Goddess is supposed to inspire him and he shakes his head and leaps frantically round and round. Ultimately he falls down in a trance. He performs some miracles and thus commands respect.[82] Dr. Cornelia Mallebrein calls these *Kalasi* as the living Gods on Earth. The moment the *Kalasi* touches the self-created stone of goddess, he becomes possessed by her spirit and embodies her.[83] The two *Dehuris* in a small and remote village in Odisha start dancing wildly and boisterously with their hairs flowing freely, and the sound of the drums is ecstatic. Goats are sacrificed to please the goddess, to nourish her, to appease her constant hunger, and to keep her cool and calm. This system is also prevalent in many countries of Africa and Australia. The sacred man in West Africa is called *Kosio.* A band of priests carries him to the image of god. He occupies His seat. If God accepts him he trembles and dances frantically and is declared as the messenger of God. Whatever of offence he commits is not taken into account. He who neglects him is punished severely. Sacred man in Syria is called Mezzan. He is given license to commit any serious offence. Childless women accept him as temporary husband. Nobody considers this action derogatory.[84]

From the above discussion it may be concluded that, the rural folk of this region of Odisha still practice the *oshas, bratas* and other blind beliefs like worship of *kalisi* and *patuas* as the living

Gods on earth in order to cure many diseases even in the 21st century. In tales of vows, fasts and festivals, Gods and Goddesses like Dutibahana, Budhibamana, Sathi, Mangala, Lakshmi and Satyanarayan punish the non-believers causing want, disease, immature death of children and reward the believers in all possible ways. But, there is no denying a fact, that these *Osha, bratas,* fairs and festivals throw much light on the then economic, social and religious condition of the Odia people during the period under study and spread the ideas of morality, good behavior and ethics in the society.

References

1. K.B. Dash and L.K.Mahapatra, *Folklore of Orissa,* New-Delhi, 1979, p.96.
2. K.B. Dash, *Folklore of Orissa,* Cuttack, 1991, p.106.
3. Orissa Cultural Forum (ed.), *Odishara Loka Sanskruti* (Odia), Cuttack, 1978, pp.50-51.
4. L.N. Raut, *Socio Economic Life in Medieval Orissa,* Calcutta, 1988, p.74.
5. Orissa Cultural Forum (ed.), *op.cit.,* pp.50-51.
6. K.B. Dash and L.K.Mahapatra, *op.cit.,* p.96.
7. A.B. Mohanty (ed.), *Types of Ancient Oriya Prose and Poetry,* Bhubaneswar, 1969, pp.49-51.
8. Braja Mohan Mohanty (ed.), *Odishara Parbaparbani, Oshabrata, Janiyatra,* Cuttack, 1975, pp.62-65.
9. K.B. Dash and L.K.Mahapatra, *op.cit.,* p.110.
10. K.B. Dash, *op.cit.,* p.112.
11. *Ibid,* pp.109-110.
12. *Bratabali* (Odia), No author, Brahmapur, no year, pp.52-55.
13. Braja Mohan Mohanty (ed.), *op.cit.,* pp.152-153.
14. K.B. Dash, *op.cit.,* p.112.
15. *Bratabali* (Odia), *op.cit.*
16. K.B. Dash, *op.cit.*
17. N.C.Behuria (ed.), *Orissa District Gazetteers: Ganjam,* Cuttack, 1992, p.237.

18. K.B. Dash, *op.cit.,* p.116.
19. Mayadhar Mansingh, *A History of Oriya Literature,* New-Delhi, 2008, p.34.
20. K.B. Dash, *op.cit.*
21. Mayadhar Mansingh, *op.cit.,* p.39.
22. *Ibid.*
23. K.B. Dash, *op.cit.*
24. K.C. Pradhan, *op.cit.,* p.308.
25. K.B. Dash, *op.cit.,* pp.114-115.
26. *Ibid.*
27. Braja Mohan Mohanty (ed.), *op.cit.,* pp.155-156.
28. S.N. Rajguru, *Naga Itihasa,* pp.106-111.
29. N.C. Behuria (ed.), *op.cit.,* p.241.
30. Braja Mohan Mohanty (ed.), *op.cit.,* pp.240-244.
31. K.B. Dash, *op.cit,* p.118.
32. Sanchita Mohanty, "Fairs and Festivals", in: *The Cultural Heritage of Ganjam,* Bhubaneswar, 2004, p.290.
33. Bhagabana Sahu, *Socio Economic and Cultural History of Orissa,* Cuttack, 2002, p.24.
34. N.C. Behuria (ed.), *op.cit.,* p.243.
35. *Ibid.*
36. Subasini Patnaik, "*Thakurani Yatra* in Folk Culture", in: *The Cultural Heritage of Ganjam,* Bhubaneswar, 2004, p.316-317.
37. Sabita Pattnayak, Tradition of *Thakurani Yatra,* in: *The Cultural Heritage of Ganjam,* Bhubaneswar, 2004, p.322 .
38. Subasini Pattnayak, *op.cit.,* p.318.
39. N.C. Behuria (ed.), *op.cit.,* p.245.
40. K.B. Dash, *op.cit.,* p.92.
41. *Ibid.*
42. H.C. Das, "Tradition of Folk Music and Dance in Orissa", in: H.C. Das(ed.), *Folk Culture,* vol.IV, Cuttack, 1978, p.90.
43. W.W.Hunter, *A Statistical Account of Bengal,* vol.XIX (District of Puri and the Orissa Tributary states), London, 1877, p.232.
44. John Campbell, *The Wild Tribes of Khondistan,* London, 1864, p.51.
45. W.W.Hunter, *History of Orissa,* vol.II, London, 1872, p.92.

46. Report of Lieutenant Hill, Survey Department, Government of India, 2nd July 1838, in: R.C.S.Bell, *Orissa District Gazetteers: Koraput,* Cuttack, 1945, p.88.
47. W.W.Hunter, *A Statistical Account of Bengal,* vol.XIX, *op.cit.,* p.235.
48. T.J.Maltby, *The Ganjam District Manual,* Madras, 1918, p.67.
49. Report of Lieutenant Hill, *op.cit.*
50. P.Mukherjee, *History of Orissa,* vol.VI, Cuttack, 1964, p.485.
51. C.R.R, John Campbell to Secretary to Government of India, 13th April 1853.
52. L.S.S.O'Malley, *Bengal District Gazetteers:* Angul, Calcutta, 1908, p.22.
53. *Ibid,* p.22.
54. G.E.Russel's Third Report, 11 May 1837, in: *Orissa District Gazetteers: Koraput,* Cuttack, 1945.
55. J.G.Frazer, *The Golden Bough,* London, 1963, p.573.
56. L.S.S.O'Malley, *op.cit.,* p.22.
57. Sitakanta Mohapatra, *Meriah* "Sacrifice: Community Participation in Ritual murder", in: Kulamani Mohapatra(ed.), *Folk Culture,* vol.V, 1978, pp.214-220.
58. Selections from the Records of the Government of India, vol.V, Calcutta, 1845, p.13.
59. J.G.Frazer, *op.cit.,* p.574.
60. John Campbell, *op.cit.,* p.126.
61. J.G.Frazer, *op.cit.,* vol.I, p.505.
62. Selections from the Records of the Government of India, vol.V, Calcutta, 1845, p.117.
63. M.P.Dash, "Cults, Customs & Superstitions of Orissa", in: Sitakanta Mohapatra(ed.), Folk culture, vol.II (Folk ways in Religion, Gods, Spirits & Man), , Cuttack, 1978.
64. Bhagabana Sahu, "*Kedu* Sacrifice in the Khond Tracts of Orissa in the Second Half of the 19th Century", in: *Research Journal* of Berhampur University, vol.IV, December 1984, p.136.
65. Ashutosh Bhattacharya, *Folklore of Bengal,* New-Delhi, 1978, p.57.
66. Sitakanta Mohapatra (ed.), *Folk Culture,* vol.II (Folk ways in Religion, Gods, Spirits & Man), Cuttack, 1978, p.194.
67. Ashutosh Bhattacharya, *op.cit.*
68. *Ibid.*

69. K.B.Dash, *Folklore of Orissa*, Bhubaneswar, 1991, p.4.
70. Maguni Das, "*Asubha Sanketa*" in: *The Samaj* (Odia daily), 7/8/1982, p.5.
71. K.B.Dash, *Lokagalpa Sanchayana*, part.IV, Cuttack, 2008, p.666.
72. Maguni Das, *op.cit.*
73. Chakradhara Mohapatra, *Utkala Gaunli Gita*, Cuttack, 1959, p.641.
74. K.B.Dash and L.K.Mohapatra, *Folklore of Orissa*, New-Delhi, 1979, p.91.
75. *Ibid.*
76. *Ibid.*
77. K.B.Dash and L.K.Mohapatra, *op.cit., p.92.*
78. K.B.Dash, *Folklore of Orissa*, Bhubaneswar, 1991, pp.135-136.
79. *Ibid.*, p.41-42.
80. N.Senapati, *Orissa District Gazetteers: Puri*, p.796.
81. K.B.Dash, *op.cit.*, p.53.
82. *Ibid.*
83. Cornelia Mellbornne, *Living Gods on Earth*, Calcutta, 2008, p.31.
84. K.B.Dash, *op.cit.*, p.51.

6

Folk Arts and Crafts

The history of the folk arts and crafts of Odisha in general and south Odisha in particular goes back to the hoary past.[1] The antiquity of this art can be traced to the pre-historic caves and rock-shelters found in the different places of south Odisha. This amply proves the artistic inclinations of the early inhabitants of this region.[2] Archaeological monuments, literary and religious documents bear evidence of mural paintings and drawing of a folk type that were in vogue in the ancient days. But, folk art is a higher form of culture in comparison to primitive art.[3] Even today, they decorate the walls of the houses with various paintings and drawings during the wedding ceremonies and other auspicious occasions like *Ushas*, *Vratas* and religious functions.

South Odisha particularly the district of Ganjam has to its credit a rich heritage of art and crafts. It is known for its exquisite handicrafts. Folk arts of south Odisha may be broadly divided into nine categories i.e.

1. Mural Paintings,
2. Cloth or *Patta* Paintings,
3. *Ganjapa* Paintings,
4. Scroll Painting,
5. Palm-leaf drawing,
6. Tribal Painting,

7. Tatooings,
8. *Alpana* and
9. *Muruja* Drawing.

It is imperative to discuss these folk art traditions of south Odisha in detail in the following pages.

Mural Paintings

The tradition of Odissi painting had broadly three streams:

(1) The Puri School centred round the Jagannath temple;

(2) the southern Ganjam tradition with the celebrated art works at Buguda, Khallikote, Dharakote, Bada Khemundi, Ghumsar, Paralakhemundi, Tekkali, Manjusha and the;

(3) third style was the Champamal School, primarily in and around Sonepur and Sambalpur.

The first two schools resembled each other aesthetically and even thematically. The functional inspiration was religious with royalty as the sponsoring agency. In fact, kings and temples were inseparable in contemporary society, and paintings adorned temple walls as much as royal palaces. The *Champamal* School was somewhat different aesthetically, and art historians speak of its resemblance to Indonesian art. One does not, however, know the precise channel through which Odisha had travelled to Indonesia (notably Java) in those times.[4]

The southern Ganjam tradition dominates in south Odisha murals. This region is famous for the exquisite mural or ritual paintings. The walls of the houses, palaces, *mathas*, temples, *bhagabat tungis*, place where the wedding couple sit, the wall where the idol of the presiding deity of the household is placed, are generally painted with floral decorations like lotus and lilies, birds like peacocks, swans and parrots, animal's like elephants, bulls, tigers, lions, *Navagunjara*, *Purna-kumbha*, palanquins, banana trees, the man playing with conch, man playing with drum, man playing with *mahuri*, twin fishes and *alasa kanyas*.[5]

Among the folk paintings, the murals of *Osakothi* shrines are significant. These shrines are meant to house *Tetisikoti Devata*

(Thirty three crores of deities of Hindu pantheon). At least ten to twenty images and maximum of one hundred gods and goddesses, heroes of epics and legends are depicted along with their attendants and relatives. The murals, thus, represent the macro cosmos in a reduced or condensed scale. On an *Osakothi* mural, the entire *kutumba* of the goddesses does *ubha* i.e. appears with sons, daughters, *vahanas*, mounts and vehicles with full associates, insignia and pomp. This goddess or *Thakurani* is then considered to be the *Adimata*, the primordial *Mother*, the mother of the universe.[6]

The worship of *Mangala*, celebrating maritime activity and the safe return of ships from distant voyages, is a popular theme painted on the exterior walls of various structures, particularly in Puri and Ganjam districts. In these paintings, *Mangala* is generally associated with a lion and a swinging science is often included. *Mangala* is also the deity worshipped in the *Khudurikuni* festival celebrated in the month of *Bhadrab* (August-September). According to the underlying maritime legend:[7]

- Taapoi was the apple of the eyes of her seven merchant brothers. This became an eye sore of her seven sisters-in-law. When the brothers went to far-off islands for trade, she was tortured by her sisters-in-law(except the youngest one). Every day she worshipped the goddess *Mangala* for the safe return of her brothers. They returned safely and punished their wives for their mischief towards their only sister.[8]

Since *Taapoi* used to offer *khuda* (broken rice) to *Mangala*, which she collected by begging, *Mangala* was known as *Khudurukuni*. Today this festival is celebrated only by the unmarried girls of Odisha. They worship of *Khudurkuni* on all Sundays during the month of *Bhadrab*. A clay image of *Khudurkuni* is installed and worshipped in the house of one of the fasting women. The image is immersed in the river after the last ritual. Scenes of the *Taapoi* legend are often included in the *Osakothi* murals painted on the walls of temporary shines in Ganjam district.[9]

The *Osakothi* wall painting marks the site where the *eaka kutumva,* the joint family of *Thakurani* recites. If the painting has an outer border, it is understood as a 'compound wall' that surrounds the temple complex. If it is divided into compartments, they are meant to indicate the chambers and houses of the various gods and goddesses forming the great family. Sometimes, the mural is laid out around a large central *ghara* (Space) on the wall that is reserved for the prominent image of the Goddess *Mangala* or *Siva Nataraja*; this central position is also called *thana* or niche, as encountered in the temple, where the *Parsva Devatas* are placed prominently in the façade and normally receive worship and special attention.[10]

Two kinds of paintings are discernible in these murals. First, the diagrams, mainly lines and dots in white powder or rice paste that are called *jhoti* or *Chita* and produced by the women of the household and second, the figurative ikons, usually painted by a specialist on cloth *(patta)* or wood or directly on a wall. Both forms are prevalent in villages of south Odisha and are used in different seasons on different occasions.

Almost all the *Sakti* and *Mahakali* images in south Odisha are painted with frightening figures of *Mahishasuramardani, Mahakali,* demons and other devotees. Some of the mythological themes are illustrated on these temple walls. The *Kothisala (Osakothi* shrines*)*, the *Dandakali* temples and the *Akhadas* of south Odisha are very famous for the mural paintings. Mural painting or *Bhittichitra* is still seen in almost all parts of Odisha . Particular types of paintings are drawn for occasions like marriage. The *kothaghar* (the room for the bride and bride-groom) is very delicately decorated with different motifs. Usually there are four birds and a pair of parrots and a *Purna kumbha* in the paintings in a *kothaghar.* There is a particular caste known as *Chitrakaras* who perform this job with zeal and skill. One of the most interesting aspects of the mural paintings is that, these have survived without any renovation which helps us to determine its time and style. It goes to the credit of the solid and persistent tradition of art that it is almost impossible to discover the slightest modern or western elements in these murals.[11]

The pictorial art of Odisha during the period was very rich, exciting and vibrant. It is interesting to note that in Odisha when the temple building activities have stopped, paintings have gained momentum.[12] Most of the walls of the temples of south Odisha were painted with beautiful mural painting. These temple murals are extremely lively. Most of the temples of 17th and 18th century Odisha with exquisitely painted walls are the variable picture galleries which attract the tourists even today. Two such important paintings-the *Kanchi Vijaya* by Gajapati Purshottam Dev depicted in the *Jagamohana* of the main temple and the *Budha Vijaya* in the *Jagamohana* of Laxmi Temple inside same complex are found in the temple of Lord Jagannath at Puri.

The paintings of Viranchinarayana Temple, Buguda are a landmark in the history of mural paintings. The paintings have been done on the outer walls of the main temple, encircled by a *verandah*. The *Ramayana* paintings dominate the walls. It is believed that the painters being inspired by the *Vaidehisa Vilasa* of Kabisamrat Upendra Bhanja have composed the *Ramayana* paintings. The other paintings of this temple include the scenes from *Krishna leela, Dasavatar* and the Puri paintings. The entire south wall contains the Krishna *Leela* Paintings, the North wall, the Puri painting and rest of the walls are decorated with *Ramayana* paintings. The most important *Ramayana* motifs are Lakshmana and Jambavana, *Ravanara Chhatrabhanga,* Rama and Sita on *Chitrakuta, Bharata bheta* and Rama Ravana *Yuddha.* In these paingings, the actions of the figures are dramatic and the human proportions are elegant. One is reminded of the waist of Rama in the *Chitrakuta* paintings and the manner he paints vermilion mark on the forehead of Sita. The delicacy of the hand gestures are superb. Similarly, the way in which Bibhisana directs his gaze at Ravana in the distant sky is very powerful in the *Chhatrabhang* painting.[13]

The puri painting with the temple of Jagannath is a graphical rendering of the pilgrim town of Puri conceived as an aerial view. The painting served as a religious destination to thousands of pilgrims, who wished to visit Puri but were unable to perform the journey. Such practices seem to be very old tradition which is even found with Jains and Buddhists. Many interesting details such as the temple of Puri, the idols of Jagannath, Balabhadra and Subhadra, *Rosaghara, Baisipahacha, Sweta-Ganga, Adapa Mandapa, Raja Nahara, Devasnana Mandapa, Dola Mandapa* have been shown.[14]

The mural paintings of the region throw flood of lights on the socio-religious and economic life of the people. The mural paintings of Puri and elsewhere decidedly betray muslim influence, ofcourse, primarily in the depiction of demonic characters. Hiranyakashipu in the Dasavatar paintings wears striped paijamas and pointed half shoes. The same kind of dress is also found in other demonic characters like Jambabahan and Bibhisana in Ramabhiseka paintings. Banasura in Ushavilas, Mahisasura in Shaktipurana are dressed in muslim court style. This influence is conspicuously absent in Ganjam paintings, because all the craft centres of south Odisha had never been under the muslim rule directly at any stage of history. Similarly, the large number of depiction of *Boitas* (boats) in the Khudurukuni osha and Ushakothi murals proves that the people of this region maintained a flourishing maritime trade with the countries of South East Asia.

Cloth or *Patta* Painting

Cloth or *Patta* painting was another popular art of the period. Icon paintings on small strips of cotton cloth were a speciality of Odishan pictorial art. *Patta* paintings were very popular during the later part of the Muslim period. The artists drew a variety of figures i.e. landscape, scene of *Darbars*, towns and forests, temples, Gods and Goddesses and walls with different colours over a thin plank and a layer of very fine white pasted clothes. According to O.C.Ganguli, "this form of pictorial art of folk significance is not only unique in the history of Indian painting but is unparalleled in the history of any form of European Painting".[15]

Some of the interesting features of these paintings are given below. The painting could both be read either from left or right. Blank space was not appreciated and the background space was filled up with decorated motifs of flowers, buds, etc. Half figures were never shown in a composition. The figures are shown in full from head to toe.[16]

The human figures which are found in Odishan paintings have their prototypes in Odisha sculptural art particularly of the temple of Konark. The swelling bosom, rounded hips and the shapely limbs are the typical Odisha female ideal which almost conforms to the types of females we see in Odisha .[17]

The architectural set up consisting of living houses, palaces of kings, courts, living apartments of the region, pavilion, arbores, chariots and temples form another important aspect of Odishan paintings.[18]

In short, it can be said that, the pictorial art tradition is very much living in this part of the country. This has been largely possible because of the distinct character of its social structure, religious beliefs of the people and the existence of the families of native painters called *Chitrakaras.*

Ganjapa Painting:

The *Ganjapa* painting or the paintings on playing cards is another form of folk art. The Zamindari estates of Digapahandi, Chikiti, Dharakote, Sheragada, Ghumusar, Paralakhemundi, Manjusha, Tekkali are famous for this art. Beautiful *patachitra* images of kings, queens, elephants, lions, tigers, chariots, *nabagunjar,* fishes, conch, floral decorations, different kinds of birds and horses were painted in the playing cards like filigree works of Cuttack. [19]

Previously there were 148 or 120 playing cards in this *Ganjapa* play. Now it is confined within 96 playing cards. This *Ganjapa* art is also widely prevalent in village Raghurajpur of Puri and Sonepur of Subarnapur District. While the art on *Ganjapa* cards of Raghurajpur are dominated by *Dasavatara* paintings, the different scenes of *Ramayana* dominated the *Ganjapas* in Sonepur area, and the pictures of fish and conch dominated the *Ganjapas* in Ghumusar area and different kinds of flowers, birds, and the pictures of *Astamallah* are dominated in the Chikiti, Badakhemundi and Paralakhemundi areas. The art of entire house of cards are divided into ten categories; therefore it is also known as *Dasarangi*. This art is also prevalent in Andhra Pradesh, Rajastan, Kerala and Karnataka besides the south Odisha. [20]

Scroll Paintings:

There is a community in Odisha known as *Chitrakaras,* meaning painter. There was a time the practice of paintings on canvas was made by the *Chitrakaras* but now-a-days, it is done either on thick pieces of cloth or on coarse handmade paper. Painting on canvas has been a very old practice in Odisha and there was a class of painting scrolls known as *Yama-pata* which used to be exhibited in different festivals or *melas* very widely, depicting the sufferings of sinners in hell after death. Even today, the tradition is being continued by the inclusion of some scenes of sufferings of sinners in hell in the scrolls painted on diverse mythological themes.[21] There was a class of people known as *Patuas* who also engaged themselves in this art.

Patua, a well-known term in Bengal and Odisha is derived from the Sanskrit word *pata* meaning a cloth. *Patuas* are the people who paint on *pata* or cloth.[22] *Patuas* were of a low social origin or class of people who were not admitted either into the Muslim or Hindu community. They also do not belong to any particular aboriginal group. Members of this community form a social group of their own. Though they show more inclination towards the Muslim religion than the Hindus, they earn their livelihood by painting and exhibiting episodes from Hindu mythology as represented by the *Ramayana,* the *Mahabharata,* the *Bhagavata, Mangal Kavya,* or any folk god or goddess, and entertain the people by exhibiting their paintings accompanied by the chanting of appropriate narrative verses. They draw the episodes on a canvas about 3ft. wide and up to 40 ft. long. They paint the various episodes one below the other; and the canvas is rolled while carrying it from place to place or when stored. When exhibiting paintings, they gradually unroll the scrolls and explain each event to the public by means of songs which they themselves compose, in their own way.[23]

The canvas used for the paintings is specially prepared for the purpose. The surface is made smooth and suitable drawing by coating it with a thin layer of clay mixed with cow dung. Five primary colours, i.e. white, yellow, green, grey, carbon, black, and red, are mainly used. In rare cases, gold leaf and gold dust, silver leaf and silver dust are also employed. Boiled seeds of tamarind made into paste with water and mixed with powders of different colours are used in the painting. The artists know the proportion of each item of mixture and also how to make the brilliance of colours of their painting long lasting and vibrant. The paintings are bold, vigorous and spontaneous. Sometimes objects like forests, trees or flowing rivers are drawn symbolically. The lines of the drawings are broad and always deeply coloured.[24]

There are a particular class of painters known as *Jadu-patua. Jadu* means magic and these painters are supposed to perform *Jadu* or Magic. They originally came from a tribal group of people living on the western borders of Bengal, Bihar and Chhotanagpur region who painted scenes of tribal social life for their livelihood. Now, of course, they have also started painting Hindu mythological themes. Originally, their profession was to approach the members of any tribal family where some death had occurred recently with a painting supposed to represent the deceased. The painting used to be complete in all detail except the iris of the eye. The relatives of the deceased would be told that the departed soul was wandering aimlessly in the air, not knowing where and how to go without the iris of its eye. Therefore, if adequate money and presents were given to him, he would put the iris of the eyes in the painting and the soul would not have any difficulties in going its own way. The tribal used to believe in his story and offer him money and presents, and after that the *Jadu patua* used to put the iris of the eye in the painting, and give other necessary finishing touches.

The *Jadu-Patua* paints animals, or folk-deities riding big animals, on scrolls. The paintings of the animals are remarkable in the sense that they still exhibit primitive characteristics, being vigorous, native and direct, free from any symbolic implications or ambiguity. [25]

Palm-leaf Itching or Drawing:

The palm trees which are abundantly found in south Odisha provided ample opportunities to utilize the leafs of these trees for palm-leaf itching or palm-leaf drawing. Every part of it is useful, its leave especially so, as these were used for writing when paper was not yet invented. Perhaps this is the reason why palm-leaf manuscripts are found in Odisha and Andhra in large quantity.[26] Its counterpart in North India is *Bhurjapatra.* Today these leaves are still useful for many other purposes. They are the main material for roofing in every village. Once upon a time, ear ornaments, i.e., *kammas* and *tatankas* were made of palm leaves, which are used today for making rain coats, umbrellas, baskets, doll boxes, fans, mats, sail materials and other sundry objects. The strong and fine fiber of palm trees is used for preparing flower baskets, boxes for ornaments, vermilion, mirrors, and vanity bags.

Palm-leaf drawing constitutes an important section of our folk-art. The practice of drawing on palm-leaves with the help of *lekhani (Iron stylus)* was in vogue since the medieval period. A visit to Jayadeba State Museum at Bhubaneswar. Raghunandan Library at Puri and Utkal University Library, Bhubaneswar and the Archival Cell of Berhampur University Library and many other places would enable one to see the painting on palm leaves. [27]

Odisha has the largest collection of palm-leaf manuscripts or *pothis* many of which were illustrated in colour. Generally they deal with puranic themes either only as written composition or accompanied by etchings which could be black and white or painted in colour. *Pothi* writing and painting is a special art of

Odisha. Seasoned palm-leaf writers wrote on the surface of the palm-leaf which required an iron stylus to write or to itch. In fact, the character of *Odia* alphabet being rounded can be traced to this.[28] Generally, the script writers were also the illustrators. There was perhaps a professional class of such painters or illustrators known as *lipikaras.* The *pothis* of very early periods seem to have been lost. What is available now are the works from 17th century onwards. [29]

It appears that this art might have its origin in early medieval period. But, from the evidences available, it is known that by 17th and 18th century this art was becoming more popular than before. There were several reasons behind its popularity in 17th, 18th and early part of the 19th century. Firstly, the Odi*a* literature grew richer during the period. The artist now found it easier to illustrate the drawing with Odia language. The influence of Odia literature on the palm-leaf artists is evinced from the fact that, the artist has taken materials from the Odia literature like *Bhagabat Gita* of Jagannath Das, *Vaidehisha Bilasa*, ,*Labanyabati* and *Rasika Harabali* of Upendra Bhanja, *Sarbanga Sundari* of Lokanath Das, *Ushavilash* of Sisu Sankar Das, and legends and episodes like *Tapoi, Kanchi-Kaberi* etc. Besides, *Ramaleela*, *Krishnalila* and *Prahallad Nataka* were depicted as these were much popular among the masses. Perhaps that is the reason why illustrated manuscripts are found in large quantity in 17th and 18th century than before. [30]

Another reason which encourages the practice of drawing on palm-leaves was the royal patronage. Any artist who could draw pictorial art on palm-leaf and present it to a king was destined to receive suitable presentations and money. As a result there rose a class of artists drawing art on palm-leaves at various places of the region The artist could retain that art in his family through generations. This often was found not only a hobby but also a source of livelihood.[31]

The artist has used a permanent colour which has very slightly faded in spite of the worn out condition of the manuscripts.

Dasavatara (Ten incarnations of Lord Vishnu) paintings on palm-leave is special feature of this art. *Gita Govinda* illustrated palm-leaf manuscript is another brilliant specimen. The two manuscripts depicting marriage scene of Lord Siva and Parvati, attended by Brahma and Vishnu makes Siva as a great god. The palm-leaf drawing took the same trend as was manifested in mural painting. In some of the palm-manuscripts, the building of *setu-bandha* by Lord Rama for fighting with Ravana, the worship of Rama's *Paduka* (Sandals) by Bharata, and Biswamitra taking Rama and Lakshmana for the purpose of killing *Tadaka* are depicted marvellously.[32] The palm-leaf manuscripts depicting *Krishnaleela*, with *Kaliadalana* are abundantly found in different villages of south Odisha. Here we find various plants and trees. The peacock, deer and cow are playing. The cow boys are happily moving in the midst of them.

The human figures on the different palm-leaves depicted majestically, landing a life-like gesture. Depiction of birds and beasts with a background of excellent natural scenery show the high quality of Odishan palm-leaf art. Love scenes are graphically depicted. The marriage ceremonies, with its social background, throw much light on the social structure of those days.[33]

Thus, the art of drawing and sketching on palm-leaves was very popular in south Odisha during the 18th and 19th centuries. It will be no exaggeration to compare the palm-leaf drawings of the period with the sculptural master pieces of the Konark temple and the mural art of the 19th century Odisha .

Tribal Paintings (*Idital*):

South Odisha has the largest concentration of tribals forming about one-fourth of its total population. It is the home land of a number of different tribal communities. Leading an isolated life from the mainstream of modern civilization, the tribals are lamentably the most backward classes in the state. Their socio-economic life was peculiar compared to those of the tribes elsewhere. Peculiar still are their marriage customs, festivals, religious rites, rituals and cultural performances which might exhibit to the world the distinct nature of their life. [34]

Odisha's tribals have created a high level of visual art. Odisha has sixty two tribal communities and is virtually an open-air ethnic museum. The wall-paintings of the *Sauras*, more popularly referred to as icons or pictograms, have a ritual base. They have creepers, trees, birds and animals as their primary motifs. *Saura* icon-making is, thus, a religious-ritual act.[35]

They have a deep sense of aesthetic expression. They have their own paintings, sculptures and various artifacts which are associated with their way of life. Most of their artifacts are bounded with their blind beliefs and superstitions. For example, the *Saura* cult of the dead and spirits reflected in the *Saura idital* or *ittal* (painting), the *Kandh's* dreads of *Bhimul* find expression in decorated walls, doors and in tattooing. The *Bonda* dormitory also serves as galleries of remarkable wall relics and paintings.[36]

An important and characteristic feature of *Soura* religion is the custom of making drawings on the walls of houses in honour of the dead, to avert disease, to promote fertility and on the occasion of certain festivals. The preponderant presence of wall painting is the main custom of *Soura's* religious-cultural canvas. It is popularly known as *idital.* The word has been probably derived from the roots of the *Soura* language *id* which means "to write" and *tal* means *Kitalan* or wall. Thus, *Idital* means "Writing on the wall". But according to Verrier Elwin *idital* means ikon which may be made by anyone who knows how; he need not be a priest, but the artist who becomes adept achieves a sort of dedicated position and is known as the *Ittalmaran* or wall-writing-man or in fact an artist. Many of the *shamans* also combine this art with their regular professional duties. These paintings are mainly connected with the cult of fertility.[37]

Origin of the *Idital:*

The origin of *idital* can be discerned from the following paragraphs,

Once upon a time there lived an old couple of *Lanjia Soura* community who were simple and unattached in nature. But, the villagers disliked them because they were not taking part in the village meetings and they were wondering in the forest naked and losing their hair up to the waist.

One day the man dreamt that his father was crying and asking that why his son had not given him a house to live and food to eat. Yuyusoom has driven the father away. *Ratusoom* is not ready to permit him to enter into the other world. Therefore, the hopeless father is wondering in that jungle. He is getting no rest. Thus, the son should build house for his father and provide food to eat as soon as possible, lest his family will suffer from terrible fever. The old man got up and informed all to his wife with the advice of the kind hearted old woman, the old man made a stage by burying pillars at the corner of their house and in front of which *salap juice* and colored cloth were placed.

On that night again, the old man dreamt his father who again said, "My son, the ancestors do not live in this cottage, nor they were satisfied by the *salap juice* only do make a wall painting in your house. Dipping a stick into sun-boiled rice gruel makes beautiful quadrilateral structure. Keep yuyusoom and ratusoom in this picture and worship us. Keep some food in a small earthen pot and wine in the *zerisual* (Pot used to drink wine) near the picture. A red hen should be sacrificed. Then only I will have everything".

"On the next day the old man arranged all the required material .As per the instruction of his father he made a beautiful art inside the wall of his house by the sun dried rice gruel. Several deities are picturised including *Yuyusoom* and *Ratusoom.* In front of the *idital* a basket full of rice covered by a new cloth and some wine on a *zerisul* are placed. The old man worshipped his ancestor, gave his salutation and sacrificed a red hen before the drawing."

After that the couple was lived happily. The old man became the *Kudammar.* He cut his front hair and made a knot with the long hair at the backside. He put on a strip of *loin cloth,* one part of which was hanging down at the backside like a *lanja* (tail).Since then they lived happily, and known as *Lanjia Saura.*[38]

Another story hints that *idital* has direct impact on fertility. The myth is as follows.

One *Gandlu* with his beautiful wife, *Sarami,* were living in the dense forest of *Gungsangada* along with other *Lanjia Souras*. They were living happily earning their livelihood from the forest. But, the only sad story is that they were childless even after five years of their marriage. Deciding to find out the reason, they visited to the *Kudamboi* (their deities) taking some boiled rice in a leaf cup. The *Kudamboi* desired to know about their arrival. Both the couple impressed their grief saying that they were childless. The *kudamboi* received the rice from them. Worshipping the *idital* invoking her *euda* (spirit of the dead) husband she could foretell that, if the couple will sacrifice a hen, a goat and a hog in the name of *youngsoom* by making a "*Kukudam idital*" they will have a child. The couple agreed and came back to home.

All the necessary materials were arranged. The couple invited an *iditalmaran* (the artist). One day during evening the *iditalmaran* came and slept that night near the wall meant for the picture. He did not take food. The ghost came in dream and directed him how to draw the *idital.* Early in the morning, taking bath, *iditalmaran* began to paint with a bamboo stick dipping down in the sun-dried rice gruel. He completed it at the middle of the day. Then, *Gandlu* arranged a hen, a hog and a goat for sacrifice. He went to the *Kundamboi.* The Kudamboi came, worshipped the *idital,* and sacrificed the animals meant for the purpose. Finally, she hung out an earthen pot containing different types of grains from the root in front of the *idital* and informed all that it must not be touched.

After someday Sarami conceived and the couple became happy. They informed to the *Kudamboi* and asked her for further steps. They *Kudamboi* said, "Bring the child to me after its birth".Though nine months passed away Sarami never gave birth.

So *Gandlu* rushed to *Kudamboi*, *Kudamboi* made worship, sacrificed a hen before the *youngsoom* and Sarami gave birth.

After the celebration of *Kukudam*-the birth rite, the child suffered from fever once and again. The Kudamboi, by seeing "*Puchuna*" (fore tell things by counting sun dried rice) and invoking her *Euda* husband, told Gandlu that his child would recover of only he would sacrifice a buffalo to his ancestors. *Gundlu* made an *Idital* sacrificed a buffalo after which his child got cured.[39]

Classification of Tribal Wall Painting

The wall painting of *Sauras* varies from place to place and for various purposes. Sometimes different pictures are painted for the same reason while at another only one picture is painted for different purposes. But, very often the *iditals* are drawn in accordance to the order of the ancestors and deities. The supernatural powers direct the *Kudamboi, Kudammar.* The *iditalmaran* (the painter) or "*the karyee*" know how to make the painting. Thus, there exist the differences.[40]

In case of incorporal marriage, the incorporal spirit guides in dream to draw painting as per their necessity and taste. Again the *iditalmaran* has to sleep with single-minded devotion near the *idital* if he feels any difficulties while or before painting. The incorporal spirit tells how to draw the painting. In case; the *idital* has already been started it is anointed partially or entirely to put the necessary changes. But whatever may be the case, the *iditalas* are made of different structures only to satisfy the various deities for various purposes. The *iditals* are drawn with personal interest and knowledge of *Kudamboies. Kundammarans* and *iditalmarans.*[41]

The icons are also drawn by the *kudan,* i.e. the priest or the sorcerer of the village. He is the person who has the traditional hereditary right to know the art of detecting the spirit and prescribing the rituals leading ultimately to the painting of the icons on the mud walls. The *kudan* has right to appropriate the object that are offered to the spirit at the time of propitiation ceremony. It means the rice, the *handia,* or *rice-beer,* the fowl and sometimes also a share in the goat sacrifice on the occasion.

The icon is always drawn in the morning. After finishing bath the *kudan* comes to the house where the icons is to be drawn. The housewife prepares some powder out of white rice, adds water to it and makes a white paste. After it is done, she gives this white paint over to the *kudan* to start drawing the icon. The women prepares this paint after her bath with empty stomach.

The day before the icon is drawn, a portion of the wall is given a clean wash in a solution of locally available red earth and water mixed together. The icon drawn on the wall is kept as such until it is repeated next year.[42]

The priests of *Lanjia soura* community express that the Goddesses and incorporal spirit are harmful to their community. They want to fulfill their desires by creating harms to the contemporaries. To satisfy them, *iditals* are painted and worships are offered. Therefore, according to different types of deities, ancestors, and spirits, diseases, calamities, injuries, festive occasions, etc, there are different types of *iditals*.

Kudamboi Idital:

Kudumboi idital is painted on three different rectangles squares joined by margins. Unlike other *Idital* man and women are shown busy with their daily chores. Outside rectangle square canvas an esoteric tree is painted with a group of monkies on branches poking at beehive, two peacocks are shown painted on the top all symbolizing invoking good monsoon. This *idital* is painted in the name of *kudang* on the occasion when one desires to be a *Kudamboi*. Generally, if drawn in the months of *Falguna* and *Chaitra* (April and May) it is believed to be very powerful.

Kurualsoom Idital:

Kurualsoom Idital contains a procession of ethereal beings shows various innerative sequences of man and nature. This painting is drawn to ward of pests and insects that destroy farm cultivation and the crops. It is usually painted in November.

Aamgansoompur Idital:

Aamgansoompur idital is painted on the occasion of *Burianad* festival, the purpose is to make offering of powdered grain out of new yield. This is meant to satisfy the ancestors. The canvas includes painting of titling farmers and other usual picture of man nature in interaction.[43]

Labasoom Idital:

Labasoom Idital is dedicated for paddy offering ceremony to *Labasoom*, the Goddess of the earth. It is believed that by drawing this painting the fertility of the land can be preserved and all the natural calamities may be controlled. It is *akinto Chita, jhoti* tradition of the caste Hindus in concept, though the painting has its usual characters of mundane world stayed put in the tribal scape.

Gongsoom idital:

The texture and structure of the *idital* has subtle difference. Here God and Goddesses are invoked through this *idital* for prevention of diseases that usually visit the Saora people.

In the *Saura* Paintings, the spirit of deadman lying on a cot attended by *chaparasis* and physicians occupied the major attention. All other figures like monkeys, trees, tigers etc. were meant to protect the beautiful nature around intended for the spirit to enjoy. They also depicted agricultural operations, pregnant women, potter families, and Gods seated on elephants.[44]

The Kandhs were no less artists either. Of course, the inconvenient atmosphere and general poverty had considerably discouraged their artistic achievements. Side by side, the actual rules of the tribes and castes worked to restrict greatly the materials they could use for the purpose. So in a rude state of Kandh society, the variety and development of art was limited and stationary.[45] Even then there were a few of them who usually in bronze or iron. Pottery and weaving was usually avoided.

The aboriginals including the Kandhs were generally restricted by custom or taboo and had to find satisfaction of their artistic impulses in the decoration of their own bodies. The custom of adorning the skin by tattooing had survived among the Kandhs. The designs which the Kandhs used to tattoo their bodies in elicited admiration from others. Furthermore, the manner in which the *Kuttia Kandh* dancers decorated themselves with white and red stripes exhibited their artistic genius.[46] The hair-do of the Kandhs of the nineteenth century testified to their artistic mettle. Even the hair pins used by the Kandhs which were made of *Sambhar* bone were quite attractive. Their other ornaments like beads, ear-rings, nose-rings, anklets, bangles and necklace demonstrated their artistic skill.

The tobacco-tubes and tobacco cases used by the Kandhs speak of their sense of artistic beauty. The tobacco-cases were made from a single node of bamboo and ornamented with the fine point of a knife. It was rubbed with oil and ash.

The Kandhs displayed their artistic skill on bronze. These bronze artefacts of the nineteenth century can be found in the Madras Museum, the Victoria and Albert Museum of London and in the Tribal Research Institute of Bhubaneswar. These bronze artefacts can be put under four categories. The first category of bronze artefacts was used in human sacrifice. The second category included lineage-group emblems, the third included a bride's dowries; and the fourth category was used for various purposes.[47]

The Kandhs used to make figures of elephants, peacocks, dolls (i.e., humans), fishes and the like in brass. Those were kept in their houses. They made special offerings to them at the time of affliction or sickness in the household or in connection with a recent ancestor's death. The other bronze articles of the Kandhs which invite admiration were bulls, horses, tortoises, cobras, deer, leopards, axes, pots, vessels, figures of musicians and ornaments. The bronze figures of the Kandh mother with facial tattooing and the baby preserved in the Victoria and Albert Museum of London is a fine specimen of the Kandhs' bronze-art.[48]

But, the Kandh wall painting of south Odisha presented a different style. The wall decorations and the wood-carvings in the houses were distinguished features of Kandh-art. Wall panting on the veranda of Kandh houses and their paintings for *Bhimul Pennu* were quite impressive, although those were lacking in perfection and finesse.[49]

The background of the paintings was of smooth dark earth, only rarely smeared with cow dung, but sometimes washed with a red clay against which the white designs stood out sharply. These paintings were the most evanescent of all; once made, no one ever looked at them; sometimes those were rubbed out and new thinly plastered that it is used to be quickly washed away during the rains and worst of all, the entire village was shifted every few years, the houses were broken up, and the labour and art forgotten. The wood-carvings, particularly those on the doors of Kandh houses were good specimens of Kandh art. Sometimes these carvings were done by the *Panas*. The figures of peacocks, elephants and the hunting scenes carved on the doors were quite impressive. Thus, the Kandhs were not at all backward in the field of art and architecture. Of course they did not prize them.[50]

These were painted in honour of *Bhimul Pennu,* their deity. Like the *Saura* paintings, the motifs in these paintings were guided by dreams. The elephant with rider in these paintings symbolized the cult of fertility.

Generally, the paintings are made with white colour on the background of a red wall. Grinding sun-dried rice, a paste is made adding water. The painters use bambostick as the bruss. The painting is drawn on the red wall with the rice paste. The *Lanjia Souras* who formed the largest population among the *Souras* of south Odisha preserve their antiquity of painting in pictorial tradition.

Thus, the tribal paintings are emotional aesthetic expressions of the tribal communities. With ritualistic significance these paintings play a prominent role in the socio-cultural life of the tribals of south Odisha.

Tattooing:

Tattooing is another kind of folk art in south Odisha. This art is an ancient tradition of south Odisha.[51] Almost all the tribal man and woman tattoo their bodies for decorative purposes. The villagers also consider tattooing a mark of beauty. A small star either on the chin or the cheek, a flower design on the forehead, or the name of the beloved on the forearm, adds a certain charm to any village woman. There is fȯlk song in Odia, wherein a vivacious girl asks her beloved to have the figures of Sita's footprints and Rama's arrows tattooed on her thighs, by paying four and a half *annas.* Able-bodied men and wrestlers tattoo their forearms, biceps, thighs and chests with different designs and figures of lions, eagles, serpents, Hanuman, clubs, swords and full-blown lotuses.

The Kandh women were very much fond of this art.[52] Generally, a Kandh girl in the marriageable age got her face tattooed with some quaint designs. The tattooing was done for ornamentation of the body. It was considered so graceful an ornament that, no Kandh would accept a girl who had not adorned herself with such ornamentation.[53]

The face was tattooed with the fine lines keeping the nose as the centre.[54] Across both the cheeks, from the temple to the lobes of the ears, were drawn straight, dotted lines at right angle to one another. Then over the forehead and chin a string of small regular geometrical figures, such as triangles, circles and diamonds, were punctured. The same figures were also punctured near the lips and eyes.[55] Sometimes, the calf of the leg and the arms, hands and chest were tattooed with figures of trees, flowers, fishes, crocodiles, lizards and scorpions.[56] Some tattoo marks were also said to have represented moustache, beard and the implements used in tilling the soil for cultivation.[57]

The punctures for the tattoo marks were made with a thick needle and were smeared with a mixture of lamp-back and the juice of the plantain, after which liquid turmeric was rubbed over the tattooed surface. Nothing acidic like tamarind was to be eaten until the punctures had been healed. The operation was performed by Kandh women. They were known to have been paid four *annas* for each case of tattooing.[58]

There is a particular caste known as *Pacchabotlavaru* whose profession is tattooing. The women of *Kela* caste also expert in this art. While tattooing the artists sing different kinds of folk songs in order to lessen the pains and divert the attention of the victims.[59] With the spread of city-based culture, tattooing is gradually, declining; the only motif in tattooing which continues to flourish is the writing of the name of one's beloved on the forearm.

Alpana:

Alpana or *aripan (Jhoti* or *Chita)* is an important branch and most celebrated form of folk art.[60] No domestic function like Osha, Brata, Marriage and Thread ceremony can be observed without this art. This type of art is prevalent almost in all parts of the region. *Jhoti* or *Chita* is solely a monopoly of women folk.[61] *Alpana* or ritual drawing are made on the mud floor of the house or in open courtyards on the occasion of any ceremonial worship. On the occasion of marriage, the wooden seats *(pidha)* of the bride groom and the bride are also decorated with *Alpana* designs. The latter is drawn on the floor or on the wall, the specimen of which can stand equal to the *alpana* or *aripan* of Bengal. Line drawing is an ancient art which has been fully preserved in all the houses of south Odisha.[62]

Here also the subject matter is comprehensive and various objects like *Kumbha* (pot with coconut) flowers, leaves, trees, fruits, fishes, peacocks, snakes, elephants, tigers, astral bodies, and gods and goddesses are depicted. Some of the *aripans* are drawn for specific *pujas* and festivals like Lakshmi *Puja, Diwali* etc. There are particular *aripans,* like the *swastika,* which are made for special occasions like childbirth. The most important *Jhoti* according to local opinion is found at the *ishta* or *ishana* shrine, the innermost family shrine of a south Odishan house. This is the place of daily worship by the woman of the household. The most essential constituent of the shrine is the white line-drawing on the wall.

It can be a complex *mandala* diagram in the shape of a lotus, a square of a five-pointed 'house' or merely some white speckling of the wall. The *Ishta* shrine in the rural Ganjam also contains the *ishta devi,* the family goddess of the household and possibly a symbol of the tool with which one acquires one's livelihood. Only women perform the worship of these guardians of the house at the *Ishana* shrine.[63]

Laxmi is the goddess of wealth. She is the consort of Jagannath and her powers and grace have been described in great detail through narration of episodes in that of the *Lakshmi Purana.* On every Thursday in the month of *Margasira,* Lakshmi is worshipped in every rural household.[64] A special *jhoti* mural is made annually for the Goddess Lakshmi on each Thursday during the month of *Margasira* (November/December), the *guruvara day* being consecrated to this Goddess. The line-drawing is executed by the women and girls of the houseghold or by the wife of a professional painter. It can extend beyond the wall on to the ground and contain motifs considered auspicious and connected with the Goddess Lakshmi, with prosperity and wealth, such as *Padmamandala* (a lotus made of circles), *Lakshmipada* (Lakshmi foot prints), *Dhanasinsa* (bunches of paddy rice), and *Dhana amara* (rice bins).[65]

This white mural can spread over many walls, inside and outside the house, and they are regarded a signs of welcome for the Goddess. Without these emblems, *Lakshmipuja,* the worship of the Goddess Lakshmi, is not possible. The place of worship is normally the innermost corner of one of the living rooms. The elegant-looking footprints of Lakshmi are painted right from the outside entrance of the house to stimulate the image that she has condescended to walk into the house and bless it. The painting is done with rice-paste and water. The patterns of the moving feet vary depending on the artist's vision and normally they are small, delicate feet symbolising grace and beauty. On this occasion the mud walls of the houses are also painted with various floral designs. In the night before Thursday, the women-folk in every house prepare the rice-paste and paint *Jhoti-chita* on the walls and the floors before retiring to bed.[66]

Lord Balabhadra is considered as the principal deity of agriculture. To celebrate the occasion of Balabhadra's birth *(Gamha purnima)* white line-drawings are made on the walls of the *guhala* or cow-shed which is a popular custom prevalent in the farmers' community of south Odisha . The place is first given a coating of *geru*, red ochre, before the motifs auspicious for Balabhadra are drawn. The images of *Balada* (bullocks), *sagada* (bullock cart), *Dhana bila*, (rice fields), in addition to heaps of paddy and various ornaments are drawn on the walls and floors. *Sindura* (vermillion) dots are applied to the painting and *duchaula*, rice in meals, is offered by the farmer while the women of his household sit inside the cow-shed and sing *hulahuli*.[67]

As protection against any evil influence, the doors of private houses, temples and *matha* institutions are marked with a special *jhoti* containing an iconic representations of Ganesha and Ekapada Bhairava. Vermilion and sandalwood paste marks along with *duchaula* offerings are painted on these doors and walls. A Sanskrit *sloka* with a protective connotation is inscribed on a palm-leaf and hanged from the roof.

The ingredients are normally rice paste and water with requisite dilution. Here the fingers are the brush. Sometimes, a small piece of cloth or beaten of sticks is used as brush along with the work of the fingers. The walls which are washed with earth and cow-dung and are dried quickly, absorb the moisture from the diluted paste leaving the designs intact. The paste is applied with the fingers and sometimes *sindur* or other colouring matter is used. In recent years, various kinds of lentils (*dal*) have been used.[68]

The *aripans* are not meant to last long and they are usually removed after the festival or the particular occasion is over. Here also some of the patterns and objects depicted are traditional and the symbolism is significant. Unmarried girls wishing to have good husbands have their particular *aripans* for *Tulasi-Puja* or *Janhi Osha*.

In the evening a particular drawing known as *sandhya aripan* is done for the worship of *Sandhya Devi.* For the Goddess of Welfare, *Kalyan Devi,* an *aripan* with symbols of the sun, moon and stars is drawn. Lotus flower with five petals represents the *puja* of *Saptarishis.* Births are marked by *aripans* made distinctive by the *Swastik* figure which is believed to shower blessings on the newborn.[69]

Young girls are taught the art of drawing *aripans* with care by the older ladies of the family. The wall decorations are often exquisite and delineate great capacity of the rural women to innovate and change within the broad frame-work of certain conventions and traditions. These in turn they imbibe from their mothers, grand-mothers or may be wives of brothers before their marriage. There is, thus, an informal professionalism which is traditionally passed from one generation to another. It is so in many other forms of folk art in Odisha . Though the *aripans* of Mithila are more cosmic in significance and more delicately expressed, the *Jhoti* or *Chitas* of south Odisha are simple and ordinary and marked with the absence of excessive delicate ornamentation.[70]

Muruja Drawings:

Muruja drawings are done on the ground with sand powder by the women of a household in front of a *tulsi chaura,* the sacred basil plant in the month of *Kartika* (October/November). This is considered the most sacred season of the year. Only widows observe this *Kartika Vrata* by drawing *pancha varni muruja,*five-coloured drawings with white chalk stone powder, turmeric powder, red, blue, pink and green are added if seven colours are required. Each motif receives a vermilion dot. *Duchaula* is offered and sometimes a *dhupavati* lamp is lit. The intricate and often very beautifully executed motifs include *bagabaguli,* the male and female crane, which symbolize the month of *Kartika* as being sacred and austere. This bird is said to abstain from eating fish during these weeks and is thus a vegetarian for this period. Vaishnava deities like *Rai Damodara, Radha Krishna, Jagannatha* with *Balabhadra* and *Subhadra* are also included as well as emblems like the chariot, the swing, the *nisuni* (ladder) motifs are drawn by which to ascend into heaven and the sacred *tulasi kshetra.*[71]

Thus, we mark some special features in the Odishan folkart which are worth mentioning. Firstly, there is a remarkable continuity in the classical, folk and tribal art-forms. Right from the cave paintings through the medieval religious and ritual-oriented or classical paintings to festival-based folk paintings and tribal paintings there is a continuity which even the modern Odishan painters use in their art idiom. Secondly, Odishan Art has always treated all art-expressions as a commonly and never made water-tight compartments for them. As a result of this, what is illustrated on palm leaves or *pattas* or on mud-walls or temple walls as murals are also the themes written about in literature, sung or danced and sculpted on stones. The parallelism which is noticeable in palm-leaf or *Patta* paintings and the temple sculptures, classical literature and song traditions is indeed remarkable.[72]

The traditional mural paintings were primarily in temples and monasteries, royal palaces and the large houses of the nobles. Nothing much of the last item, however, are now available. In medieval times, that art of painting was extremely popular both in royal courts and also in the folk tradition and religious tradition to convey the ideas of gods, their lives or the history of kings etc. In fact, a manuscript of 13th century mentions the various schools and traditions of paintings and names them as fourteen. The *Rajas* and *Maharajas* considered it a matter of prestige to have a *chitrakar* or *chitralekha* who could draw and paint. The tradition of Odissi painting had broadly three streams:

(1) the Puri school centred round the Jagannath temple;

(2) the southern Ganjam tradition with the celebrated art works at Buguda, Khallikote, Dharakote, Khemundi, Chikiti, Ghumsar, Paralakhemundi, Tekkali, Manjusha etc. and the third style was the Champamal school, primarily in and around Sonepur and Sambalpur.

The first two schools resembled each other aesthetically and even thematically. The functional inspiration was religious with royalty as the sponsoring agency. In fact, kings and temples were inseparable in contemporaneous society and paintings adorned temple walls as much as royal palaces.[73]

Folk art, on the other hand, drew its sustenance from the life of the folk; it partook of the energy, the elegance, the vivacity and the jest for living that characterize the life of the folk. Art creation had no set theory to guide it; no formal, intellectual hypothesis that governed it. It was open-ended, tentative, informal, communitarian. Art creation was often a group activity. Often too, it was a celebration of life, of joys and sorrows. It was never divorced from life, never far from it, as its centre was a concern for the group; intimate linkage with the gods, the ancestors and above all nature.[74]

Thus, Odisha has a rich repository of folk paintings. The folk and tribal paintings of south Odisha present a wide, variety, a rich and complex heritage. It is heartening to note that, though the folk dance, folk-tales, folk music are fast disappearing and declining from the Odishan society, the folk art tradition of south Odisha are continuing with great vigour and became popular day by day outside Odisha and even abroad.

Crafts:

South Odisha is also noted for its folk crafts. Each village of this region is a centre of rural craftsmen like blacksmiths, carpenters, stones sculptures, bamboo and cane workers, weavers, potters, etc. The silk industry at Berhampur enjoys traditional reputation for centuries. The kings of Mohuri estate invited the *Deras* of south India to promote silk industry at Berhampur even before the coming of the East India Company.[75]

There are three distinct types of crafts evolved over the years in this region. They are the folk crafts which are created by the people for their personal use, by the village craftsmen for a limited use and the specialized crafts which fetch international reputation and foreign money. The variety of folk embroideries which are popular all over India is an expression of folk traditions which kept alive by women folk of this region.

The idol of *Gram Devatas* or village gods made of clay, wood or stone, which are prepared by village craftsmen, display an expression of the people's religious beliefs. Specialized objects made by village craftsmen for particular occasions like the *Deepavali, Gamha Purnima, Durga Pooja,* the *Manabasa-Gurubara,* the *Sahi yatra* and *Thakurani yatra* are designed to answer the needs of a particular festival. There are craftsmen who specialized in creating textiles and ornaments which meet the requirements of a particular section, drawn from each community with its own distinctive design.[76]

Secondly, there are crafts which have been developed around religious centres. These cater to the needs of the religious institutions and the ceremonies associated with them and the pilgrims. Many important religious places have become specialized centres for particulars crafts. For instance, Nuapada, Pitala, Kabisuryanagar, Kodala and Bamokoi are famous for making fine *saris* and bamboo works, Belaguntha for bell-metal fishes, Paralakhemundi for horn and ivory works, Chikiti for wooden deities and musks, Kodala and Mathura for stone-carvings, Chikiti and Badakhemundi for *Ganjapa* and mask making, Buguda and Bhanjanagar for *pattachitra* and puppet making.[77]

Thirdly, there are crafts which have been developed in the weekly markets known as *hattas.* Places like Aska, Balipadar, Chandiput, Chandragiri, Gumma, Kanchili, Ichhapur, Bellaguntha, Surangi, Chikiti, Badakhemundi, Kabisuryanagar, Narendrapur, Hinjilicut, Jagmohan, Kanchuru and Berhampur are known for coir, bell metal and huge image making like *Kali, Raja Rani, Sapua Sapuani* (made of canes and clothes) cottage industry which prepares various kinds of mats and household potentials and instruments used for music and *kirtan* parties and even idols worshipped at temples.[78]

The brass fish made by the craftsmen of Bellaguntha are mostly exported abroad to fetch foreign exchange for a few specializing families. The carpenters of Paralakhemundi have earned international reputation for making a large variety of toys and decorating articles with the help of horns which can be well preserved in the houses. The industry based on horns received royal support and some of the craftsmen migrated to Cuttack for the sale of horn works which are now meant for exports. Maharaja Krushna Chandra Gajapati Dev, the founder of modern Odisha state was in fact responsible for elevating this household industry into an exportable craft.[79]

The folk crafts of south Odisha during the period under review may be broadly divided into five kinds. These are as follows-

Pottery:

Pottery and Terracotta was the earliest art of the human civilization. It is one of the earliest skills developed by man in the handling of clay. The soft alluvial clay was needed and coiled into container. Lumps of clay were hand-moulded into toys or the deity that was worshipped. Thus, moulding with clay became an intimate part of the lives of people of different villages of south Odisha. It was the women who worked on clay. Even today wherever pottery is shaped by coiling or moulding, it is done by the women.[80] In Jarada, Chikiti, Rayagada, Kotepad this art of pottery and terracotta are famous. Women shape the pottery by coiling. Only later when the wheel was discovered, men took over the task of making pots. The movement of the wheel and the pressure of the hands on the clay made new shapes and forms. The potters of today still create this art form which were made 5,000 years ago.

The clay-cart and the bulls-on-wheels are toys with which children play, known as *Arjuna Ratha.* Different kinds of animal and birds, flower vases and different pots with majestic designs are prepared by the potters of different villages of south Odisha. It is remarkable how little technique and designs have changed over the millennium.[81]

The wheel used for throwing the pots is like the primitive one resting on a peg dug into the earth. The potter slaps the prepared clay in the centre of the wheel, forms it into a cone and rotates the wheel with a stick held in his hand. After it has gathered momentum, he opens the clay with his hand and pulls the form upwards. The movement of the wheel, the pressure of the hands, creates the form a pot carrying the imprint of the circular movement and the potter's own creative skill. With a string, he severs the finished pot from the lump of clay and gently lifts it with both hands. In the rhythm of creation there is a fascination which grips both the creator and the onlooker. For a moment, the potter identifies himself with the rhythmic movement as if it was the rhythm of life and he was *Prajapati.* The severing of the finished piece form the lump of clay with the deft movements of the hand and the final phase when the potter lifts the finished form gives the impression as though the pot was a new-born child: the process is expressive of the creator's identification with form created by him.[82]

Though glazing was known in India even centuries ago, the finest pottery of the unglazed varieties are found in the different villages of south Odisha. Faience, a form of glaze, is found in the Harappan pottery. Even beads with different patterns were created out of it. It is pertinent to observe that, despite an early knowledge about the manufacture of glazes, glazed pottery as such was not highly developed in this region during the period under review. This may happen because the use of pottery by Hindus as a domestic object for everyday use was restricted. Earthen pots were used as water containers or as containers for grains or oils. Some special dishes were cooked in pottery, but no one ever ate out of pottery dishes. If they were used while eating at all, they were used only once and after that discarded, for it was not considered hygienic to re-use them. It is probably because of this factor that glazed pottery was not developed in this part of the country.[83]

Each area has its own distinctive forms of water pitchers. Local traditions and the type of available clay influence the shapes and the decorative designs. The potter, *kumbhar* or the *Kumbhakara* is an integral part of the society of south Odisha . He creates not only pottery vessels but also images for worship during seasonal festivals. He also creates toys for children, and large terracotta figures which are offered to deities to propitiate them, or to beseech them for a boon.

Terracota:

In the rural areas, it is fairly common to see terracotta animal figures placed under Pepal trees or in shrines. The clay figurines carry marks of *sindhoor*, auspicious red powder, the maoli thread, as well as the largest offerings to the deities. When the gods and the ancestors are propitiated or appeased through offerings, good luck is assured. Usually a large banyan tree with its roots reaching down creates multiple arches in the villages of the region which gives the appearance of a natural shrine of gods and goddesses. Nestling beneath are kept hundreds of elephants, horses, lions and even a carved wooden goddess, conjure up a mystic atmosphere.[84]

In most cases, these terracotta figures are made by potters, the *kumbhars*, but in some cases, the worshippers create their own deities. In some areas it is the women of the household who create these forms as part of their *Sadhana*, their prayer. It is a common sight in the villages of south Odisha to see the *sanjhi* figures made on the walls of clay huts during *Navaratri* celebrations. The goddess is created out of clay pieces and is worshipped by the people.[85]

Woodwork:

Woodcarving and wood work is another major area of folk craft.[86] The tradition of wood-carving in India existed even in ancient times. The early stone-carved temples which have survived the ravages of time bear eloquent testimony to witness the influence of folk art on wooden structures of the temples. Scenes from *Ramayana, Dasavatara* in wood carvings are found in the temple of Biranchi Narayan in Buguda.[87]

The *Matsya Purana* mentions that every home should have a door-frame in carved wood as a sign of welcome to visitors. This tradition of carved wooden frames and carved wooden balconies supported by brackets of animals, birds and human forms, is a part of the architectural design of homes, palaces and temples, as well as other community places built all over India.[88] South Odisha is no exception to this custom.

South Odisha which abounds in extensive forests with a variety of wood available in them has a rich tradition of wood-carving. Here we get a product range that extends from palanquins, carved doors and windows to toys and articles of daily use. Etchings and use of colour heighten the beauty of the products.[89] The palaces, temples, *Bhagabat Tungis* and the houses of the rich people were decorated with a variety of wood carvings. These carried large carving of mythical figures such as *garuda,* the *vahana* of Vishnu, in the form of the half-man and half-eagle, and Hanuman the monkey-god, crocodile, the *vahana* of Ganga, and the lion, the *vahana* of Durga. Besides these, the carvers created a *simhasana,* lion's seat, on which the celestial image was placed. The Elephants, *Garudas* made of wood is still produced by different districts of south Odisha for use in worship at homes.

Carpentry in Ganjam was of superior quality and the skilled carpenters were invariably engaged by the rulers of the Zamindari estates for building carts for car festival and other religious functions, frames, altars and swings used in the temples and furnitures in the palaces. During the *"Thakurani Yatra"* at Berhampur that occurs in every alternative years as initiated by the Zamindars of Mohuri, the craftsmen of Berhampur and neighbouring areas remain busy in building wooden carts fairly big sized to accommodate large images of mythological Gods like Lord Rama, Lord Parsurama, Jwalamukhi, Laxman, Arjun etc. The painters and decorators remain busy for about a month to beautify the images seated on the carts that are located at central places of Berhampur particularly in the *bazzar* area. Interestingly the carpenters prepare a beautiful wooden ship fixed to a high platform representing the maritime tradition of Ganjam. On *Kartika*

Poornima the carpenters like their counterparts elsewhere prepare a variety of decorated boats that are floated on the seas, rivers and tanks.

One of the carpenters of Digapahandi made one wooden dancing girl in such a way that clad with a *sari* and could easily walk with the help of the carpenter himself from his workshop to the gate of the palace. The carpenters of Dharakote once prepared the wooden statue of a wood-cutter with the help of springs in such a manner that its elastic hands could hold the axe and help cutting woods. This kind of statues were fixed by the Zamindars in the jungles to attract tigers from distances for the purpose of hunting.[90]

In south Odisha, wood-carving developed under a dual influence: the influence of North and that of south India. This can be seen in temple carvings and in the carvings of *Rathas* for religious processions.[91]

Wooden-carved bowls, ladies, churners, jars and chapatti-rollers are an essential part of our everyday life. Each area has shops where these objects are made and sold. Those made to be given to brides, as part of their dowry so as to help them set up their new homes, are specially designed and decorated with colourful carvings. These articles add a special charm to their household chores. It would not be wrong to say that wood-carving are closely linked with the lives of the rural folk.

Mask Making:

Mask-making is another folk art of south Odisha. The mask required for *Prahallad Natak, Bagha Nacha, Gai-Rama Nacha, Sapa-Sapuani, Kela -Keluni, Raja- Rani, Ghoda Nacha* etc. are prepared by a people of special class known as *Chitrakaras.* The *Rajas* of the *Zamindari* estates of south Odisha used to patronage the *Chitrakaras* and craftsmen engaged for the purpose of mask making. The *Chitrakaras* were also hired in large number during festival occasions like *Dussehara, Oshakothi* and *Thakurani Yatras.* The *Rajas* of Paralakhemundi, Dharakote, Athagada and Chikiti provided many sorts of incentives to the *Chitrakaras* particularly in the palace town. [92] Mask is an essential element of this dance as the dancers impersonate various gods, animals, birds, hunters, etc.[93] Besides such masks, the full-sized masks of various gods and goddesses and, different animals and birds required for the dance and *Thakurani yatras* as already mentioned in the preceding chapter are also prepared and beautifully painted by the craftsmen. This craft provides livelihood to many families, particularly in the ex-Zamindari estates of south Odisha.

The masks are made of dark clay found on the bed and banks of the different rivers of the region. The masks of special quality are made out of very trivial items like waste paper, tamarind seeds, cow dung, clay, etc. and the artiste make them living and elegant by the touch of their brush and colour. The clay model of the character is fixed on small wooden planks and allowed to harden. Muslin gauze is pasted on it and over the gauze two or three alternate layers of paper and muslin are pasted, the top being coated with a thick layer of the clay. Sharp instruments, like those used by a mason, are used to carve out noses and eyes. A particular facial expression is painted into the masks, some of which, especially those representing gods, demons etc., are highly artistic and deeply symbolic.

There are certain *Chitrakara* families in the Ex-Zamindari estates of south Odisha like Chikiti, Paralakhemundi, Badakhemundi, Humma, Polosora, Buguda and Khallikote who were experts in the art of mask-making. *Chitrakaras* of Chikiti are well-known for their excellent masks of Lord Nrusingha which are vivid and vibrant and used in the *Prahallad Natak.* These masks are also used for different dances.[94]A large number of these masks are sold outside Odisha and even India from where they are produced.

In some of the folk dances and indigenous tribal and semi-tribal dances, masks are worn by the dancers. The most prominent of such dances are the *Prahallad Natak* and the *Thakurani Yatras* of different places of south Odisha. The dancers depict entire dramas with the help of the hands and feet.

However, with the popularity of Television serials and drama program, the art of mask making is gradually declining.

Puppet Making:

Puppet dance, or *Kandhei-nach* as it is called in south *Odisha,* is a very popular form of folk entertainment. Sometimes life-size puppets made of wood, representing different characters of folk and classical legends, are made and public exhibition of their 'dance' is given on festive occasions and during any time of the year. The skillful movement of the inanimate puppets in the hands of the artists holds the audience's attention. Like actors and actress of flesh and blood, the puppets look lively.[95]

The puppets are made of wood and carved and painted by the village carpenters. In south Odisha puppet making has developed as family art down the centuries. The puppets are kept unclothed in a basket but beautifully dressed up before they are introduced in a performance. For development of this art, no rich patronage was necessary. The support of the village folk helped it to flourish.[96]

Considering difference in design, mode of manipulation and presentational techniques, puppets are basically of four types: glove-puppet, rod-puppet, string-puppet and shadow-puppet. Glove-puppets known as hand-puppets, are the simplest, but that does not mean they are less fascinating. Rod-puppet is an extension of glove-puppet, but often much larger with a full-length rounded figure supported and manipulated by concealed rods from below. String-puppets are also known as marionettes. The performance of shadow-puppets is known as shadow-play or shadow-show, but these type of puppets are not known to the people of south Odisha. Of these, two types of puppets only prepared by the carpenters of this region. The rod puppets are much smaller in size usually they are about 12 to 18 inches. Most of these puppets are have joints at the neck and possess two shoulders. While the head of the puppet figure is attached to a rod by which it is manipulated, the hands are usually tied to strings. Thus elements of rod and string puppets are combined in this form of puppetry.

There are special classes of artists who prepare these puppets or *Kandheis* for this puppet dance or *Kandhei-nacha.* The artists prepared the puppets either by wood or by rags. Village Bada Kodanda near Bhanjanagar and Pitala near Aska and Narendrpur near Berhampur are famous for this *Kandhei* artists.[97]

In recent years there has been a growing interest in folk art forms all over the world. In a sense this can be looked upon as an attempt to return to the roots, to discover the true source and significance of art in the universal modes of aesthetic perception intimately linked with the business of living. Folk art, drew its sustenance from the life of the folk; it partook of the energy, the elegance, the vivacity and the jest for living that characterize the life of the folk. Art creation had no set theory to guide it; no formal, intellectual hypothesis that governed it. It was open-ended, tentative, informal, communitarian. Art creation was often a group activity. Often too it was a celebration of life, of joys and sorrows. It was never divorced from life, never far from it. At its centre was a concern for the group; intimate linkage with the gods, the ancestors and above all nature. In fact, they all were part of the environment man lived in.

Metalware:

The flexible metalware fish and snakes of Bellaguntha and Nuapada are an exclusive craft of Ganjam District. The body of the fish is made flexible through the following process. Brass sheets are beaten to make them extra thin and malleable. They are cut into narrow strips and welded to a cylindrical shape. The radious of each such cylinder varies along a gradually tapering scale. The cylinders are indented on one side by chipping away slowly and carefully with a small chisel. Then these foils are inserted one into the other and a thin line of stitching along the fins is done with brass wires to join them. The head and the tail are beaten out separately and joned.

Flexible snake is also made in the same process. The flexible Brass fish is made so well that they give movement and create an illusion to that of real once.

Stone Sculpture:

The Stone sculptures of Mathura and Athagada are of high artistic and aesthetic value. Stone carving, temple building, traditional, massonary and occasionally chariot building are the traditional professions of Sutradharas. The sculpture carve bull, image of idol out of a huge block of gneiss stone, which proves the excellence of artistic character. All the stone carvers are from a single village known as Mathura in Polosara block. There are near about 100 families of stone carvers there. In addition, a few of them who had gone on the assignment of temple building have settled in different places of Odisha.

Textile Applique:

The appliqué works of Ganjam District can be traced back like all other handicrafts to rituals. During Jatras, during various festivals like Dolpurnima, Thaku 8 rani Yatra, in folk dances like Ghoda Nacha, Thia Nacha, Rama Lila, Rasa Lila, Danda Nata and in marriage processions, the images of animals arev required to be represented. The mask of animal i.e. bull, tiger, horse etc are made out of paper, cloth, wood or cane and printed. Now comes the appliqué work which covers the cane frame of the animal. Besides, the other products of the appliqué works are small fans, wall hangings, table cloth, canopies, umbrellas etc. The artistes are located in the village of Dharakote Block, Barapalli and Buguda etc.

Luckily in Odisha, life has never strayed too far from the ancient folkways of living. This is partly due to history. Odisha was one of the last regions of the country to be conquered by the British and the modernizing influence of British rule had a comparatively late start. The folk art remained undistorted, unalloyed for long and it is only in the last few decades, with the pace of modernization and industrialization, that there have been little changes on these forms.

From the above discussion, it is inferred that, the folk art and crafts of south Odisha are very artistic, lively and vibrant. It supplied livelihood to a large number of families and entertainment to the travellers, tourists, poets, onlookers and the lovers of beauty. The folk arts and crafts are an integral part of life of the people, despite rapid social and technological changes taking place. Today there is a tremendous interest in the rich heritage of folk tradition. Immense in its variety and range, this tradition reflects the amazing diversity of the people who have created it. This clearly indicates that, how the arts and crafts of imaginative rural folk can be related to the day-to-day living, their legends, myths and festivals. It explores the rare and native genius of the folk people. Thus, the opinion expressed by O.C.Ganguly, may be regarded as a just conclusion "This form of pictorial art of folk significance are not only unique in the history of Indian painting but are unparallel in the history of any form of European painting".

References

1. P.C. Raychoudhury, *Folklore of Bihar*, New Delhi, 1976, p.163.
2. *Ibid.*
3. K.B. Das and L.K.Mahapatra, *Folklore of Orissa* , New Delhi, 1979, p.117.
4. Sitakant Mahapatra, *The Rainbow of Rhythms*, Jagatsinghpur, 2005, pp.149-150.
5. *Ibid.*, p.149.
6. Dinanath Pathy, *Traditional Paintings of Orissa* , Bhubaneswar, 1990, p.
7. T.E.Donaldson, *Tantra and Sakta Art of Orissa* , vol.I, New Delhi, 2001, p.45.
8. Biswarup Das, *Orissa: Social, Cultural and Religious Aspects*, New Delhi, 1985, p.52.
9. T.E. Donaldson, *Tantra and Sakta Art of Orissa* , vol-I, New Delhi, 2001, p.45.

10. Dinanath Pathy, *The Murals of the Gods and Goddess of Orissa,* New Delhi, p.
11. *Ibid.*
12. Bhagaban Sahu, *Cultural History of Orissa,* New Delhi, 1997, p.108.
13. Dinanath Pathy, *Orissa Murals,* Delhi, pp.18-20.
14. *Ibid.*
15. B.B. Jena, *Orissa – People, Culture and Polity,* New Delhi, 1980, p.102.
16. Dinanath Pathy, Orissa Murals, Delhi, p.
17. K.C. Panigrahy, *History of Orissa ,* Cuttack, 1980. pp.430-431.
18. *Ibid.*
19. Prabhasini Sadangi, '*Ganjamara Ganjapa*' in: *Mardaraj*(Odia), Khallikote, 2010, pp.57-59.
20. Bhagabana Sahu, *Socio-Economic and Cultural History of Orissa,* Cuttack, 2002, p.80.
21. Ashutosh Bhattacharyya, *Folklore of Bengal,* New-Delhi, 1978, p.156.
22. K.B.Dash, *Folklore of Orissa,* Bhubaneswar, 1991, p.92.
23. Ashutosh Bhattacharyya, *op.cit.,*p.156.
24. *Ibid.*, p.157.
25. *Ibid.*
26. S.RamaRao, *Folklore of Andhra Pradesh,* New-Delhi, 1971, p.
27. Bhagabana Sahu, *Cultural History of Orissa,* New-Delhi, 1997, p.110.
28. Sitakanta Mahapatra, *The Rainbow of Rhythms,* Jagatsinghpur, 2005, p.154.
29. *Ibid.*
30. B.C.Ray, *Orissa under the Mughals,* Calcutta, 1981, p.152.
31. *Ibid.*
32. Bhagabana Sahu, *Cultural History of Orissa,* New-Delhi, 1997, p.111.
33. *Ibid.*
34. Bhagabana Sahu, '*Kedu* Sacrifies in the Kandh Tracts of Orissa in the second half of the 19th century', in: *Research Journal of the Berhampur University,* vol.IV, December 1984, p.133.
35. Sitakanta Mahapatra, *op.cit,* p.155.
36. Department of Tourism Government of Odisha, *Tribal Heritage of Orissa,* Bhubaneswar, 1991, no page.
37. Verrier Elwin, 'The art of Ikon', *in:*Sitakanta Mohapatra(ed.), *Soura Painting,* New-Delhi, 2009, p.2.

38. A.C.Sahoo, "*Saora* Script and Wall Painting" in: *The Cultural Heritage of Ganjam,* Bhubaneswar, 2004, p.352.
39. *Ibid.*
40. Verrier Elwin, *op.cit.,* p.7.
41. A.C.Sahoo, *op.cit.,* p.355.
42. Sitakanta Mahapatra, "*Saora Icons as Pictograms*", in: *The Rainbow of Rhythms,* Jagathsinghpur, 2005, p.167.
43. A.C.Sahoo, *op.cit.,* pp.355-358.
44. *Ibid.*
45. A.Duff, "Goomsur; the late war there-the Kandhs of Hill Tribes" in: *The Calcutta Review,* vol.v, no.ix, 1846, p.45.
46. Verrier Elwin, *The Tribal Art of Middle India,* Bombay, 1951, p.10.
47. M.Barbara Boal, *The Kandhs,* Warminster, 1982, p.200.
48. W.Taylor, "On the Language, Manners and Rites of the Kandhs of the Goomsar Mountains" in: *Madras Journal of Literature and Science,* vol.v, Jan-june, 1837, p.41.
49. Dinanath Pathy, *Orissa Murals,* Delhi, pp.12-13.
50. Verrier Elwin, *op.cit.,* p.15.
51. P.K.Pattnaik, *Lokakala-Chitakuta* (Odia), in: *Mardaraj,* 2010, pp.132-136.
52. M.A.Sherring, *The Tribes and Castes of the Madras Presidency,* no place, no year, p.202.
53. L.S.S.O'Malley, *Bengal District Gazetteers: Angul,* Calcutta, 1908, p.66.
54. H.H.Risley, *The Tribes and Castes of Bengal,* vol.I, Calcutta, 1891, p.408.
55. L.S.S.O'Malley, *op.cit.,* p.66.
56. R.V.Russell and R.B.Hira Lal, *The Tribes and Castes of the Central Provinces of India,* vol.III, London, 1916, p.472.
57. C.F.MacCarties, *Madras Census Report,* Madras, 1881, p.97.
58. L.S.S.O'Malley, *op.cit.,* p.66.
59. P.K.Pattnaik, *op.cit.,* pp.133-137.
60. P.C.Roy Choudhury, *Folklore of Bihar,* New-Delhi, 1976, p.166.
61. Ashutosh Bhattacharya, *Folklore of Bengal,* New-Delhi, 1978, p.154.
62. Sitakanta Mahapatra, "Folk Art of Orissa: Continuity in Visual Tradition" in: *The Rainbow of Rhythms, op.cit.,* p.176.
63. Dinanath Pathy, *Art, Architecture and Paintings of Orissa,*

64. Sitakanta Mahapatra, "Folk Art of Orissa: Continuity in Visual Tradition" in: *The Rainbow of Rhythms, op.cit.*, p.175.
65. Dinanath Pathy, *Art, Architecture and Paintings of Orissa,*
66. *Ibid.*
67. *Ibid.*
68. Sitakanta Mahapatra, "Folk Art of Orissa: Continuity in Visual Tradition". in: *The Rainbow of Rhythms, op.cit.*, p.178.
69. P.C.Roy Choudhury, *Folklore of Bihar,* New-Delhi, 1976, pp.166-177.
70. *Ibid.*
71. Sitakanta Mahapatra, "Folk Art of Orissa: Continuity in Visual Tradition" in: *The Rainbow of Rhythms, op.cit.*
72. Sitakanta Mahapatra, "Temple Murals *and Patta* Painting" in: *The Rainbow of Rhythms, op.cit.*, pp.147-148.
73. *Ibid.*
74. *Ibid.*
75. Prahllad Panda, "Art and Craft in Ganjam", in: *Mardaraj*, Khallikote, 2007, pp.16-17.
76. Dinanath Pathy, *Art, Architecture and Paintings of Orissa,*
77. Prahllad Panda, *op.cit.*,
78. Padma Charan Padhi, *British Trade and Tariff Policy in Orissa,* (Unpublished Ph.D thesis submitted to Berhampur University in 1998), pp.129-130.
79. Prahllad Panda, *op.cit.*
80. Jasleen Dhamija, *Indian Folk Arts and Crafts,* New-Delhi, 1970, p.39.
81. *Ibid.*
82. *Ibid.*
83. Odisha Cultural Forum, "*Loka kala*" in: *Odishara Lokasanskruti(Odia),* Cuttack, 1978, pp.169-173.
84. Jasleen Dhamija, *op.cit.*, p.42.
85. *Ibid.*
86. Sitakanta Mahapatra, "Folk Art of Orissa: Continuity in Visual Tradition" in: *The Rainbow of Rhythms, op.cit.*, p.185.
87. Brushaketu Dash, "*Katha Konarkara Bindhani*" *(Odia),* in: *Mardaraj,* Khllikote, 2010, pp.67-69.
88. Jasleen Dhamija, *op.cit.*, p.44.

89. Sitakanta Mahapatra, *op.cit.,* p.185.
90. Prahllad Panda, *op.cit.,* p.17.
91. Jasleen Dhamija, *op.cit.,*p.44.
92. Prahllad Panda, *op.cit.,* p.15.
93. P.C.Roy Choudhury, *op.cit.,* p.168.
94. Dinanath Pathy, *Art, Architecture and Paintings of Orissa,*
95. Jivan Pani, *Living Dolls: Story of Indian Puppets,* New-Delhi, 1986, p.10.
96. K.B.Das and L.K.Mahapatra, *Folklore of Orissa,* New-Delhi, 1979, pp.131-133.
97. Prahllad Panda, *op.cit.*

7

Folk Medicines and Methods of Treatment

Folk medicines and the folk method of treatment form a fascinating chapter in the history of folk culture of south Odisha. Talismans, sorcerers, folk-medicines and cure deities have been of much interest to the scholars of folklore studies. The village folk have their own medicines and methods for curing different ailments of the body and the mind. Magical powers are often attributed to village physicians known as *Vaidya* some of whom are adept in *Ayurveda*, the indigenous Indian system of medicine. Though they are illiterate, they acquire this knowledge of medicine through tradition of transmission from generation to generation. They are more acquainted with its practice than its theory. Some of them know single-herb cures. This chapter gives a vivid account of folk medicines and the folk method of treatment.

In the primitive days the vast majority of settlers in the region under study were cut off from any kind of formal or rational medical care. The competent physicians were also remained beyond the reach of a vast segment of the population. Being deprived of these benefits, the rural folk used folk medicines derived from time honoured and age-old traditions.[1]

Even after new and better treatment became available, the folk clung tenaciously to folk remedies handed down from generation to generation. Many such remedies survived well into the twenty-first century and even constitute a part of home treatment practiced in remote areas of the mountains.[2]

As far as recorded history goes, the earliest instances of rational medical knowledge are to be found in the *Rig Veda* and the *Atharva Veda* both of the second millennium B.C. But there is much evidence to show that the *Ayurveda* was preceded by an earlier medical knowledge developed by the builders of the Indus Valley civilization. The Aryans developed it by taking of the beliefs and practices of the black-skinned indigenous people speculating and experimenting freely in their own way, learning much and unlearning only that which was patently wrong.[3]

The medical knowledge of the pre-Aryan Indians has been so thoroughly mixed, diluted and absorbed into the Ayurvedic system that it would be an almost hopeless task to attempt to separate the earlier knowledge which survives only in some *tantras* and in the non-Ayurvedic medicine still practiced by otherwise ignorant medicine men throughout India, employing inorganic remedies, secret herbs, animal products and venoms. In the beliefs and practices of the primitive aboriginal tribes of India also a store house of this ancient knowledge can be discerned.[4]

The reputation of medical skill possessed by nomadic tribes, can also be attributed to this primitive knowledge. Some examples of ancient *Dravida* medical lore are believed to have survived intact without debasement in the non-Ayurvedic systems of medicine still surviving in parts of south India and are found codified in existing treatises in Tamil and in other south Indian languages. The fragmentary remnants of *Agadatantra* (use of poisons and venoms in curing diseases and treatment of bites of poisonous animals and poisonings) found in various ancient works and of *Bhutavidya* (black magic and treatment of mental diseases and possessions) found in Vedic lore and in Ayurvedic treatises, as will be discussed later, testify to the existence of lost branches of non-Ayurvedic medical knowledge incorporated in the *Ayurveda*. In the *Ramayana*, Ravana, the demon (non-Aryan) king is said to be a master of many sciences including medical science and the prince Laksmana resuscitated from a mortal injury by the medical skill of the monkeys, that is dark-skinned aborigines (6th canto; *Laksmana,* already dead by the *saktibheda,* is revived by a rare plant prescribed by a learned doctor from among the monkeys).[5]

This is how the folk medicine and folk treatment of disease originated. J.G.Frazer who called it as "Occult Science" acclaimed a worldwide recognition.[6]

In the folk medicine and folk treatment of diseases no degree holder or qualified persons are required. The folk people use different types of herbs, roots, fruits, leaves and jells for the cure of different diseases. They practice it from generation to generation by oral transmission. There are mainly six forms of folk medicines, which are as follows:

1. Juice (*Rasa*):

The leaves of the certain trees are grinded and the juice are extracted from it and given to drink to the diseased persons. By this method several diseases are cured. The leaves of *tulasi, bela, masanga* are mainly used for this purpose for the cure of cough, jadish, diabetics, typhoid, etc.[7]

2. Powder (*Churna*):

The powders of leaves, fruits, roots, barks of different trees are prepared mixing with *sunthi, pippali and jira.* This mixed powders are given to the affected persons for the cure of indigestion, *amlapita* and various belly diseases.

3. Quath:

Quath is the extraction of different commodities boiled in water. Different kinds of herbs, fruits, leaves, roots and barks are jointly boiled in water. When three-fourth of it is evaporated the rest one-fourth is used as Quath for the cure of different diseases. *Triphala pachana, Dasamula pachana, Anantamula* are some of the examples of this *ayurvedic* system.

4. Paste:

Paste is another type folk medicine which cured cuts, skin diseases and used for healings. It is also known as *Kalka* or *Prolepa.* Here also different type of roots, leaves, barks, fruits of the plants are collected and prepared a paste which was applied in the affected areas for the disease of different skin diseases and healings.

5. *Hima*:

Hima is a kind of drinking which is prepared by immersing the fruits, roots, leaves, barks of different trees and creepers for a long time in the water. Usually, these things were drowned in water in the night and used to drink it in the morning after filterisation.

6. *Phanta*:

Phanta is the extract of different kinds of herbal items boiled in water and given to the patients after filterisation. Although the most illiterate people of the remote villages of south Odisha in the tribal hill tracts of this region have not heared the names of Charak and Sushruta the famous physicians and the founding fathers of *ayurveda* of ancient India but they used all the above forms of *ayurvedic* medicines for the cure of diseases.[8]

The *Vaidyas* and *Boyas* who are well informed about herbal plants and roots, supply herbs to village physicians. The barber women who attend to maternity cases in the village also know of many herbs and leaves that cure wounds and cuts. Almost all the elderly women in the village know the cures for ordinary ailments of children, like cough, cold, dysentery and eyesore. Serious diseases like epilepsy too come under the purview of locally available prescriptions. There are village physicians who are capable of curing jaundice, breast abscess, asthma, and rabies etc. with single herb. They also know the cures for snake-bite and scorpion sting. They use either medicine or magic, sometimes both, as antidotes to these poisons.[9]

Veterinary doctors among the village folk cure many cattle diseases. The new sprouts growing from stumps of the great millet, castor-oil planet etc. are poisonous. Village cattle generally die in number on eating these sprouts in season. Therefore, every village has at least one person who knows the cure for the different affliction which cattle are subject to. They use medicines as well as magic and fire cures for these purposes. Knowledge of folk medicine, especially herbal and magic, being closely guarded secrets, is imparted towards the end of the physician's life to only one person, who is either his son or his disciple.[10]

Henry H. Presler has rightly remarked in his *Primitive Religions in India,* "Men look out upon the same universe and interpret it differently. The different interpretations are partly due to different ways of knowing, partly different environments experienced, partly to individual leaders. Accordingly, alternatives exist to the primitive or rural folk in medicines and treatment".[11]

To the illiterate folk nothing was perhaps more astonishing than disease, which naturally attracted his most careful attention as it sometimes led to death. With an imperfect knowledge of its cause, he naturally turned to supernatural means in order to counteract it. He invented charms and amulets, cultivated magic and witchcraft, and developed the idea of cure-divinities. He believed that if he could propitiate certain invisible spirits supposed to be responsible for various diseases, he would be free from their attacks.[12] Same theory is also applicable to the tribals. An important characteristic feature of *saura* religion is the custom of making drawings on the walls of houses in honour of the dead, to avert disease, to promote fertility and escape from natural calamities.[13] To satisfy the evil spirits and gods, sacrifice of animals and birds is believed to be efficacious and thus it is looked upon as a bargain or give and take between god and man. The community worship of *Durga* or *Kali* has a tremendous hold on the masses.[14]

They view injury and disease in terms of cause, diagnosis, and cure. Causes recognized by them may be natural, human, or supernatural. Diagnosis may be by inspection, inference, or religious ritual. Remedies may be empirical (scientific), magical, or religious. A *Vaidya* is a medical practitioner specializing in administering herbs, in message and in applying heat and poisons. The *Vaidya*, as a type, does not resort to supernatural power to cure injury and disease. The point is that the illiterates regard the *Vaidyas* assistance as different from that of their *Panda* or low status priest, as secular, not sacred. The modern dispensary with its rows of bottles and pill-boxes appears equally secular to the illiterate. To suppose that, the cure affected in a modern hospital would make the world-view of most primitives is illogical. That, supposition betrays ignorance of the people, natural remedies play in the primitive's own therapy.[15]

Villagers are conservative in their outlook. They take every element of the past dictated by the tradition as sacred trust and consider a little digression from it a sin. They believe in ghosts and spirits, witch-craft and sorcery and approach the fetish gods and goddesses for solution of their problems. Old customs bind them like chains, and check their progress. Their age-old superstitions make them prey to virulent diseases; stifle any development of scientific or rational outlook. They do not understand this and retain most of the savage customs and superstitions, coarse and repulsive to the civilized, in their religious rites and ceremonies. Of course, no nation however civilized, is proud of shaking them off altogether.[16] Diseases is considered to be a punishment for sin and a normal result of the neglect of one's responsibilities towards the supernatural world. Crop failure, flood, drought and other calamities are regarded as distress to be dealt with when they appear in accordance with traditional techniques.[17]

The rural folk personified the natural and cosmic forces as gods and their influence was considered supreme in causing and curing illness. Water was the primordial element of the rural people. In the waters is the nectar of immortality and in the water is the potent curative powers. Divinity was also conferred upon plants with healing powers. The spirit of Evil (*Ahira Mainya)* and other demons bring all diseases which can be cured by exorcism, *mantras* (holy chantings), sacrifices of cattle and also by *baesajas* (drugs). Innumerable plants with healing powers are associated with the 'water' (which is not only the primordial element but also a source of health) and with *haoma,* the liquor of immortality. The cosmic elements rule over the human body and cause its functions and malfunctions, the human body being the microcosm of the universe. Three types of medicine men are distinguished; those who practice with the knife, with plants and with the holy words, the last class being the most esteemed.

To avoid or escape from all the above factors the folk people devised several methods like spells, cure-deities, magics, therapies, amulets and medicines. These are discussed below.

The Sorcers:

The common people of Odisha strongly believe in the efficacy of magic and are afraid of witches and sorcerers. Some tribal groups like the Santals in north Odisha are well known for the practice of sorcery and witchcraft.[18] The Kandhs of south Odisha are the greatest magicians and their women are the worst of witches.[19] In the folk beliefs magical powers are wielded by some persons with special training in magical lore and practices. Some others, in a way, exude evil magical power at the sight of beautiful, lovable or covetable objects, animals, crops or even presentable human beings. These occult powers are known as the evil eye (*nazar*) or evil touch. People suffering from stomach and minor ailments, cows not yielding milk, plants not yielding sufficient crops or women not paying amorous attention all are taken care of by practitioners of magic in the villages. Very often magical means are applied against the possible harms of the evil spirits or goddesses. For example, a child going out of the house is usually anointed with a particular paste, usually a mixture of cowdung and colyrium to ward off evil spirits. Exorcism of Goddesses of disease or spirits of epidemics is effected with the help of magical objects and recitation of magical spells.[20]

That the people believe in contagious magic is amply proved by some popular superstitions. For example, filing of one's nails, cutting of one's hair or the shedding of milk teeth are disposed of very surreptitiously, as a sorcerer can do magical-harm to these wasted parts of the body and thereby harm the whole body of the concerned individual.[21]

Sorcerers or witch-doctors are a special type of people who are known locally as *Ojhas, Guniyas, Sakhas, Vaidyas, Maits* or in different other names. They are not confined to any caste or class group. Among the tribals different groups are experts in dealing with different types of diseases. Expert magicians of the Chotanagpur area are known as *Maits.* These *Maits* come of Korwa, Bhumihar, Baiga, Dusad and Panka communities. In Bengal these people come from different caste groups.[22] Different sorcerers of different groups are specialists in different treatment, as for example, *Sauras* are expert in dealing with evil spirits. Kandhs are experts or specialists in the treatment of drowned, night goblin, labour pain and pain in mother's breast. They had a particularly strong belief in that exercise of the art which enabled witches to transform themselves into tigers, leopards, wolves and so on, and in this shape to attack human beings or their cattle.[23] They believed that witches had the faculty of transforming themselves into tigers then called as *Pulta Bagha.* John Campbell himself had come across such cases of *Pulta Bagha.*[24]

The *Guniyas* of general Hindu caste are specialists in driving away ghosts and curing a patient from the snake-bite or from the biting of scorpion, bees, dogs and jackles. In this treatment they use spells, herbs and other materials. They also advice foods which a patient will have to take for quick remedy. In need, they advice their clients to arrange for worship of a cure deity and for which they also prescribe articles to be needed. Thus in treatment of ailments, magical rites, medical treatment and worship go hand in hand.[25]

The sorcerers and witch-doctors, it is believed, prevent fire from burning, can stop or bring rain, find out thieves and stolen articles, cure a patient from snake-bite or from biting of scorpion, bees, dogs, jackals, drive away ghosts, and evil spirits, relief stomach disorder, headache, toothache, bleeding, boils and resins, dysentery, diabetes, eye problems, inflammation, hives, kidney troubles, measles, mumps, sudden weeping of babies, pains of abdomen, bone fracture, labour pain, barrenness, indisposition, mental troubles and what not. They also treat small pox, cholera, fever, cough, cold, cattle diseases; can stop evil from the practice of witch-craft, ward off evil spirits and ghosts and advise their clients how they should appease guardian and cure deities. It is for all these powers that sorcerers or magicians or *Ojhas* are very much respected in the folk and tribal society. They regard these people with the same amount of reverence as they have for different guardian and cure deities. In need, their service is also commissioned by the sophisticated people of India.[26]

Different spells are used for curing different diseases. Generally the male members of the society practice sorcery, but a few female members also practise it. The womenfolk who practise it, is called *Dahani* or *Dankini*. Some people practise magic. It is an institution to them where, there are both professional and non-professional magicians and exorcists. Professional one learns the art of sorcery or magic from a *Guru* or a preceptor. Non-professional exorcists are generally those persons who are informed in a dream by a deity or a spirit to act as advised and he acts accordingly. He cannot generally teach the art of magic, or his secret, it is his own specialization. But a professional exorcist learns the art by practise. He got his training from a teacher or from the appropriate authority. This can also be learnt in hereditary way.[27]

Many exorcists maintain their-family tree, but there are some exorcists who do not bother for this. They move like mad man. They are whimsical too. They work according to their sweet will. They are semi-professional and professional. Professional exorcists may again be divided into two types. The one, who earns his livelihood as his main source of income and the other type of professional exorcists practises this in spare time. Therefore, he is not fully dependent on exorcism for his livelihood. Thus, he is liberal in monetary affairs. In a sense, he is akin to non-professional exorcists.

Generally the fair sex does not practise exorcism, but among the non-professional group female exorcists are not uncommon. In this case they receive medicine through a deity or a spirit in a dream, and practise with that. They generally do this as public service or for general well-being and not for their personal gain. Although exorcists who receive medicine in dream are not allowed to do business with that, yet, there are people who make propaganda with that and earn a lot of money by such medicines. Since the common men have high esteem for such medicines, these people exploit their sentiment, by advertising their medicines as gifted one by a deity or a saint.[28]

There are some women who practise witchcraft. Among the tribal communities like the Santals, the Mundas, the Kandhas, Sabaras etc. this is widely practiced. Generally barren women or old and decrepit deformed, infirm wives or widows practise witchcraft. But whoever practices it, she does it in secret. A witch can change her form, Witches are sometimes cured by the oil of the castor plant, by shaving their heads, by cutting their foreheads, by tearing the holes in the ear lobes, or by a shoe beating, or by being compelled to eat unmentionable things.

Medicinal property needed for an exorcists or an *Ojha*, who act according to the advice of a deity or a spirit, are sanctioned by the deity or spirit themselves. The person who treats a patient with medicine endowed with divine powers or the medicine he receives in a dream, there might have some special drug prepared from indigenous products for his treatment. The drug generally vary from the drugs prescribed by a professional one. But, on a close observation it has been observed that there are many common native products for country made drugs for both the groups of professional and non-professional magicians. These products are: oil, water, mustard seed, grass, *sindur* or vermilion, particular herbs and roots, barks, leafs, flowers, stones, bones, magical cord and other things.[29]

It is believed by the folks and tribes that all disease in men and animal are caused by the mischief of some evil spirits or due to the curse of a guardian deity. If, therefore, these spirits or deities are appeased properly and the evil spirits can be driven away by force or so, there will be no danger of disease. Keeping this in view, the magic-doers or *shaman* apply charms, amulets consecrated water, salt, oil, *jharphuk, totakas, tuktak* etc. use talisman, practise contagious magic at the crossing of three, four or five rods and so on. They also advice their clients to invoke guardian deities and in such worship they often prescribe birds like pigeon, cock and animals like he -goat to be sacrificed.[30]

Magical Property:

In the magical practice as well as in the worship of deities different things or substances are used. A magician or an *Ojha* may use a single product for different purposes as for example, consecrated water or salt or oil may not only be applied for determining the cause of affliction, but also, these may be used as folk medicines for curing fever, headache, toothache and many other diseases.

Magical puff along with muttering of incantation or magic-lore, use of talismans, tieing of medicinal herbs and roots etc. with black cord or red thread in any part of the body to counter evil spirits are used. Charms or spells are also used to win good luck, to win in a litigation, to have prosperity as well as to avert bad luck and diseases of various kinds. Applications of consecrated water, turmeric, mustard-seed, *durba*-grass and others are common practices of the exorcists for remedy from different diseases. Beating an evil spirit with shoe, broom, etc. are made to drive it away. Tieing of magical rope, consecrated water, water dipped by stone etc. are used for curing many disease including biting of animals, snakes, dogs and for curing barrenness and other female diseases. These are also used for relieving labour pains, birth control, to ward off child death, to cure a rickety child, to cure a mother whose issues die after birth and so on. For the same purpose amulets are also used. Magical rites are also practiced for the treatment of cattle disease and getting back lost animals. Magic-lore is utilized for killing an antagonist person or enemy and for what not. It is thus observed that *mantras* or charms or spells are common items of the magic doctors along with water, mustard, *durba*-grass, turmeric, herbs and roots, some particular flowers, bone of a dead man who died in accident, bone of a cat or dog, magic cord, amulets and the type materials.[31]

Cure–Deities:

In the worship of cure deities also there are some common procedures. Here also common objects such as unboiled rice, fruits, banana, sweets, *sindur*, flowers, sacrifice of animals or birds etc. are necessary. Folk deities have some common pantheons which consist of spirits of the dead ancestors, defined heroes and natural objects. There are different kinds of gods and godlings both benevolent and malevolent with different functions. For the recovery of any illness, for the birth of a child to a barren woman, for the fulfillment of wishes of votaries, every now and then, folk gods and goddesses are worshipped. Objects of offerings and mode of worship are such as are coming down from generation to generation.[32]

It should be remembered in this connection that the popularity of a cure-deity depends upon the nature of the disease it represents. For example, though fever is a common disease of frequent occurrences, the divinity which represents it is not popularly worshipped. But small pox which breaks out only casually has well-developed cults. The more virulent is the disease, the more ardent becomes the followers of the cult.

When small pox breaks out in epidemic form the village folks take the vow that they would worship Sitala, its presiding deity, for recovery. They say: "We worship there O goddess Sitala, who is seated on an ass and without any clothes on." She is provided with a broom and a pitcher. Her head is adorned with a winnowing fan. She sprinkles nectar on those who got emaciated with eruptions. It is believed that by broom the deity sweeps the affected person head. Orthodox Brahmin priests, in general, do not officiate as priests of the deity, but now-a-days, a class of priests is found to worship her in some places. This priest belongs to the Brahmin caste. Her worship may be held in private or public. For her worship begging from door to door with singing songs or ballads for collecting the ingredients is found on many occasions. Sometimes women make *manasika* or a vow promising *Puja* to the goddess to invoke her aid in averting small pox and on the fulfillment of the vow they invoke her. She is also invoked for overcoming barrenness.[33]

The Goddess of Small-pox (**Sitala** ***Devi***): Of all the cure-deities, the cult of the deity of smallpox is the most widely distributed throughout India. In south Odisha the cult has its own local characteristics, which are as follows:

When smallpox breaks out in an epidemic form in some villages, the villagers take the vow that they would worship the presiding deity of the disease, Sitala (literally meaning 'the cool') as soon as it will show a sign of abatement. They attribute the disease to the wrath of the deity who is believed to be of an extremely malefic character. The villagers do not even mention the name of the disease directly out of fear for it, and refer to it as the 'grace of the mother'. While nowadays on the occasion of worship of the deity, images answering the description as found in her prayer formula are made, about four decades back no images were worshipped but offerings were made to the symbols representing the deity. This is the practice even today in some permanent shrines for the deity, where daily worship of the deity is held.

As a rule orthodox Brahmins would not officiate as priests of the deity, though nowadays, for economic reasons, their services are also available. A class of community known as *Mali* or *Roula or Desari* generally officiates as priests. They also prescribe various quack medicines for the disease. In the absence of any specific medical treatment people approach these native doctors for the cure of this disease. These 'doctors' not only prescribe quack medicine, but also offer worship to the presiding deity of the disease on behalf of their patients, on payment of a prescribed amount. Animal and birds are sacrificed and even *Pana* (Juice) and *Pithas* (Cakes) are offered to these goddesses for cure of these diseases.

The Goddess of Cholera (*Grama Devati*): Next in virulence to smallpox is cholera, which is known as *Haija* or *Jhada-banti* or *Badi* in Odisha. The deity supposed to be presiding over this disease is known as *Grama Devati* or *Thakurani* .

When Cholera breaks out in epidemic form, the villagers try to pacify the deity supposed to be presiding over the disease by worship, generally accompanied by animal sacrifices, sometimes on the outskirts of the village under the shade of some lonely trees. The services of a priest generally hailing from the lower castes of Hindus are requisitioned. The worship is performed with conventional ingredients, though red colored articles are preferred. A piece of red napkin, vermilion, and red flowers are offered to the deity. Animals and birds are sacrificed and the blood of the sacrificed animals is sprinkled over the food offerings to the deity. No food offering can be carried home after the worship is over. This must either be consumed at the very place of worship or thrown away beyond the border of the village. No orthodox Hindu would partake of it; in fact even the common people hesitate to do so. In normal times no other public worships of the village gods are held, but if an epidemic breaks out or there is scarcity of rain, special worships, as prescribed, are held. On such occasions the festive aspects of the celebrations are kept in abeyance, but due care is taken for observance of the rituals in their minutest details, for they are meant for propitiation of the angry deities.

In Bengal the deity which is worshipped in cases of outbreak of cholera is known as Raksha Kali, meaning "the saviour Kali". Evidently, the name has been Hinduized in recent times the worship of this goddess is conducted by Brahmin priests in temporary shrines built outside the village.

Cholera is also another virulent disease. Its presiding deity is known as Olaichandi. Exorcists also perform rites in warding-off this disease. These exorcists are of two types – one acting for the well-being of mankind, and the other doing business with his magic. When he fails to satisfy his clients by warding-off the disease, he sometimes collects some clothes of a cholera patient and by uttering incantation claims to have 'confined' the disease spirit into it. After that, he carries the cloth to a neighboring village, and washes it in secret in the tank from which drinking water of the village is drawn. In no time cholera breaks out in that village.[34]

For skin disease there are different folk cults. Diseases like leprosy, boils and itches are clearly distinguished from one another and for each type of skin disease different deities are believed to be presiding over. The sun god, is believed to be the presiding deity of leprosy. He is worshipped in different names i.e. Biranchi Narayan and Surya Narayan in different places like Buguda and *Arka Kshetra*(Konark) on different days and *Tithis* like *Magha Tila Saptami* and on Sundays of *Magha* and *Pausha* by the women-folk as a deity of the skin disease. Cakes made of rice powder, milk, curd and vegetables including arum are needed for His worship. Likewise, the favour of different *Pirs* or Muslim saints are sought for to ward-off different diseases.[35]

The village folk not only worshipped the deities but also worshipped trees, stones and the such type of things. Originally there was no temple for gods. Even now for the folk cults generally there are little permanent shrines or temples. Among the folk cults who have been up-graded as higher cults, there are temples or permanent places, for them. But host of them are found scattered everywhere and are represented by stones, clay images etc.

In ancient times huge shady trees were supposed to be the abodes of some unseen powers or gods. So, they were worshipped for curing diseases as well as for good luck. This ancient practice is still in vogue in south Odisha. Thus the village folk worship *Neem* tree (*Azdirachra indica*) as it is believed goddess of small pox inhabit in it. When a person suffers from pox, the leaves of this tree are used in several ways to lessen or to relieve of his ailment. The oil extracted from the *Neem* fruit possess much medicinal value. The temperature of the patient, it is believed, goes down if the oil is applied to his head and the lower part of his feet. Its flowers have blood purificatory properties. The leaves of Neem are also used to drive away the evil spirit. It is believed that the smoke and fire of this wood are powerful enough to resist a devil or a ghost. *Sheora* tree (*Streblus asper*) is worshipped for propitiating the spirit. They address the *Sheora*, on the top of which, they believe, *Vana Durga* or the goddesses of the forest resides, as *Sakhi* (friend). *Vana Durga* is also worshipped for fertility. The banyan tree is worshipped for immortality. [36]

Some folk people now take modern medicines, wear amulets and take magic doctor's help together, to cure illness. They also use herbal medicine, as for example, *buettneria herbaccarox*, in treating broken bones, *Acacia pennat's* young leaves is given for body pain, headache, fever and other diseases. *Ekephantopus scaber linn* is used to suckling children suffering from fever, *Melia azedarach* – leaf juice is used for womb troubles and to encourage conception in women. *Tectona grandislinn's* oil obtained by distillation of wood chips cures eczema and ringworm, *Orthosiphon rubincundus beneth* is applied to wounds of cattle, *Gynandropsis pentabhylla*, leaf juice is used in ear ailments, *Tamarindus indica* is used to make baby children healthy, three handful of leaf juice given in a weak for three. *Wedelia calendulacca* leaves are taken for jaundice, Dhelakata, the juice or the leaf is applied with common salt in any eye sore, Nelakutui, the root paste prepared on a particular stone cures eye catarach. The medicinal herbs are considered ineffective without the accompanying *mantras*. These *mantras* will have to be recited by the *Ojha* at the time of herb collection, at the time of preparation of medicine and at the time of medicine administration.[37]

The Spells (*Mantra*):

Magic-lore or spells or *mantras* which comes to the users through oral transmission from magicians of different castes and sub-castes, have no linguistic uniformity. These spells are small but powerful; to ward off diseases or unpleasant behavior of a person, or to win fortune in any way. Witches and imposters have always held a competition with physicians. Sometimes medical physicians face enormous difficulty in treating a patient of the rural community. It is not only the physician but also common men are treated badly if they visit a place where a patient is suffering. As soon as an outsider visit that place he is considered as a devil or a spirit and thus receives torture and suffering. Urban patients with rural bent of mind or having faith in tradition in general and rural patient in particular, place more confidence in the oracles, magical-puff, amulets, herbs and roots, consecrated water, salt, mustard etc., and the juice of fruits, branches, roots or skins of a few tree for remedies than in the prescription of a medically trained doctor.[38]

The techniques of folk medicine, various incantations formulate and practicing rites and rituals generally differ from community to community, but the articles needed for magic and worship do not differ much.

Different magicians may utter different charms or spells for achieving an object, that is to say, for one particular purpose there are different *mantras* of different magic-doctors. Since these *mantras* or spells are not found in written form they vary from person to person according to dialectal influence. So there is various magic lore or charms among different people for the cure of a particular disease. Also, worship formula for invoking different cure deities are different, in the manner, different drug manufacturing concerns produce different types of patent medicines for the treatment of the single diseases. As there are different spells for a single purpose, so sometimes a single spell is practiced for curing different diseases, as for example, to stop baby's cry consecrated salts or consecrated oil may be used.

It is to be remembered here that, in the folk and primitive society, the art of curing diseases, as well as that of healing injuries, do not always confined to a professional person. It is practiced indiscriminately by all persons. The persons who have experience and position in society and who are given some weight and importance to their advice do give free medical advice like a physician. The womenfolk too apply native and folk medicine for curing diseases of their sons, daughters and relatives as well as of themselves.[39]

Thus, *Mantra Chikitcha* is a very popular form of folk medicine. There are certain people who cure the different diseases through the *Mantras*. Some of the specimens of the *Mantras* which are collected from different areas of south Odisha are given below:

1. "*Durga mohara maa. Mu phunkai khandara ghaa.*
   Raha rakata sukhu ghaa. Narahu boli kahara agyan,
   sri durgankara koti koti agyan".[40]

(This is applied for stopping the bleeding after every cut.)

2. "*Thanahara dui gotau. Amukai i.e* (Referring the name of the wife of the person) *thanahara yehi khani jau. Jau boli kahara agyan- Hari Sahadebanka koti koti agyan.*"

(This *Mantra* is applied to cure the breast diseases.)

3. "*Aum Hari Sahadebaya namaha, aum Hari Sahadebaya namaha, Hari Sahadebaya namaha, aum amukai i.e* (Referring the name of the cattle) *goruthare je poka podiachi jhada ansari goda poka, na padu boli kahara rana, patale srihari sahadeba thakurankara koti koti rana.*"

(This is applied for cure of cattle diseases.)

4. "*Aum Kali charei chi chi kare somodra raje. Hanumanto dakadie dhaa dha asi bhage*".[41]

(This *mantra* is applied for cure of migraine.)

Witchcraft:

The Kandhs are firm believers in magic and sorcery.[42] Certain painful experiences in their day-to-day life like diseases, deaths and the like led them to believe in the existence of an invisible spirit. It was believed that this spirit could be appeased by the chanting of some formulas which amounted to the practice of some techniques of canalizing the power for good and evil. This practice is called magic or sorcery.[43]

This was professed by one who claimed to possess the power to work marvels, not through the aid and counsel of the supernatural powers but by certain occult faculties and devices. Persons who professed it belonged to either of the sexes. Alfred Lyall has described such persons as crazy Charlatans. However, the man who did it best in the southern Odisha was called the *Chemru Mousa.*[44]

The rural folk used to believe that the witches and devils roamed about chiefly at night-time.[45] According to them, the soul used to wander during sleep. A case has been cited by F.Faweett that on one occasion a dispute arose owing to a man discovering that another Kandh, whose spirit used to wander about in the guise of a tiger, ate up his spirit and he became ill.[46]

However, for the detection of such persons (witches?) several ordeals used to be performed.[47] Sometimes the *Desari* was called upon to examine the *panji* (palm leave manuscript) and name the person suspected to be the witch.[48] The witch-doctor or *Desari* was believed to have controlled those ill-willed forces and so he alone would be able to control them.[49]

However, in a Kandh village the medicine-man was an important personality. Unlike the priest whose office was hereditary, the medicine-man was promoted to begin his practice as the result of a series of spiritual experiences with a Goddess who, having guided him into his profession, remained there after his mentor and mediatress with the Gods. He was respected by the tribe who regarded him as one specially chosen by a Goddess. He was also accredited with possessing supernatural powers and being a sorcerer. His functions were chiefly to counteract the harm of evil spirits as manifested by inauspicious omens and the various illnesses that plagued the inhabitants.[50]

Of course all those beliefs were nothing more than superstitions. In all such beliefs the geography of the region and its environment plays a crucious role. Placed beyond the pale of communication with the plains, the rural folk especially the tribals remained buried in ignorance, superstition and prejudice.

The Amulets and Magic Cords:

The folk people also believe in amulets and supernatural agencies. They frequently prescribe the most disgusting and absurd medicines such as the heart of a mule ripped up alive, a portion of the lungs of a man who had died a violent death. It is also due to the influence of supernatural agencies that the folks believe, a dead man's hand could dispel tumor of the glands by stroking the parts nine times, but the hand of the man who had been cut down from the gallows was the most officious. To cure warts one had nothing to do but to steal a piece of beef from the butcher, with which the warts were to be rubbed; and as it rotten the warts would wither and fall. The chips of a gallows on which several persons had been hanged, when worn in a bag round the neck, would cure the malarial fever.[51]

Folk medicine in all regions relies upon the potency of mystical cords and riddles to facilitate labour pain. Ties the knot with the injunction 'Shut your eyes and fear nothing, take this in your hand or any other suitable part of your body on any Saturday or Wednesday after performing worship to Goddess Kali or other deity, no harm will happen to you." Sometimes it is asked to hold it in a way unseen by others. Magic cords with knots, is believed to make teething easier for bodies, if tied on a hand or waist with a coin. Gird up one's loins with magic cord save him from many diseases. A stone with a hole in it, suspended at the head on the bed, would effectually stop the nightmare. There are too many medicines of these types which need not be repeated here.[52]

The Bone:

It is believed that the bone of the head of a cow or a black cat, and vultures or a man died of an accident have strong magical powers. These can do good and bad both. Besides utilizing these, it is also believed by the folk that the blood can be snatched away by charms, dislocated bones can be cured by magic spells, evil spirits or enemy can be averted by magic puff, pregnancy of a barren woman is possible by *mantra* or by *batichalan* or *hatchalan* and the type of magical act, snake-bite and other biting can also be cured that way.

The effect of bones for cure is a magical practice. The strength of imagination in effecting wonderful cures has been observed in all ages. A halter that had served hanging a criminal was an infallible remedy for a headache, backache.

Magicians having magic bones were believed to be able to raise the gods of the upper and lower world, and compel them to answer questions. The power of medicinemen to inflict disease and death, to cure all disorders, to make known the distant and future events, to cause rain, hail and tempest, to stop excessive rain, to call up are also powerful enough to convert a living one into a stone, a man into an animal or a tree, and they themselves could take the forms of a tiger, a dog, a jackal or so. They could handle every kind of serpent without danger. These powers, the folk people believe are not obtained by art, but imparted to certain person.

Magicians have their instruments the bone of a dead man or the skull. Generally these are considered more powerful if these come from a man died on an accident on any Saturday or Tuesday in the dark half. Some bones of animals like cat, cow, etc. (the bone of a black cat has great magic power) are important for their purpose. Of course these bones too need to be duly sanctified by rituals before they are used for such acts.[53]

The Water:

The folk people have strong believe on the curative power of water. The water of hot springs as is found in Taptapani (near Digapahandi in the district of Ganjam, Odisha), and other places are potent with curative strength. It is believed that the bathing in Taptapani can cure all kinds of skin diseases including leprosy. The salutary medicinal effects of sea-bathing are acknowledged. Sea water taken internally has been beneficial for several maladies and is freely drunk by various savage tribes as health drink. Rivers have various qualities of recovery. Many use the waters of lake.

Water of particular places produces various morbid affections; and to this cause have been attributed goiters, cretinism and other distressing diseases.[54]

Presentation of Silver Eyes and Ears:

Presentation of silver and golden eyes and ears, nose and tongues to the gods and goddesses is a very common practice among the rural folk of Odisha . If a villager suffers from the eye or ear disease, he promises to offer the silver or golden models of the same to Lokanath or the notable Gods and Goddesses of the region. He earnestly believes that His mercy will cure him more effectively than any medicine. This practice is not peculiar to Odisha only. In Bengal, Goddess Kali is presented with the same models in the same way.[55]

Folk Method of Treatment:

Almost all the tribals of south Odisha are a superstitious folk who believe that the diseases are mostly caused due to the wrath or displeasure of a deity or ancestral spirits.[56] Even any mishap or accident is ascribed to the indignation of different *Penus* (Gods) and *Dumbas.* They had many queer myths and their imaginations were fed with various fantasies. That was because of their living in rugged mountains and dark forests.[57]

They, therefore, make every effort to appease these supernatural agencies who are associated with different deities, spirits etc. A functionary known as the *deshari* who normally belongs to their own community plays an important role in the diagnosis and treatment of disease. On the basis of certain symptoms or divination he diagnoses the disease. On the other hand, the *Bejuni,* who is a *shamanin* and who is also supposed to cure disease, traces out the deity behind the disease. In order to do this she performs necessary rites, gets into trance, realizes hallucinatory revelation, sacrifices animal as per the demand of the deity or spirit. Thus, when the *deshari* diagnoses diseases with local herbs and roots perforated with divination, the *Bejuni* diagnoses the disease only through necessary rituals and divinations.[58]

Medical Therapy:

Though all the diseases are considered to be the outcome of the wrath of deities and spirits, the *Kandhs* and the *Sabaras* still consider some of the minor diseases like fever, headache, cough and stomach pain etc. to be the result of natural causes and skin diseases to be due to contagious. But diseases which are incurable and prolong for number of days are ascribed exclusively to the obsession of spirits and deities. It is believed that due to commitment of immoral action or complete violation of the social customs a normal person is destined to suffer.[59]

The *Deshari*, who mostly uses herbal medicines, collected from the nearby forests, applies them in following manner for different diseases.

To stop bleeding, *Latchiri-creeper* is made paste and anointed over the wound. Immediately after the preliminary aid, paste of leaves of *Drayakala* plant or *Luhatarchi* plant is applied at the wound. For quick recovery from a fatal injury warm turmeric paste is also applied.

For any sort of burn injury, cow dung is applied immediately. Later on, the bark of *Manda tree* is soaked in water for a day and then grinds to prepare a sort of paste which is applied on burn bruises for healing up.

In order to lighten the pain of a sprain, castor-oil is boiled with turmeric paste and applied three to four times a day over the sprain. Sometimes a paste prepared out of *Bishalyakarani* is applied over the sprain after heating it up. And upon this sort of balm, a tender banana leaf is covered and tied up with a piece of cloth for a day or two in case of bone fracture.[60]

The southern part of Odisha is a land of high hills and dense forests. It is infested with gigantic snakes like *Ahiraj* (King of snakes), *Pythons*, *Sankhachuda* and poisonous snakes like *Cobra, Tampa, Chiti* and *Boda.*[61] When the people are caught by snake bite they never go to any hospital *Kabiraj* or *Vaidya*. They themselves are petty doctors. Roots of *patala garuda* and *Fapana* plant are grind together and applied over the wound caused either a snake or a poisonous insect. As an antidote to the poison, caused by venomous snakes, roots of a creeper, locally called *gadda*, is grinded and orally administered.

For healing up of fracture, *Hadsikula creeper* is also used by the Kandhs. A tender portion of the creeper is collected and then it is grind to a thick paste which is evenly applied over the fractured bones, which is then tightly fastened by placing two pieces of split up bamboo on either side of it.

For cure of eye-diseases, the Kandhs use turmeric paste. It is wrapped up in a small piece of cloth and then frequently heated up for giving hot compression to the eyes for healing. In case of vomiting, *Bhusanda* (roots of *Patal Garuda*) is grind up and then orally taken, for cure of diarrhea pulverized root of *Kumdi* plant is taken along with water.

Roots of *Anahinga* plant, *Bachha* or *Daja* plant and arrow-root (*Badhra*) are grind together and diluted with *Mahua* liquor (*Irpi Kalu*) in order to prepare a lotion which is anointed over the entire to get rid of fever.

Seeds of *Tralu* tree are collected. The skins of the seed are taken out. Root of *Ketkaya* plant is mixed with entire substance is diluted with water and used twice a day to get rid of cold.

For cure of indigestion, the roots of *Sarumaricha* plant and roots of *Bhusanda* (*Patal Garuda*) plant are grind together and taken with water three to four times a day.

Roots of *Kumdi* plant and roots of *Bhusana* plants are pulverized together and then mixed with water. It is taken three to four times a day. It is a curative for any sort of gastro-internal disease.[62]

Modus Operandi of *Deshari:*

Similarly each Kandh of the region, more or less, knows certain remedial measures when he is susceptible to minor sufferings. His open-air movement, less liking for confinement in his houses and frequent movement in hills and forests tend him to pick up basic knowledge of certain medicinal herbs and roots which either he gathers or brings immediately for treatment. Only when his personal knowledge falls he approaches the practitioner. In almost all the big villages there are one or two *Deshari* who are consulted even in odd hours.

The practitioner verifies certain symptoms after checking the palpitation of the right wrist of the female and accordingly diagnoses the disease. Eyes and tongues are not checked only stomach is pressed after due checking the practitioner diagnoses the disease and prescribes the medicine.

The practitioner is the custodian of indigenous herbs and roots. He, after due checking, takes out appropriate herbs or ready-made medicine, utters some magical spells solemnly and puffs on the medicine as well-as on the patient three to four times. It is believed that the *Ghungi Penu* is worshipped by the *Deshari* and appeased with adequate sacrifices so as to acquire the knowledge of the art.

A *Deshari* is supposed to know the medicinal effect of required roots and herbs available in the area along with charms and spells. The post becomes hereditary if the son is competent. If not, any man who develops the art becomes *Deshari.* A woman *Deshari* is not found in the area.

Deshari does not demand any fee for the treatment. The patient pays only a nominal fee of 25 *Naya Paise* for the medicine, and when cured, he pays what he likes as gift either in kind or cash.

Deshari does not undergo any formal training to learn the art. The post is also not hereditary. If the son likes, he learns some spells and charms to appease the *Penu* in connection with different treatment.

The status of a *Deshari* is in no way inferior to those of other religious functionaries of the village. As a folk doctor of the village, he is highly esteemed and given higher status in the society.[63]

Mental Therapy:

Therapeutic treatment through magic is also practiced by individual effort in this region. *Bejuni* or the *shamanin*, through white magic takes up treatment of mental illness. People also believe that through magical diagnosis the diseases can be cured and therefore, attach much importance to it.

It may be stated at the outset that *Shamanin* as such, is actually a part of religious nexus because it is through a ritual process the end is achieved. The key idea is to ward off the evil spirits and deities as well as to appease them with appropriate rites and sacrifices. Through this appeasement when the desired end is achieved, it may be called sympathetic white magic.[64]

For harming an enemy also the services of a *Shamanin* is sought. The type of occultism which she uses for infliction misfortune and harm on a target person is called *Peshini.* Such an art may be termed as contagious or black magic. It is not public but secretly practiced lest the party may be bewitched by more experienced practitioner.

However, only when medical therapy fails, the people take recourse to magical therapy, that is, they approach the *Shamanin* to take up the treatment.

Shamanins are organized on the basis of their respective tutelary spirits, whom they worship. In each group the *Pat-Bejuni* or the chief *Shamanin* takes the lead in divinations or in the performance of rites, who supposed to have gained proficiency in the art after rigorous training. Though there are male *Shamanins*, their number is much less. When they act, they adorn themselves with ladies garments.[65]

Modus operandi of the *Shamanins:*

The symptoms of the disease are ascertained first by the *Shamanin.* The *Pat-Bejuni* tests the external symptoms of the patient. From the very look of the patient, she can guess the type of disease which the patient is suffering from, and then determines the main causes of sufferings. Afterwards she resorts to the procedure of divination and invokes appropriate spirits and *Dumbas* of the ailment leaving aside other spirits and *Dumbas.*

The *Pat-Bejuni,* along with her assistants, starts supplicating sundried rice balls separately in winnowing fans with magical spells and charms so as to trace out the concerned spirit which has done the harm. In case, the spirit remains unidentified even after long recitation, *Pat-Bejuni* jumps off and starts dancing. Immediately the disciples follow her. While dancing she is possessed by the spirit. It is believed that the real spirit who is causing harm gets into her body. She ultimately gets into trance and starts talking to the spirit on behalf of the patient in that state of trance. She vows to placate and appease the spirit with whatever sacrifices the spirit desired to have. After that she gets back her senses and prescribes for ritualistic articles to be offered to the spirit. Accordingly rites are performed and sacrifices are given.

If, even after this, the patient is not cured, a more efficient *Pat-Bejuni* is consulted, who performs rites more elaborately and offers more sacrifices. And if after this the patient is not cured, the matter is left to be decided by the Earth-Goddess known as *Dharani-Penu.*

Shamanins are generally paid nominal fees. At the individual call she collects about 250 to 500 grams of sundried rice given by the head of the household, heads of sacrificial animals, that is, head of a chicken, a fowl or a goat and a nominal fee of Rs.1 to Rs.25. On communal worship, a group of *Shamanins* participate and the entire mass of sundried rice and the kills are equally distributed. In terms of money, each *Shamanin* gets about Rs. 55/- if she participates in the communal festival. In exercising white magic a *Shamanin* is rewarded as per the nature of benefit received by the beneficiary. For performing black magic a *Shamanin* is paid about Rs.60/-.[66]

Medical Care:

No special attention is given to a patient by the inmates of the house as they remain busy always. The patient usually sleeps on the floor covering the body with a piece of cloth. Mainly the housewife cooks food for the patient. No special diet is given other than ragi-gruel. Rice is not usually given when patient suffers, but it is given when the patient recovers. In case, any one visits market, buys cheap biscuits and bread for the patient. But it is very heartening to note that during the period of recovery the patient is not given liquor to drink.

These people in general were neither health-conscious nor taken proper care of their health. Even when they are sick, they either work or leisurely walk. But, only in acute stage, they seek for treatment. The acute stage is only ascribed due to wrath of the deities and spirits. Normally when indigenous efforts are failed, they prefer to succumb to the alien medicines like allopathic. But, illness or death during old age is not accounted for the evil effort of deities and spirits.[67]

In the whole circle of the occult sciences, there is scarcely anything more abstruse or intricate than the mythical science of sorcers. The use of them has occasionally received much opposition from incredulous individuals while on the other hand; it has stood the grind with firmness amidst the change of ages. Amongst mankind in general, there is much of talismanic belief. This belief prompted the folk to undertake various treatments, even to such diseases, which should receive the attention of a scientific oriented physician, with folk medicine. As for example, leprosy is considered as one of the most terrific maladies inflicted on mankind. Tribal people and to some extent a few rural folk believe that, the leprosy is due to greatest sin and crime like to intercourse with one's nearest relative with whom it is tabooed, or for the crime of cutting a young *sal* tree or *segun* tree or killing a calf or a cow or other domestic animals. To murder a child or burn a grain-*gola* and ignore the village *panchayat* or behave disrespectfully to the elders and to deity cause this disease. It is not a chronic disease and the sin or the crime of the father may be shared by his son or others so it may pass on from generation to generation.[68]

It has been observed that the people in general know many native medicines for ailments like cuts, pains fever, headache, etc. For complicated diseases a native doctor or a village medicine man or even a scientific doctor is always called for. He prescribes native drugs or scientific medicine or performs exorcism.

From the above discussion, it seems that the rural folk of south Odisha still continue to rely on indigenous method of diagnosis and treatment in spite of their cultural contact with the west and the people of the towns. But, towards the end of the period under study, they have started availing of the allopathic treatment available in the dispensaries and hospitals installed by the Christian Missionaries and the Government. But, due to inaccessibility of the region, the insufficient number of dispensaries, lack of medical staff, the proper nonfunctioning of the medical institutions and the people's apathetic attitude towards allopathic treatment made the folk treatment of diseases a common feature in this area.

Our search has shown that, since the population is very heterogeneous in the villages of the region, one should not be surprised to see the activities of the *Gunias, Desharies, Bejunies, Shamanins, Exorcists, Kalisis, Witches* (which are termed as leaving gods) for the cure of diseases and preparation of folk medicines. Although much data are not available to prove this it is an established fact that the system is still going on in the remote villages of course not in a large manner.[69]

The Folk medicines, witchcrafts and magic cords have not only weakened by the forces of modernization, but have, on the contrary, been fortified, so that it plays a significant role even in the determination of the character of the rural and tribal folks. In spite of great advancement, rural folk believe, even today, that a disease can be cured not by medical treatment alone but by divine aid as well through sorcerers, witch-doctors, charms, *jharaphunka,* amulets, talismans, incantations and cunning men who treat all maladies by spell. Besides, the summoning of ghosts and spirits, the worship of cure deities also play an important role for this purpose. Added to this, local cults, *pirs* also have their due share in curing diseases.

In spite of the spread of education and industrialization in south Odisha, sorcery and witchcrafts, and the system of animal and bird sacrifices for the cure of diseases and epidemics which thrived in social life during the 19th and second half of the 20th centuries, have continued till today in a lesser form. This was one of the important reasons for the backwardness and poverty of the rural folk of the region.

References

1. P.S.Fisher, Folk Medicine, in: *West Virginia Historical Society Quarterly*, vol.x, no.4, January, 1997, p.11.
2. *Ibid.*
3. A Concise History of Science in India
4. *Ibid.*
5. Balaram Das, *Jagamohana Ramayana,* 6th canto, *Lanka Kanda*, p..
6. *Folklore and Folk life in India,*
7. Orissa Cultural Forum, *Odishara Loka Sanskruti,* Cuttack, 1978, pp.174-177.
8. *Ibid.*
9. Lakshman Mishra, *Gan Baida (*Odia*),* Cuttack, 1958, p.17.
10. Ibid.
11. H.H.Presler, *Primitive Religion in India,* Madras, 1973, p.211.
12. Ashutosh Bhattacharya, *Folklore of Bengal,* New-Delhi, 1978, p.50.
13. S.K.Mohapatra (ed), *Saura painting,* New-Delhi, 2009, p.1.
14. P.C.Roy Choudhury, *Folklore of Bihar,* New-Delhi, 1976, p.19.
15. H.H.Presler, *op.cit.,* p.211.
16. K.B.Das, *Folklore of Orissa,* Cuttack, 1991, p.3.
17. Ganesh Chaubey, *Folk gods of Bihar,* in: Bihar in folklore study, Calcutta, 1972, p.2.
18. K.B.Das and L.K.Mohapatra, *Folklore of Orissa,* New-Delhi, 1979, p.87.
19. Varrier Elwin, *Tribal Myths of Orissa,* vol.II, London, 1954, pp.554-555.
20. K.B.Das and L.K.Mohapatra, *op.cit.,* p.87.

21. Ibid.
22. Sankar Sen Gupta, *Folklore and Folk life in India,*Calcutta, 1959, pp.151-152.
23. H.H.Risley, *The Tribes and Castes of Bengal,* vol.I, p.408.
24. John Campbell, *A Personal Narrative of Thirteen Years Service Amongst* The Wild Tribes of Khandistan for the Suppression of Human Sacrifice, London, 1864, p.44
25. Sankar Sen Gupta, *op.cit.*, p.152.
26. M.N.Hotta, "*Phulbani Kandh Sampradayara Lokavidya*" (Odia), in: *Biswabharati Dipika,* vol.VIII, Santiniketan, 1987, pp.15-43.
27. Sankar Sen Gupta, *op.cit.*, p.152.
28. Sankar Sen Gupta, *op.cit.*, p.152.
29. *Ibid,*pp.153-154.
30. *Ibid.*
31. *Ibid.*
32. Ganesh Chaubey, "Folk-gods of Bihar", in: *Bihar in Folklore Study,* Calcutta, 1972, p.156.
33. J.G.Millingen, *Curiosities of Medical Experience,* London, 1939, p.32.
34. Ashutosh Bhattacharya, "Cure Deities of Bengal", in: *Folklore,* vol.III, no.2, February-March, Calcutta, 1962, p.11.
35. P.K.Maity, "Dharm Thakur of Bengal and his Association with Human Fertility", in: *Folklore,* vol.xiii, 3rd March, Calcutta, 1971, p.5.
36. Ashutosh Bhattacharya, "The Cult of Tree deities of Bengal", in: *Indian Folklore,* vol.I, no-4, October-December, 1958, p.7.
37. S.K.Jain, "Medicinal Plantlove of the Tribal of Bastar", in: *Economy of Botany,* vol.xix, Calcutta, 1965, p.27.
38. Sankar Sen Gupta, *Folklore and Folk life in India,*pp.161-162.
39. *Ibid.*, pp.162-163.
40. K.C.Pradhan, *Odia Loka Sahitya o Loka Sanskruti(*Odia*),* Cuttack, 1995, p.57.
41. Orissa Cultural Forum, *Odishara Loka Sanskruti,* Cuttack, 1978, p.180.
42. John Campbell, *op.cit.*, p.44.
43. L.P.Vidyarthi and B.K.Rai, *The Tribal Culture of India,*Delhi,1977, p.244.
44. D.F.Carmichael, *Manual of the District of Vizagpatam, in the Presidency of Madras,* Madras,1869, p.104.

45. T.J.Maltby, *The Ganjam District Manual,* Madras, 1918, p.73.
46. E.Thurston, *Castes and Tribes of Southern India,* vol.III, Madras, 1909, p.405.
47. H.H.Risley, *op.cit.,* vol-I, p.408.
48. D.F.Carmichael, *op.cit.,* p.104.
49. S.Pearce Carey, *Dawn on the Kond Hills,* London, 1936, p.20.
50. Watts Neville A, *The Half-Clad Tribals of Eastern India,* Bombay, 1970, p.63.
51. Sankar Sen Gupta, *op.cit.,* p.163.
52. *Ibid,* pp.163-164.
53. *Ibid,* pp.164-165.
54. T.J.Maltby, *op.cit.,* p.50.
55. K.B.Das, *Folklore of Orissa,* pp.49-50.
56. Kamaladevi Chattopadhyaya, *Tribalism in India,* New-Delhi, 1978, p.7.
57. N.R.Patnaik, "Studies in Superstitious Beliefs, Myths, Witchcrafts, Sorcery and Sacrifice of the 19th Century Orissa", in: *Orissa Historical Research Journal,* vol.XXXIII, nos. 3-4, pp.129-130.
58. *Ibid.*
59. N.Patnaik and P.S.Das Patnaik, *The Kondhs of Orissa,* Bhubaneswar, 1982, p.177.
60. *Ibid.*
61. K.B.Das, *Folklore of Orissa,* p.123.
62. N.Patnaik and P.S.Das Patnaik, *op.cit.*
63. Ibid.
64. Ibid.
65. Ibid.
66. K.B.Das and L.K.Mohapatra, *op.cit.,* p.87.
67. N.Senapati (ed), *Orissa District Gazetteers-Koraput,*
68. N.Patnaik and P.S.Das Patnaik, *op.cit.* Sankar Sen Gupta, *op.cit.,* p.171.

Conclusion

British conquest of Odisha was the culmination of their diplomatic policy to link the two seats of their administration i.e. Calcutta and Madras. Odisha was one of the last regions of the country to be conquered by the British. South Odisha may be regarded as the epitome of the East India Company's unsympathetic administration. Perhaps, no other part of India received, so scant an attention from the Government of East India Company as this region. It had no roads, no railways, no navigable canals, no hospitals, no colleges till the 80's of the 19th century. This led to the late introduction of western education, late establishment of large scale industries and late start of other modernizing influences. Of course, it was just like a boon for the people of south Odisha so far as folk culture is concerned. This also had its beneficial effect on this part of the country to allow the different aspects of folk culture to survive in their original and relatively pure forms without distortion and disturbances for a long time.

The Odia culture as such, including the folklore traditions, has a distinctive character because of the fact that Odisha is geographically so situated that for centuries it enjoyed the status of being the meeting ground of the north and the south. The Vindhya range of mountains divides India internally into two halves. The northern part, called *Uttarapatha,* owing to repeated invasions, developed a culture different from that of the *Dakshinapatha,* the southern part. The coastal plains of Odisha became a link between the two. Thus Odisha had the privilege of shaping its own culture integrating the elements of both. It will not be difficult to discern the synthesis if the various aspects of Odishan culture like music, dance, art, literature, religious thinking etc. are carefully examined.

Owing to the isolation in which this region has remained for so many ages, the peasantry have retained old world ideas and fancies to a great extent than any other Aryan people of India. Predominantly an agricultural country, it has a rich and glorious tradition of folk songs, folk music, folk-tales, folk dances, and theatres, ballads, folk festivals, folk arts and crafts which are known for their distinctive quality and vitality throughout the world.

More than ninetyfive percent of south Odishan population lived in villages during the British period. But, the villages were deprived of any sort of social entertainment of giving pleasure through radio, television, telephone, printed books, calculators, computers, modern drama, audio-visual show and orchestra, and the villagers felt extremely isolated. So they found their own natural way of life by singing folk songs, staging folk dances, folk theatres, preparing folk-arts and listening to folk-tales. This was the natural flow of life among the rural unsophisticated and unlettered people who wanted intimate communication with the main purpose of enjoying life out of isolation and sufferings. This media of expression is like a flow of river which is still flowing in the veins of rural folk as a social institution.

Endowed with rare scenic beauty by its soaring mountains, terraced valleys, lush green forests, murmuring streams and waterfalls, sweet sounds of singing birds, golden sea-beach with rolling blue lagoons, amazing charm of the lake Chilika, picturesque landscape, and the varied tribal life, this part of Odisha is a veritable paradise of nature lovers. It occupies a prominent place in the folk culture of India. South Odisha in general and the district of Ganjam in particular is regarded as the cradle of the folk-dances of Odisha. This seems true to a great extent in case of south Odisha- an open ethnographic museum of aborigines and village folks who are emotional in nature and creative in spirit.

South Odisha is very rich in folk literature. Folk literature is the first unwritten literature of the world. It is the root of the elite or sophisticated literature. It forms the source and supplies resources for the progress of learning, language and literature of a nation. Literate, illiterate, sophisticated and unsophisticated all are the lovers of the folk-tales and folk-songs. It goes from mind to mind, mouth to mouth and generation to generation. The tradition of general literature is chiefly found to be in the written form and is preserved in that form. But the literature that composed by the folk people was meant not to read, but to be listened, to be recited and to be sung. It is also known as oral literature. Oral literature are of many kinds: folk-tales, legends, folk-songs, proverbs, *dakabachanas*, riddles, sayings and similes.

Among them, folk-tales form the most interesting and fascinating part of the folk literature. Folk-tales of south Odisha may be divided into the following classes: a) tales of gods, giants, ghosts and witches; b) tales of birds, beasts, reptiles and fish; c) tales of adventure; d) tales of typical questions and answers; e) tales raising problems and their solutions; f) morals translated in one's life; g) tales of humour and satire; h) tales of sea voyage reminding us of the golden age when Odisha had an overseas trade-relationship with many nations of the world.

Folk-tales have their roots in the hoary past when men acquired the power of articulate expression. He proudly gave out his heroic feelings in case of hunting a ferocious tiger or lion or killing his inveterate enemy or narrated his pitiable lot in course of storm, flood, and famine or earthquake. But, a folk-tale is a fully imaginary piece which may not bear any relation to the real fact of life. However its educative value was tremendous. The creative and imagination power of the children increases to a high degree by listening these folk-tales. The morals of the folk-tales show the way for right action, right conduct and right livelihood.

Proverbs are essence of life of the people and may be defined as "pearls of wisdom". A nation's real character is known through its proverbs. Its struggle for existence, its humour and mockery, its taste for beauty, its art and learning, its peculiarities may, to a great extent, be known from proverbs. It is the very foundation of any great language. When it is neglected, the foundation is shaken to its root. Proverbs throw a flood of light on the socio-economic and cultural life of the people. Proverbs are the shortest expressions of the longest experiences of life. The proverbs of south Odisha are not only innumerable but also popular which is used by the people very often in their talks.

Folk literature is incomplete without a study of riddles. Riddles are puzzles. The riddles are simple exercises to awaken and sharpen the human intellect and are particularly popular among the children. Like all other branches of oral literature riddles also are the creation of rural people. Asking and solving riddles (questions) is still one of the ideal forms of mental recreation for the rural-folk, young and old. Through the riddles one can make out many salient facts regarding the social customs, manners and inhibitions of the people.

South Odisha has been the cradle of many folk dances and songs. The daily life of an average Odia from birth to death finds an expression in the folk-songs. The people of this region in general are emotional in nature and creative in spirit. They sing a variety of folk-songs which can captivate the minds of all the art loving people of the world.

Folk-song is the traditional heritage of those people who have an unsophisticated way of life in a particular society and who usually give a free expression of their sentiments through their songs. It is through folk-songs and folk-music that we come to know the inner life, the culture, the social and an environmental set up of a community, whether living in far off jungles or in highly industrialized towns.

South Odisha mostly comprise of villages. Villagers lead busy lives. They do not compose to sing in their leisure hours. They sing when they plough fields, harvest crops, row boats, drive carts, herd buffaloes, husking paddy and feeding their children, and busy in tattooing. They sing to break the monotony of hard work or of a long journey on foot. Folk-song is a spontaneous overflow of the people that live in a more or less primitive condition outside the sphere of sophisticated influences.

The term "folksong" implies that there is an element of spontaneity as well as simplicity in it. It springs from the common man's natural desire to give spontaneous expression to his feeling and emotions in so far as these can be expressed through musical forms. It would, therefore, be improper to expect a high degree of polish or finesse either in the composition or in the melodious quality of such songs. It is the earliest poetry of any people, unpremeditated and unwritten, fresh and simple, genuine and natural. It is popular because it alludes to incidents connected with people's lives. It carries the voice and vocabulary of the masses.

Songs are sung to teach the child to walk, to dance, to drink milk, to eat food, to play. To learn counting, to be industrious and good-natured a child receives home education through folk-songs which are unforgettable and everlasting. The songful atmosphere at home and in the village helps him, even indirectly, to become a musician, an artist, or a litterateur.

The themes of the folk songs normally comes from every day life of the community, their joy and sorrow, hope and despire, feeling and imagination, love and sufferings.

Music forms the core of folk songs, folk ballads and folk dances. The music is heard in the nook and corner of the rural life specially in folk festivals which are the unique characteristics of Odia's cultural life. From the above analysis it is clear that folk music preserves the tradition longer than the sophisticated music.

The folk songs of south Odisha are broadly divided into four classes, viz.

(a) those sung by women exclusively,
(b) those sung by men exclusively,
(c) those sung by men and women jointly,
(d) and those sung by boys and girls.

The first category may again be divided into-songs of husking, tattoo songs, songs of tears, play songs (*puchi geeta*), swing songs and lullabies. They charm with their naturalness and deep poetic emotion. The second category includes-ploughman's songs, boatman's songs, cartman's songs, herdsman's songs, snake-charmer's songs, songs of *Yogi* (*Chakuliya Panda, Natha yogi* etc.), battle songs (*Ranapa gita*). The third category covers- *Baunsarani* songs, love songs. The last category includes children's songs, love songs, etc.

The songs which are sung in doing some kind of work or labour are known as work songs. These includes The songs of the snake charmers, songs of *Chitakuta Keluni*, songs of Cartman, ploughman's songs. The songs of tears or the *Kandana Geeta* are most pathetic and heart touching. Songs of *Yogis*, swing songs, prayer songs, songs of snake-charmers are the speciality of Odishan folk-songs.

The folk-songs may not soar high in their imaginative flights. They may not have the ostentation of classical music with its flourish and elaboration. But deep in their heart, there is a melody of pure joy. Further, the songs and ballads not only reflect the cultural and economic conditions of the people but also portray the social and religious condition of the rural people as a whole.

But the pity is that folk-music and folk-songs are fast disappearing from this region mainly due to the increasing impact of urban modes of living on the rural life. The fast growing industrial development and new means of entertainment like the cinema, television, etc. are making considerable changes in the styles of folk-singing. There is danger that the fountain source of our past traditions and cultural heritage may soon dry up. So the steps may be taken to preserve the folk-songs in the form of VCD, DVD, e-library, etc. otherwise the traditions of the centuries will disappear from the society very soon.

Folk theatre is the theatre of the masses and is also called the village theatre. It preserves, rejuvenates and inspires the cultural achievement of the people. It forms the source and supplies resources for the progress of theatrical art. The mainstay of the folk theatre is its dance, language, art, music- be it ritual, religious or secular. Regarding the folk dances of Odisha John Boulton has rightly remarked that "It is a literature that walks and talks before our eyes".

The district of Ganjam which forms the core of south Odisha is the cradle of many folk-dances and theatres. Among the folk-theatres of south Odisha *Prahallada Nataka* is very popular. The theme of the play centres round the love and devotion of *Prahallada* to *Hari* (Vishnu) in the face of stiff resistance of his father Hiranya Kasyapu, who tried his utmost to dissuade *Prahallada* from uttering the name of Vishnu. The theme finds occurrence in the *Nrusimha Purana* and *Vishnukesari Purana*, composed in 15th and 16th centuries. The story narrates the emergence of Narasimha, the man-lion *avatar* of Vishnu, from a stone pillar of the royal court to mangle and kill Hiranyakasyapu, the demon-king. The play contains as many as 42 Sanskrit *Slokas* and 11 Odia *Slokas.* There are 126 songs which use 35 *Ragas* and 6 *Talas.*

Music is the life breath of *Prahallada Nataka.* It not only provides the base but also determines the dramatic structure. Both vocal and instrumental music at appropriate places intensify the dramatic effect. It is so popular in the district of Ganjam that there are now more than 112 groups.* *Prahallada Nataka* is quite akin to *Prahallada Charithram* of Tamilnadu and draws heavily upon the traditional music of Odisha which, though influenced by both the Karnatic and Hindustani systems of music, has a distinctive character of its own. This proves that the influence and impact of south India is clearly discernible in many of the folk dances and folk theatres of Odisha.

In almost all the regions of this country various forms of ballad singing forms are prevalent. South Odisha has a special form of ballad singing which is known as *Dasakathia.* This is a unique form of ballad singing that aesthetically blends elements of theatre, classical Odissi music, highly sophisticated Odia and Sanskrit poetry, wit and humor.

Although *Dasakathia* originated in the southern part of Odisha, especially in the district of Ganjam, it has now spread to the other parts of Odisha, Surat and even Rangoon.

No country has such a wide range and variety in performing art tradition as India has. Again, in this country, Odisha perhaps has the richest and the strongest traditions in performing arts. South Odisha is proud of having at least six highly evolved folk-dances and theatres. These are *Dasakathia, Prahallada Nataka, Ranapa Nacha, Bharata Leela, Radhaprema Leela, Rama Leela, Krushna Leela,* and *Kandhei Nacha*(puppet dance). Odisha is the only state in which all the four styles of puppet theatre- glove, rod, string and shadow- traditions are still surviving. Odisha is perhaps next to Kerala in the richness of theatre traditions. In Koodiattam and Kathakali, the classical theatre tradition survives in Kerala, but in Odisha the *Sangeetaka* style of Sanskrit theatre has become extinct. The folk traditions such as *Thakurani Yatra, Prahallada Nataka, Dandanata* and various kinds of *leela* plays etc. are still prevalent in rural Odisha.

Like many regions of this country, Odisha too, has scores of different traditions in folk and tribal dances and music. Thus the heritage of Odisha in performing art is as rich as varied.

People of south Odisha are more conservative and superstitious than the people of other regions of Odisha and even the neighbouring states. From the moment of birth to the funeral ceremony, his life is an eventful journey of social ceremonies, rituals and festivals. They take every element of the past dictated by the tradition as sacred trust and consider a little digression from it as sin. They observe many fairs and festivals throughout the year either out of their superstitious beliefs or religious bent of mind. Among them *Oshas, Bratas, Kalisi, Patua,* human sacrifice (it was suppressed by the British in 19th century), walking on burning charcoals, on the edge of the swords, beliefs in spells and witch-crafts are worth mentioning. But, there is no denying the fact that these *Oshas, bratas,* fairs and festivals throw much light on the economic, social and religious condition of the Odia people during the period under study, and the spread of the ideas of morality, good behavior and ethics in the society.

South Odisha particularly the district of Ganjam, has to its credit a rich heritage of art and crafts. It is known for its exquisite handicrafts. Folk arts of south Odisha may be broadly divided into nine categories i.e.

(1) Mural paintings,
(2) Cloth or *Patta* paintings,
(3) *Ganjapa* paintings,
(4) Scroll painting,
(5) Palm-leaf drawing,
(6) Tribal painting,
(7) Tatooings,
(8) *Alpana* and
(9) *Muruja* drawing.

Art has been almost a part of the daily ritual in the life of the people of south Odisha. This extends all the way from plastic arts like wall paintings, *Jhoti, Chitta* or *Muruja* to earthen pots of stylished artifacts. The tribal paintings of south Odisha are also very lively and vibrant. In the *Saura* paintings, the spirit of deadman lying on a cot attended by *Chaparasis* and physicians occupied the major attention. All other figures like monkeys, trees, tigers etc. were meant to protect the beautiful nature around chiefly intended for the spirit to enjoy. They also depicted agricultural operations, pregnant women, potter families, and Gods seated on elephants.

Thus, Odisha has a rich repository of folk-paintings. The folk and tribal paintings of south Odisha present a wide, variety, a rich and complex heritage. It is heartening to note that though the folk dances, folk-tales, folk music are fast disappearing and declining from the Odishan society, the folk art traditions of south

Odisha are continuing with great vigour and becoming popular day by day outside Odisha and even abroad.

South Odisha is also noted for its folk-crafts. Each village of this region is a centre of rural craftsmen like blacksmiths, carpenters, stone sculptors, bamboo and cane workers, weavers, potters, etc. The silk industry at Berhampur enjoys traditional reputation for centuries. The kings of Mohuri estate invited the *Deras* of south India to promote silk industry at Berhampur even before the coming of the East India Company.

From the above discussion, it is inferred that the folk art and crafts of south Odisha are very artistic, lively and vibrant. It supplied livelihood to a large number of families and entertainment to the travellers, tourists, poets, onlookers and the lovers of beauty. The folk arts and crafts are an integral part of life of the people, despite rapid social and technological changes taking place. Today there is a tremendous interest in the rich heritage of folk tradition. Immense in its variety and range, this tradition reflects the amazing diversity of the people who have created it. It explores the rare and native genius of the folk people. Thus, the opinion expressed by O.C.Ganguly may be regarded as a just conclusion "This form of pictorial art of folk significance are not only unique in the history of Indian painting but are unparallel in the history of any form of European painting".

Folk medicines and the folk method of treatment form a fascinating chapter in the history of folk culture of south Odisha. Talismans, sorcerers, folk-medicines and cure deities have been of much interest to the scholars of folklore studies. The village folk have their own medicines and methods for curing different ailments of the body and the mind. Magical powers are often attributed to village physicians known as *Vaidya* some of whom are adept in *Ayurveda*, the indigenous Indian system of medicine. Though they are illiterate, they acquire this knowledge of the medicine through tradition of transmission from generation to generation. They are more acquainted with its practice than its theory. Some of them know single-herb cures.

Villagers are conservative in their outlook. They believe in ghosts and spirits, witch-craft and sorcery and approach the fetish gods and goddesses for solution of their problems. Old customs bind them like chains, and check their progress. Their age-old superstitions make them prey to virulent diseases; stifle any development of scientific or rational outlook. They do not understand this and retain most of the savage customs and superstitions, coarse and repulsive to the civilized, in their religious rites and ceremonies.

It seems that, the rural folk of south Odisha still continue to rely on indigenous method of diagnosis and treatment in spite of their cultural contact with the west and the people of the towns. But, towards the end of the period under study, they have started availing of the allopathic treatment available in the dispensaries and hospitals installed by the Christian Missionaries and the Government. But, due to inaccessibility of the region, the insufficient number of dispensaries, lack of medical staff, the proper nonfunctioning of the medical institutions and the people's apathetic attitude towards allopathic treatment made the folk treatment of diseases a common feature in this area.

Our search has shown that since the population is very heterogeneous in the villages of the region, one should not be surprised to see the activities of the *Gunias, Desharies, Bejunies, Shamanins, Exorcists, Kalisis, Witches* (which are termed as living gods) for the cure of diseases and preparation of folk medicines.

In spite of the spread of education and industrialization in south Odisha, sorcery and witchcrafts, and the system of animal and bird sacrifices for the cure of diseases and epidemics which thrived in social life during the 19th and second half of the 20th centuries, have continued till today of course in a lesser form. This is one of the important reasons for the backwardness and poverty of the rural folk of the region.

During the period under review, the values have also undergone a good deal of change. These folklore traditions are the products of a highly evolved agricultural civilization. The tentacles of industrial civilization have spread so much that its vibrations are felt even in the remotest villages. It is the Odia intelligentsia that must now decide whether and how to continue the traditions in their best health or allow them to die peacefully. It will be extremely unfortunate if these beautiful traditions are transformed to become fascinating tourist material.

From a balanced view, it can be said that the folklore traditions of south Odisha has a wide spectrum and magnitude which is perhaps unique in India. But it should be the duty of the public, philanthropic organizations and the Government to take steps for the revival and survival of many of the folk-dances, theatres, *leelas,* arts and artifacts, folk-music and songs which are either extinguished from our society or on the verge of extinction, otherwise the traditions of the century and precious wealth of the generations will be lost forever.

Appendices

Appendix-i

(Names of the Villages having *Prahallada Nataka* troups)

1. Sunathara (two groups)
2. Dhamanakhola
3. Gadagobindapur (two Groups)
4. Gobara
5. Karapalli
6. Paili Pada (Usmmapalli)
7. Sindheshwar
8. Polasara
9. Chhanamari
10. Bhusanda Pal
11. Bahada guda
12. Baragaon (BelaGuntha)
13. Pandiachuki
14. Sindha Pur
15. Allari gada
16. Sundi Kendu
17. Jayanti pur
18. Lembei (Dasapalla)
19. Sumandi
20. Karachuli
21. Pallaka sanda
22. Kathachira
23. Bhakasingi
24. Gangana Pur
25. Abhandi
26. Tanka Rai
27. Hugulapatta
28. Jagamohan
29. Kamagaon
30. Gaina Sasana
31. Khagipalli
32. Bhismagiri
33. Gothagam
34. Chancha Palli
35. Kharani pada
36. Arenda
37. Chauduri Tikarapada
38. Karadia
39. Dauni
40. Bahaka guli
41. Mundapota
42. Jharapari

43. Bamkoi
44. Padmapur
45. Dekhali
46. Naira
47. Bhalasingi
48. Bentiguda
49. Dhidhi Gaon
50. Takaswara
51. Khariaguda
52. Baula gaon
53. Murungi sasana
54. Lochapada
55. Mundula
56. Liakhai
57. Sundipalli
58. Baulajholi
59. Dhabalapur
60. Lupamayupura
61. Karadakana
62. Mandarada
63. Dhaugaon
64. Sambharada
65. Gopinath Pur
66. Seragada (Padmapura)
67. Lakshminarayan Pur
68. Gundura
69. Goudagaon
70. Sunaredi
71. Balipadar
72. Khambari Gaon
73. Sunkuru
74. Baramunduli
75. Kalasandapur
76. Kusasuki
77. Tentuapada
78. Bipilingi
79. Pranapapur
80. Malabada Pur
81. Talapada(two Groups)
82. Gaunju
83. Belapada
84. Khajuria
85. Gunapada
86. Sahasapur
87. Kalia Ghai
88. Kelajhuri
89. Chudanga Pur
90. Kukudakhandi
91. Khukundia
92. A.K.Pur
93. Maulabhanja (two Groups)
94. R.K.Pur
95. Pannada
96. Birikota
97. Karapada
98. Mandimara
99. Ludukudi
100. Pindika
101. Nuagada
102. Numanagar
103. Gothogaon
104. Krushnapur
105. Gurandi
106. Randiba
107. Khajuripada
108. Mohana
109. Kasinagar
110. Cheligada
111. Guma
112. Gopinathpur

Appendix-ii

(Names of the Villages having *Bhrata Leela* troups)

1) Khandadeuli
2) Mantridi
3) Boula Jhuli
4) Chandipadar
5) Mahisanpur
6) Kholo Khali
7) Solondi
8) Motabadi
9) Golanthara
10) K.Nimini
11) Kumar Pani
12) Krushna Chai
13) Kurula
14) Gothagam
15) Karatali
16) Biranchipur
17) Tala Sakara
18) Buduli
19) Amurutuli
20) Jhagadei
21) Mundamarei
22) Digapahandi
23) Gudiapalli
24) Khariaguda
25) Gallery
26) Harigada
27) Turumu
28) Kulada
29) Chhamunda
30) Kamasar
31) Kadua
32) Panchabhuti
33) Birikote
34) Baragoam
35) Khukundia
36) Ambapua
37) Khamarapalli
38) Bhaliakhai
39) Agajholo
40) Gulia
41) Malasapadara
42) Gajalabadi
43) Jagamohana
44) Gunthapada
45) Kampa Nuagoan
46) Kabisuryanagar
47) Bhagabanapur
48) Gudiapalli

Appendix-iii

(Names of the Villages having *Dasakathia* troups)

1. 1.Bhanja Bihar,
2. Erendra,
3. Khandara,
4. Nuapalli (Purushottampur),
5. Satanala,
6. Sumandal,
7. Belagaon,
8. Nagaradiha,
9. Lathi,
10. Haladiapadar,
11. Ambapua,
12. Handighara,
13. Marudi,
14. Kalasandhapur,
15. Balasi,
16. Digapada,
17. Kodala,
18. Babanapur,
19. Pitala (Ramachandrapur),
20. Polosara,
21. Baulagaon,
22. Duarasuni,
23. Koradakana,
24. Singapur,
25. Kansamari,
26. Phulta,
27. Nunipada,
28. Polasapur,
29. Pattapur,
30. Jilunda,
31. Bhejiput,
32. Podamari,
33. Samantarapur,
34. Sorada,
35. Sankuda,
36. Jamuni,
37. Sadangipalli,
38. Ladigaon,
39. B.J.Pur Sasan,
40. Patrapur,
41. Tentuapada,
42. Beguniapada,
43. Sunabeda,
44. Gudiapalli (Budhamba),
45. Baliarsingpur,
46. Chirikipada,
47. Hatikhala(Badagada),
48. Mathasarasingi,
49. Pattapur,
50. Pattigada,
51. Thuruburai,
52. Takarada,
53. Gandala,
54. Sapuapalli,
55. Sunyaramachandrapur,
56. Chandramadevipur Sasan, 57. Old Berhampur,
58. Hinjilicut,
59. Narendrapur,
60. Digapahandi,
61. Badagada,
62. Bandhaguda,
63. Tulasipur(Khallikote).

Appendix-iv

(Names of the Villages having *Dandanata* troups)

1 Panchabhuti
2 Gallery
3 Tarasingi
4 Jirabadi
5 Jagannathprasad
6 Mujagada
7 Patadhara
8 Lembei
9 Kulada
10 Kukalunda
11 Dhudhua
12 Gamundi
13 Belaguntha
14 Jilundi
15 Kusapalli
16 Gobara
17 Kulagada
18 Badagada
19 Surada
20 Balipadar
21 Begonia
22 Phasi
23 Angaragoan
24 Jahada
25 Jogamahana
26 Dharakote
27 Padampur
28 Manikyapur
29 Mahupadar
30 Dengabosta
31 Digapahandi
32 Pattapur
33 Patharapunji
34 Kaluapadar
35 Jarada
36 Jakara
37 Chikiti
38 Kalasundhapur
39 Bijipur
40 Panigrahipentho
41 Birikota
42 Mandimara
43 Pindika
44 Alangura
45 Nuagada
46 Parimala
47 Numanagar
48 Randiba
49 Khajuripada
50 Guma
51 Kasinagar
52 Bhudukunuagoan

Appendix-v

(Names of the Villages having *Radhaprema Leela* troups)

1. Jugudi,
2. Sandhigoam,
3. Antharapada,
4. Chachina,
5. Gudiali,
6. Golia,
7. Pudamari,
8. Pratapur,
9. Kankarada,
10. Bamakoi,
11. Solaghara,
12. Krushnapur,
13. Dura,
14. Kumarada,
15. Mundapata,
16. Rajapur,
17. Badakelajhuri,
18. Chikiti,
19. Pathigovindapur,
20. Kampa
21. Nuagoam,
22. Turubudi,
23. Koligoan,
24. Karabalua,
25. Sabulia

Appendix-vi

(Names of the villages having *Oshakothi*)

1. Kullada,
2. Baunsalundi,
3. Netagaon,
4. Dengapadar,
5. Boragaon,
6. Buguda,
7. Sorada,
8. Balipadar,
9. Kandhagocha,
10. Badagada,
11. Balisira,
12. Arakhapur,
13. Panibandha,
14. Bhetanai,
15. Polosora,
16. Devabhumi,
17. Dharakote,
18. Sundarapada,
19. Babanapur,
20. Mayurakona,
21. Magura,
22. Golamundala,
23. Mundamarai,
24. Dhaugaon,
25. Asika,
26. Baragaon,
27. Golapalli,
28. Benia,
29. Mangalapur,
30. Barasingi,
31. Pathara,
32. Kumbhari,

33. Dhabapalli,
34. Purushottampur,
35. Bairani,
36. Haridapadar,
37. Mantapada,
38. Jhadabai,
39. Ghasibili,
40. Komasasan,
41. Kharida,
42. Kumari,
43. Pratapur,
44. Karakhandi,
45. Pudamari,
46. Chhanamari,
47. Phasiguda,
48. Goutami,
49. Digapahandi,
50. Odasingi,
51. Kumarada,
52. K.Nuagaon,
53. Chikiti,
54. Lanjia,
55. Jayantipur,
56. Berhampur,
57. Karakhandi.

Appendix-vii

The villages of Khemundi having Krushna Leela troupes are as follows:

1. Kadua Mangarajpur,
2. Narasimhapur,
3. Patapabuli,
4. Pitala,
5. Chaitanyapada,
6. Patrapur,
7. Balipadar,
8. Golia,
9. Karula,
10. Chikiripada Sasan,
11. Makarapalli,
12. Jagannath Parasad,
13. Bethuar,
14. Bhismagiri,
15. Sheragada,
16. Purushottampur,
17. Surangi,
18. Buguda,
19. Khariaguda,
20. Tinigharia,
21. Kodala,
22. Chaitanyapada,
23. Jakara(Chikiti),
24. Sunathar,
25. Nandigaon,
26. Naranapur,
27. Bhairapur,
28. Podadigi,
29. Mardarajpur,
30. Ahundi,
31. Kalluha,
32. Kuanala.

Appendix-viii

(Extracts of various folk-songs)

The Cartman's Songs

1. Rama is gone and
Gone to the forest,
Run up O Baula
We have to go a long distance.
My bullocks are slow-going,
It is a rough road,
And I have to join my friend, the cartman who has gone ahead.
He (Ravana) kept Sita, a prisoner in the Asoka forest.
For what fault of her?
Baula, it is already evening.
Rama sent Hanuman to look for her.
You impudent Chandia
Why do you move so slowly
Hanuman met Sita there
And showed her Rama's ring.
We have still to cover a long distance, Baula.

2. Without oiling the cart properly, I went on driving it
(in anger) My elder brother's wife scolded me outside my house.

3. Soft plantains have been fired in butter
"Oh my *Devara*
You are too young
Do not go driving the bullock cart.
What pleasure can you get from it?
The girl of sixteen your wife-
Under whose charge will you keep her?"
"I shall keep her in charge of my little brother Hatia."

4. The song of the cartman can be heard from the cluster of trees.
The cart has now come back.

The Snake Charmer's Song

Padmabati, the queen of Kamsal, was fasting
It was the *"Dhanitiri"* fast.
O Govinda Hari,

At Kamsa's orders, Banamali went to pluck the lotus.
O Govinda Hari,
As he entered the Lake Kalindi,
The Snake Kali you stung him.
O Govinda Hari,
Unable to bear the terrible pain of the
Poisonous sting,
Srikrishna fell senseless on the water,
O Govinda Hari.
BalaDeva came and lifted him up, O Govinda Hari.
Then he called upon *Garuda* who brought nectar (from heaven)
O Govinda Hari.
As the nectar was sprinkled on his body
Banamali got up,
O Govinda Hari.

Raja Geeta

1. The Swing festival *(Raja)* has come,
And I like to see it arm in arm with my beloved.
Now I wish to decorate myself with *'abira'*
And adorn the pretty face of my beloved with the same
I will buy sweets and feed her on the swing.
She will pay the debt with her love.
I wish to kiss her round cheeks,
And (in happy modesty) she will hide her face behind the veil of her Chintz saree.
I will gladly meet her with a betel piece in the bedroom and
Make her chew the same.
The half chewed 'betel' I shall take out of her lips.
I will then look at her moon-like face, heavy with slumber.
I like to play cards with her in the moonlit night.
If my beloved be with me, I will not care a bit for any sorrow.
In the world.
If I feel sleepy I shall sleep on the lap of my beloved and
rise of birds.

2. There blooms a lily in the Lord's Lake.
O Mother dear, did you nourish me like a lily
Only to send me away to a stronger's house?

3. Sapling of banana tree.
"O Mother, you sent me (to my mother-in-law's house)
When I was but an immature girl.
From whom should I learn skill (in household work)?"
4. A red chalk on the mud shelf.
"O Mother, I would have stayed a few days more in your house,
Had it not been for my brother's wife who wants to See me go (at once)."
5. A house on the top of another house.
"Brother, you make me your own so long I am in your house.
As soon as I go out of your sight,
I also go out of your mind."
6. A round piece of stone outside the house.
At home, the rich man's daughter was reared in indulgence.
See, how she has been granted a deed of divorce.
7. The swing makes a jarring sound.
"O my dear swing, silence please,
If you keep quiet,
A golden crown shall your price be."
8. The swing murmurs.
Brother and sister, gaily we sing, when the mother calls us for Lunch.
9. The door creaks.
"O my swing, I am really ashamed to see
My co-wife's son calling me 'mother'."
10. Fruits of morning are there
"Touching your body, I swear, I love none but you."
11. The date palm tree makes a pleasing sound.
In the father's house the daughter is happy.
But in her mother-in-law's house,
She is just like an oil-pressing machine
12. Fresh is the moonrise,
Her face glistens like a mirror.
O Moon, rise up (pleasantly).
A piece of betel I shall give you.
13. I made relations in a far-off land.
Now I die of walking the long distance.
14. Dried leaves fell into the well
There is hushing sound in the field of sugar-cane

With a procession of torches the bridegroom approaches near,
Get the bride ready.

15. I pleased ginger on the curry stone.
"You gave me in marriage to a rich man.
I possess but one piece of cloth,
Which, when I bathe, has to dry on my own body?"

16. The shovel of a confectioner.
You gave me in marriage to a rich man
But in that house the cakes are counted
(For they suspect that I may eat some of them).

17. The lake's embankment has given way.
"Tell my father that he has totally forgotten me after sending
Me away.

A Snake in Charmer's Basket (A Ballad)

Father-in-law has an abounding affection for me.

So much so that he renames me as "inauspicious".

Always he asks me what caste I belong to.

Strange, he has not known my caste as yet;

And how should I describe the affection of my mother-in-law.

A vile viper she calls me.

(With her sharp nails) she scratches my soft cheeks.

The chattering of her teeth terrified me.

When she beats me, her eyes glow like fire balls.

At night she plaes a rope by my head (so that I may hang myself).

(When I wake up) I mistake the rope for a snake and get frightened.

Then I get up, spread a part of the cloth I put on, and sleep by the Distance.

How can I describe the history of the other members of the family?

The affection of each one of them will cover a book.

They always treat me as an outsider, except when I cleanse the offal.

(If I hesitate) they argue "none but your Husband has taken his meal there."

I have not seen my husband as yet and do not know if he be fair or Black.

I have been sleeping on my mother-in-law's lap since I came here.
She provides no light in the kitchen.
I kindle the coconut leaves and manage somehow – O Mother.
I use the stems of "*Chana*" as firewood and coal –O Mother.
They give me a little fire in a coconut shell and ask me (repeatedly)
If the cooking is finished.
In the dark I carry the earthen pot full of steaming rice.
If I sit, she calls me a round piece of stone.
If I speak, she says the daughter-in-law is very harsh in tone.
If in my sorrow I (sometimes) fall asleep, she remarks the Daughter-in-law is very idle.
If I shed tears (to relieve my heavy heart)
She asks, "Which of your relations is dead?"
O Mother, my voice is too feeble to speak out their (many) virtues.
They mix water in my cooked curry.
It is beyond my power of speech to describe their vice-O Mother.
They mix salt in my cooked curry (to get me insulted).
They say "The goddess of wealth had made her abode in our house.
She vanished as soon as your inauspicious feet touched the place."
Now I (desperately) look at the hills and dales and tears flow from My eyes incessantly.
What can I do?
My grandmother is dead.
My uncle is poor and helpless.
My father's (economic) condition is wretched from my very birth.
I cannot turn again to my father's house.
So I drag on (miserably) like a snake in the snake-charmer's basket.
The place where the mother-in-law's house is built, is only six cubits
Long and contains some coconut trees.
What fortune did you see in that and gave me in marriage there-O Mother?

I carried with me the utensils of Cuttack and Kantilo, utensils for the Family god from Calcutta, golden plates from Baripada,

Sofas, bedsteads, chests, painted boxes of various kinds, a Gun and different kinds of sarees from jambu and Puri.

But my mother-in-law tells me repeatedly that my father had given Me nothing (as dowry). Patiently have I borne all insults

And my heart is turned as hard as a pillar of stone.

Crossing the Ocean on a Crocodile's Back (A Ballad)

O Govindachandra, greatest among nine hundred thousand kings,

If you now turn to be a yogi, you will be immortalized for all times.

Be a yogi, be immortal and move about the kingdom.

O Managovinda1, obey my words and move about the kingdom.

You will suffer from various diseases at eighteen and die at nineteen.

Your span of life at present is only thirteen days

'Yama' will tie up (your soul) and carry you away.

The procession of "to-days" and "to-morrows" passes on Day follows day.

O *Managovinda*, I could not save you from death and now I advise

You to go to the forest.

The endless sea is before you

And you expect, the crocodile will help you to cross over it

You will fail into the clutches of death in the twinkling of an eye

Then the son said,

"O *Mukutadei*, my mother, why did you not make Me a monk from my childhood in playhouse of dust?

If you had it in your mind to make your son a slave, why did you Got me married?

Why did you put this rope round my neck?

A king or monk (I cannot but die) if death be so sure.

Why should I then be afraid of this trifling death?

Why should a king be a monk?

(if immortally be not assured?)

The kingly life is full of joy.

That of the monk is filled with endless hardship.

He begs from door to door and has to bear the scorching sun, heavy Rain and cold dew."

Then the mother said, "Go away, go away son, as a monk. Do not be Deluded by this mirage.

The house shines so long as this lamp (soul) is burning.

When it is put out, there will be nothing but darkness all around."

Govinda said, "Mother, let Podana,

My beloved queens accompany me. I shall then have the least objection To becoming a monk."

"Rodana or Podana, by whatever name.

You call a woman; she is none but a demoness in disguise.

If you are thus attracted, you will be entrapped and killed.

Do not be enchanted with their beauty.

They are nothing but *mahakal* fruits.

If you open them, you will see nothing but charcoal inside

Why are you charmed with red 'simul' flowers?

When their fruits burst, the cotton is soon dispersed."

Black Beauty

O men of good taste, please listen to these words.

Once Sarangapani in search of Radhika found her on the bank

Of the Jamuna in a sorrowful mood and asked her to talk smilingly.

Radha muttered, "So black (ugly) you, and are, why do you run after me?"

"Is it fair of you to call me black?"

For, the hair so glorious on your head is black,

So is the colour of the water of Jamuna.

From the dark palm trees are made rafters.

The black cloud rains waters,

(On which the life of all creatures depends)

The gun of the opium tree is also black,

The speech of the dark woman is sweet indeed.
Black is the basil leaf that adorns the crown of god,
So is the lamp offered to him in oblation?
With black ink are written songs (of love).
How beautiful the eyebrows (of ladies)
Look when they begin to dance
How very melodious is the song of the cuckoo, so fircely dark.
How nicely the black pupils play in the sockets of the eyes.
Mung, served first in a feast,
Sag is offered in the *sraddha* ceremony of your father.
Ladies (fair ones) long for sarees black as clouds.
The black she-parrot.
Possesses such a sweet voice;
Real beauty is not found in colour (dark or fair).
What counts most is the body's grace
You have not called me black,
Rather you have cast a thunderbolt on my head (O cruel One!)"
Struck tongue-tied for a while
Radha replied (softly), "Is there any man who can outstrip Krishna
In arguments?"

Songs of Tears (*Kandana Geeta*)

As you wash the plate, the water is agitated, O Mother.
You have given me in marriage in a distant land.
Who will go so far to being me back ? O Mother.
The flower blooms in the night of *Chaitra* and fades away in the scorching sun,
Your daughter grows pale in a single harsh word, O Mother.
Blades of grass grow with showers of dew,
I grew up with your affection – O Mother.
The branchless banyan tree spreads its shadow across the waste land,
Star clusters twinkle in the sky.

I have to leave *Gopapura* (home) today

The *suari* is now lifted

Gopapura will be out of sight.

Flowers bloomed in our garden like lamps of *Jagara*

O Mother, we are a sea of gold.

If flowers fade, the gardener will be at a loss,

When we grow pale, the mother will weep.

My father smashed my dolls and ruined my play.

He tasted the water of seven bathing *ghats* and drank the water that was fully poisonous.

Today I take my seat among so many friends in the inner court of a place.

The Boatman's Songs

1. Measureless is the depth of the river,
   (on which) a stone-raft is floated,
   Oh Mother Mangala2.
   Lend me your helping hand.
   And the raft will move itself.

2. Smooth is the surface of the lake
   Curved the river's course
   An unseasonal pumpkin flower floats away on its ripples.
   Let it float away in the river,
   But that '*Kalareiphula*' (beloved)
   Should send words (or her love)

3. I cut down the plantain tree, built a raft and sent it coursing far away.
   I do not know in which island of the world lives the only son of his parents.

4. What song did you sing in that corner of the boat?
   Would that sweet sixteen (your lady love) come to the river
   To wash rice and listen to it?

There are also some other Odia folk-songs which lend support to our assumption that the Buddhists protected the girls who were in the state of being abducted. One of them runs as follows.

1. Damarakaure	damarakau,
2. Vanaparabate	turabuthau,
3. Se vana parabat	kunchikunchika,
4. Tahire basicchi	tini munchika,
5. Tini tini pana	athara pana,
6. Bhainki dakai	kaudi gana,
7. Kaudi ganu ganu	paila rati,
8. Chor neigala	kajajapati,
9. Asa go sangata	gadhoijiba,
10. Kainchi kakudi	toil aniba,
11. Kainchi kakudi	munditi pita,
12. *Chha bohunkara*	*Chhaa duhita*

The meaning of the above song is given below:

"O, crow, O crow, thou art cawing in the forests and hills. The forests and hills are now curled. There sit three saviors (on hills and forests). Three three *panas* make eighteen *panas.* Call in your brother to count the cowries. In course of counting the *cowries* the night ends. (And) the thief *kajalapati* (king crow, *Khanjana)* takes away the cowries. O, friend let us go to bathe. (And) bring the little cucumber after plucking them. The top-part of the cucumber is of bitter taste. The six daughters-in-law have got six daughters.

Thus, the Buddhism once abolished the sexual union that was unfettered by moral consideration of social expediency can be gathered from the following Odia folk-songs:

> "Megha barasila tupuru tapuru kesura maila gaja
> Keun raijare rahile mo raja telingi vaida vaja"
>
> "The rain falls in *Tapar and tapara* i.e. in drops. But Kesura or Kisora destroys the sprout. Proclaim by beat of Telinga drum which country our king now rules over".

Sankhachil mahachil	Dhobadhauiia pakshi
Ramachandra kahiyaicchanti	Sita baba duhkhi

To thantare machha thau Mo hatare kacha thau
To thanta machha millyau Mohat kacha bajra he u
Padhana yichi dhanabilaku
Mari anithita Sankhachiaku
Paikamninkara Ede bharasa
Dekhai dianti sambalapuriya khosha

"Oh, conch shell-headed kite white bird, great (*Vilva*) wood apple, Ramachandra has declared that Sita has been greatly oppressed. Let no the fish remain in your beak to be rotten and be the bangles in my hands as unbrittle as thunderbolt.

Glossary

Adhia	:	Prostration at the feet of God or a deity for the fulfillment of one's wishes.
Adhikari	:	Manager or Chief of the folk dance/ *nataka.*
Adimata	:	Presiding deity/ the first mother or the source mother.
Agadatantra	:	Treatment of patients from snake or poisonous animal bite.
Aghasura	:	A demon with serpent shape.
Agni Danda	:	The midnight performance of *Dandanata,* with flame/ fire.
Ahi-nakul Samparka	:	Bitter relationship.
Ahiraj	:	Large snake.
Airabata	:	The chief elephant of Lord Indra.
Akhadaghara	:	A hall meant for the rehearsal of the acrobatic dances and theatres.
Akrura	:	Minister of Kansa, the maternal uncle of Lord Krishna.
Alasa Kanya	:	Playful maiden(*nayika*) female figures in various poses decorating the exterior façade of the temple.
Alata	:	Red colour liquid which the women used to paint their hills and toes of the feet in different ceremonies; lac dye.

Alati	:	Lighting of the candals before the god or goddesses at the end of *pujas.*
Ambakashihara	:	The golden necklace made with mango shaped pendants.
Anantamula	:	Root of a plant used for medicine.
Angi	:	Shirt.
Anka	:	Regnal year
Anna	:	One-sixteenth of a Rupee.
Antapattia	:	Waist belt.
Anthakudi	:	A barren lady/ usually used as a word of abuse.
Arjuna Ratha	:	Chariot of Lord Arjun.
Ashan	:	Anything to sit on/A sitting item/ seat or sitting posture.
Astamallah	:	Playing cards with eight wrestlers of Kansa motifs.
Aswin/ Aswina	:	A month of Odia calendar/ the sixth Indian month (September-October).
Atavika	:	*Adivasis* or tribals.
Avatara	:	Incarnation.
Badi	:	Court yard/ backyard.
Baga-Baguli	:	A kind of tribal dance/ A sort of dance in the guise of paddy-birds.
Bagapanchak	:	Last five days of the month of *Kartika.*
Bagha Nacha	:	A dance with the mask/attire of a tiger.
Bahuti	:	One kind of ornament.
Baidhana	:	An expression of tenderness and love; Established by law/ lawful/ legal/ Constitutional.
Baigani	:	Violet colour.
Bajabandhu	:	One kind of ornament.
Bajeni/ Bejuni	:	A witch or a lady Sorcerer.

Bakala	:	Bark of a tree
Bakasura	:	A crane shaped demon.
Bakula	:	A kind of tree with fragrant flowers.
Balachappa	:	Hair clip.
Balada	:	Oxen/ a bullock.
Bana Danda	:	Forest goddess.
Bankibadi	:	Bent stick.
Bara Masaku	:	For twelve months.
Basti	:	Village site or slum area.
Bauri	:	A low caste Hindu.
Bayak	:	Instrumentalist.
Bayeni	:	Female instrumentalist.
Bazzar	:	A market place.
Bela	:	The wood-apple, the *marmelos* fruit, *Aegle marmelos.*
Beni	:	Braid/Hair style of a lady.
Besha	:	A dress, a guise, a disguise, decoration.
Bhabani	:	Goddess Durga.
Bhadrab	:	The name of an Indian month.
Bhagabat Tungi	:	The hall meant for *Bhagavata* recitation and the pedestal where the seared book is enshrined and worshipped every day evening.
Bhajana	:	Prayer songs; worship, adoration, a song in the praise of Gods.
Bhajanas	:	Mythological songs.
Bhakta/Bhokta	:	The devotees of *Dandanata.*
Bhesaghara	:	Green room/ dress room/ house to wear dress and ornament.
Bhimul	:	The ancestor or the spirit of the tribals.
Bhodei	:	Relating to the month of *Bhadraba.*

Bhurja Patra	:	One kind of leaf used for writings.
Bhushanda Kaka	:	A mythological crow.
Bhutavidya	:	Sorcery or treatment through spell.
Bhutta	:	Ghost; Goblin.
Bhuyan/Bhumya	:	The name of a tribe.
Binakar-Binakarini	:	Instrumentalists both male and female.
Bisalyakarani	:	One kind of herbal leaf used for healing of diseases.
Boda	:	One kind of snake.
Bonda	:	The name of a tribe.
Boya	:	The doctor of the *Sauras.*
Bratakatha	:	Votive tales/ story of a vow or a religious act.
Burning Ghat	:	Cremation ground.
Chadaya-Chadayani	:	Bird hunters both male and female.
Chaitra	:	The last month of the Hindu calendar.
Chakulia Panda	:	One kind of *yogi*/bagger who sings ballads moving from village to village.
Chalanti Pratima	:	The small image representing the main God/ movable image.
Champu	:	A kind of literary composition in which the same subject is continued in prose and verse.
Chana	:	Pea nuts.
Chanda	:	A subscription, a contribution/bald headed.
Chandala/ Chandaluni	:	A low caste people.
Chandamarka	:	Teacher of Prahallad.
Chandrakanti	:	One kind of cake.
Chandua	:	Appliqué/ a canopy.
Changu	:	One kind of musical instrument/ a kind of round shaped drum.

Chaparasi	:	A peon or an office messenger.
Chautisa	:	An indigenous literature.
Chedi	:	Name of a dynasty.
Chemru Mousa	:	The man who performs charms is called as Chemru *mousa* by the *Kandhs.*
Chhamundia	:	A stage/ a temporary shed.
Chhtrabhanga	:	Retreat/ Dispersion.
Chikitcha	:	Medical treatment.
Chita	:	The decorative wall/floor paintings painted by the village women.
Chita raika	:	A netted blouse.
Chitakuta Keluni	:	Women tattoo maker.
Chiti	:	A vipor.
Chitrakara	:	An artist/The painter and also a caste.
Chitrakuta	:	Name of a place/ name of a mountain in Bundelkhand.
Chitralekha	:	Lady painter.
Choukia	:	A village watchman.
Choupadhi	:	Community hall of a village
Choupadi	:	A small poem/ a poetical composition consisting of four couplets.
Cowries	:	Tropical bright shell used as money in ancient period/ A kind of marine shell use as money.
Dagara	:	Watchman or announcer; a messenger, a runner, a small cattle drum.
Dahani/Dankini	:	Lady witch.
Daitapati	:	The name of a *sevaka* of the temple of Lord Jagannath.
Dakbachan	:	One kind of proverb/idiom.
Dalkhai	:	One kind of tribal dance.
Danda	:	Street Road.

Danda	:	Physical penance/pole, stick or staff.
Danga	:	Boat.
Dasa	:	Devotee/ a slave, a servant, a bondsman.
Dasamula Pachana	:	One kind of juice prepared from the roots of the plants for cure of diseases.
Dasiri Nacha	:	One kind of dance.
Dedhasura	:	Eldest brother of husband.
Deepali	:	The container of the candle.
Deepavali	:	One of the most famous festivals of the Hindus/ The festival of light.
Dehuri	:	A *kandh* priest.
Dera	:	A caste/ weaver.
Desari	:	Astrologer of *Kandh* tribe.
Deshiya Nata	:	One kind of dance/ country-side dance.
Devara	:	Youngest brother of husband.
Devi	:	Goddess
Dhaga	:	Popular saying, proverbs, an apt saying.
Dhaga-Dhamali	:	Idioms, jokes and proverbs.
Dhana amara	:	The hall for the storage of paddy/ Rice Godown/ Godown.
Dhana bila	:	Rice field/ corn field.
Dhangada Ghar	:	The dormitory house for the recreation of the tribal youths.
Dhangada-Dhangidi	:	One kind of tribal dance.
Dharma	:	The eternal thought of the mankind. It is believed that *Dharma* can be obtained by men's perfect duties.
Dhenki	:	An instrument used for husking paddy/ a husking pedal.
Dhoba-Dhobuni	:	Washerman/washerwomen.
Dhola	:	Drum.

Dholia	:	A drummer.
Dhoti	:	White cloth.
Dhuduki	:	One kind of musical instrument.
Dhuli Danda	:	One stage of *Danda Nata* performed on the hot sand of the summer.
Dihudi	:	Rope made of straw which is kept burning during *Danda Nata.*
Doli	:	Swing.
Dolirani	:	Swing queen.
Duari	:	A door-keeper/Gate keeper/main artist of the *Bharata Leela.*
Duchaula	:	A mixture of rice, grass, milk, etc. used as sacred of ring to the Gods and Goddesses.
Dumbas	:	Earthen pots offered to ancestors by the tribals.
Dungdunga	:	One kind of musical instrument.
Durba	:	One kind of grass.
Durga Puja	:	A famous festival of Hindus/ the festival in honour of the goddess Durga.
Dussehara/Dasahara	:	A famous festival of Hindus/ the tenth day of the bright fortnight of *Aswina.*
Dutika	:	Assistant of the heroine.
Ekadashi	:	A sacred day of Hindus/ the eleventh day of a fortnight.
Fakira-Fakirani	:	Jokers, both male and female.
Gada	:	Mace.
Gadaba	:	The name of a tribe.
Gadi	:	The seat of the *mahanta*/the throne.
Gahana	:	Singer.
Gai-Rama nacha	:	One kind of dance with cow head mask.
Gamha Purnima	:	One kind of festival on the fullmoon day.
Ganda Vairab	:	A mythical bird of the Odia folktale.

Ganjapa	:	Round shaped painted playing card.
Ganthibabuli	:	Fibre made knotted wig.
Garuda	:	The name of a bird/Vehicle of Lord Vishnu
Gayak	:	The chief singer of the play.
Gayeni	:	Women assistant singer or instrumentalist.
Ghagara	:	A long skirt having seven strips.
Ghagudimala	:	A string of small bells
Ghara	:	House.
Gharamani	:	The name of a goat in *Taapoi* folktale.
Ghat	:	A landing place in the river, a ferry, a bathing place.
Ghat	:	Hill ranges/ a mountain-pass/ upland/ mountainous region.
Ghoda Nacha	:	One kind of dance/ a resemblance of horse-dance/ a dance with the mask or attire of a horse.
Ghoongura	:	One kind of ornament used for foot, usually a string of small bells.
Ghumura	:	One kind of dance.
Gini	:	A pair of small cymbals.
Gotra	:	Family or lineage.
Gouduni	:	Milk-maid/ a cowherd woman.
Gouri-Beta	:	A stuff used in *Danda Nata.*
Govinda musa	:	A rat used in the folk songs of the snake charmer.
Grama Devata	:	Village goddess.
Gua	:	Betel-nut.
Guna	:	Nose ring.
Guniya	:	A sorcerer or witch/ an exorcist.
Guru	:	Teacher or director; a preceptor/ a spiritual guide.

Guruvara	:	A day of the week which corresponds to Thursday.
Hadasikula	:	One kind of creeper or plant used for medicine.
Hadi Baja	:	One kind of instrument used by a low caste Hindu group belonging to sweeper class.
Hadi/ Hadiani	:	The sub-caste community, basically known as the scavengers; a person belonging to the sweeper class.
Hadipa	:	A saint or hermit.
Haija	:	Cholera.
Handia	:	Pot or pitcher.
Harijan	:	Scheduled caste/ God's own people, a name given by Mahatma Gandhi to the untouchables.
Hatta	:	A weekly market or fair.
Hingulai	:	The name of a Goddess.
Hiranya	:	The chief artist of the *Prahallada Nataka.*
Homa	:	A sacrifice/ a burnt offering.
Hula Huli	:	An inarticulate sound made by women on auspicious occasions/ One kind of voice uttered by the women during the time of ceremony/ festival.
Idital/Ittal	:	*Saura* wall painting/drawing.
Iditalmaran	:	*Saura* wall painter.
Ishana	:	Sacred place of the house where God or Goddesses are kept i.e. the north-east.
Ishta	:	Family deity or presiding deity of the house/ one's tutelary deity.
Itala	:	The name of a flower.
Jadu	:	Magic.
Jagamohan	:	Audience hall or frontal porch in front of the sanctum.

Jagara	:	Night awaking festival/ unsleep night.
Jagulai	:	The name of a Goddess.
Jala Danda	:	One stage of *Danda Nata* inside water of a pond.
Jalamahura	:	One kind of treatment of disease.
Janhi	:	A sort of vegetable.
Jata	:	Matted Wig/ the clotted hair.
Jau	:	Grinding made of ragi; boiled crushed food, a sort of gruel.
Jau Pedhi	:	Lac box.
Jaupata	:	One kind of costly silk cloth.
Jhada banti	:	Cholera/ purging and vomiting.
Jhadaphunka	:	Treatment of diseases through spell.
Jhaliri	:	Colourful Rexene and papers.
Jhanja	:	Cymbals.
Jhara	:	One kind of ornament.
Jhoti	:	One kind of folk paintings.
Jhumpi	:	One kind of ornament used by the women/ ear ornament.
Jhuna	:	Resin.
Jhuna Khela	:	Offering of incense fire to *Patta-Dandua* bearing the kali banner at the time of *Agni Danda.*
Jira	:	Cumin seed.
Jwalamukhi	:	Goddess Durga in ferocious mode.
Kaba	:	Waist coat.
Kabiraja	:	Village doctor/ Ayurvedic doctor.
Kachara	:	A caste/ bangler.
Kadamba Brukshya	:	The name of a tree associated with Lord Krishna.
Kajalapati	:	A black bird, a case to keep collyrium.

Kalapahara	:	An iconoclast who destroyed the Hindu temples.
Kalara	:	A bitter edible vegetable.
Kalisi	:	A person engaged for the worship of Goddesses who dance to the tune of drums and performs miracles by walking on the burning charcoals/on the edge of the swords/sitting on thorn swings.
Kali/ Kalika	:	A Goddess/ the Goddess Kali.
Kalindi	:	A lake infested by poisonous snake Kaliya.
Kaliya	:	Seven hooded serpent king which was killed by Lord Krishna.
Kamana ghara	:	The house of worship/ the prayer house for fulfillment of desires.
Kamandalu	:	One kind of begging pot (ewer).
Kamma	:	A caste in Telugu society.
Kanaphula	:	Ornament for ear/ ear ornamnet.
Kanchula	:	An ornament.
Kandana Geeta	:	Weeping songs.
Kandhas/Khonds	:	The name of a tribe.
Kandhei-Nacha	:	Puppet dance.
Kankana	:	An ornament for wrist/ a bracelet.
Kansa	:	Maternal uncle of Lord Krishna.
Kara	:	One kind of instrument.
Kartal	:	One kind of instrument/ the clapping of hands or cymbals.
Kartika	:	A month of the Hindu calendar/ the month of October-November.
Katha langala	:	Wooden plough.
Kathasua	:	Wooden parrot.
Kathatali	:	Wooden cymbals.
Kela	:	A low caste people/ a wandering tribe.

Kendara	:	One kind of musical instrument/ an one-stringed fiddle.
Khadu	:	An ornament used for wrist and toe, a bracelet, a glass bangle.
Khajuri Chanchuni	:	Date palm broom.
Khana vachana	:	A legendary female character having a reputation for her astrological prognostication/ the words of a stammer.
Khanda	:	Sword.
Khani	:	Underground store for storage of paddy/ a mine.
Khanjana/Khanjani	:	One kind of musical instrument, a tambour, a small drum struck with fingers.
Khasu	:	*Khasu* is a golden ornament used as necklace where the coins like golden lockets are joined.
Khetrapala	:	Master of the field or area.
Khuda	:	Raw-rice bran/ broken rice.
Khudurikuni	:	Name of an *Osha* or fasting.
Kirati	:	Crown.
Kirtan/ Kirtana	:	A singing party who moved from street to street reciting the name of Rama and Krishna / singing aloud in concert/ A group or chorus reciting *Bhajanas* moving from street to street.
Kitalan	:	Tribal painter.
Kothaghara	:	The village community hall where the rehearsal of the folk dance and *natakas* are conducted/ a house belonging to a community.
Kothi/Kothisala	:	A kind of folk dance/ a granary.
Koya	:	The name of a tribe.
Krutika Chandi	:	A goddess.
Kudamboi/Kudummar	:	*Saura* deities.

Kudan	:	The priest or the sorcerer of the *Sabaras.*
Kuhukamandal	:	Magic field.
Kula sabha	:	Meeting of a community or caste.
Kumaris	:	Unmarried girls.
Kumbha	:	Earthen pot with a coconut.
Kumbhakara/Kumbhar	:	The pot makers or potters.
Kundala	:	An ornament for ear/ ear ornament.
Kunja	:	A well structural wooden altar used in the *Radhaprema Leela.*
Kurma	:	Tortoise/An incarnation of Lord Vishnu.
Kuttia Kandh	:	The wild and distinct tribe living in the remote mountains of south Odisha.
Kutumba	:	Family.
Labasoom	:	God of the *Sabara* tribe.
Lambata	:	Long one/ Tall one.
Latchiri	:	One kind of plant.
Laukika	:	Relating to folk/ wordly, mundane.
Lekhani	:	An iron stylus used for writing on palm leaf.
Lipikar	:	Copyist.
Mada Kancha	:	Wine bottle.
Magha	:	A month of Hindu calendar.
Mahakala	:	A fruit with a charming exterior but very ugly having bad smell in the interior/ a poisonous fruit.
Mahanadi	:	Largest river of Odisha.
Mahavisuva Sankranti	:	The first day of Hindu calendar.
Mahuri	:	A musical instrument.
Maits	:	Sorcerers.
Mali	:	Gardener.
Maliahs	:	Hilly or forest regions

Mallavira	:	The body guard of the king.
Malyani	:	Wife of the gardener.
Mamu	:	Maternal uncle.
Manabasa	:	A festival observed on Thursdays of *Margasira* month.
Manasikadhari	:	Person having a desired goal or vow/ a person vowed in the mind.
Mancha	:	A stage.
Manda	:	A rice cake.
Mandal	:	A circular shape area used for religious ceremony.
Mandapa	:	A stage for religious discourses/ Pillared hall; a temporary pavilion erected for holding a meeting or performing a ceremony
Mangala Charan	:	Prayer for an auspicious beginning.
Mantra	:	Spell.
Mardala/Mrudanga	:	An indigenous two sided drum.
Margasira	:	A month of the Hindu calendar.
Masanga	:	A kind of grass.
Matha	:	A Hindu monastery/ a hermitage.
Mathamani	:	A kind of ornament used on the forehead.
Mathia	:	An earthen pot.
Matsya	:	Fish/an incarnation of Lord Vishnu.
Mayurchula	:	Feather of the peacock.
Mela	:	The festival or the congregation of the devotees.
Moja	:	Socks.
Monibandha	:	Wrist.
Mudi/Mudrika	:	Rings for fingers.
Mukhavina	:	One kind of musical instrument.
Mukuta	:	Crown.

Munga	:	Green gram/a kind of careal.
Muruja	:	Coloured stone powder used for painting.
Naga	:	A serpent/ snake or Cobra.
Naga Chaturthi	:	A festival where snakes are worshipped.
Nagakanya	:	A daughter of snake king.
Nageswar	:	A musical instrument used by the snake charmers.
Nagram	:	Gourd shaped small golden hair clip.
Naguni	:	Snake queen.
Namaj	:	Prayer of Muslims
Nath Yogi	:	One kind of yogi/bagger who sings ballads moving from village to village.
Nauria	:	Boat man.
Navagunjara	:	A peculiar animal having the organs of nine different animals.
Navanna	:	The festival for eating the newly produced rice.
Navaratri	:	A festival for the worship of Goddess Durga or preceding nine days of *Dasahara* (or *Dusshera*).
Nazar	:	An evil eye.
Nishan	:	One kind of musical instrument.
Nisuni	:	Ladder.
Notha	:	Nose ornament.
Odhani	:	Thin apron.
Ojha	:	A caste.
Osakothi	:	A folk dance.
Oshas/Osa	:	A *vrata* or fasting.
Paati	:	Ornament used for legs.
Padaka	:	Pendants.
Padmamandala	:	A circular shaped area painted with lotus flower.

Padmatola	:	A song sung by the snake charmers.
Paduka	:	Wooden Sandal.
Paita	:	Sacred thread.
Palia	:	Assistant singer of *Dasakathia.*
Pana	:	A low caste.
Pandavas	:	The five sons of Kunti.
Paneswari	:	Name of a Goddess.
Pani	:	Water.
Paniki	:	Native blade.
Parabha/Prabha	:	A painted Kali banner in appliqué style on a woven bamboo base.
Paraja	:	A tribe.
Parsva-Debata	:	The subsidiary Gods/ Deities connected in doctrine with the main divinity of the temple placed in niches of the central projection.
Patala Goruda	:	A kind of plant.
Patara Soura	:	A sub-caste of *Sauras.*
Pathagar	:	A library.
Patta	:	Silk cloth.
Patta Bhokta/Pata Dandua	:	Chief devotee.
Pattachitra	:	Cloth painting.
Patua	:	A person performs miracles by walking on the burning charcoals/on the edge of the swords/sitting on thorn swings.
Paunjhula	:	A kind of ornament.
Peshni	:	A witch.
Phanta	:	A juice.
Pidha	:	Sitting material/ a low stool.
Pippali	:	Kind of medicine/ the long-pepper.
Pitha	:	A sort of cake; pedestal.

Pothi	:	Book.
Prajapati	:	An epithet of Lord Brahma.
Pralepa	:	Paste/ a plaster, smearing.
Prasad	:	Food offered to the God or a deity.
Puchi	:	One kind of folk dance performed by small girls.
Puja	:	Worship.
Pulta Bagha	:	The art of converting a man into a tiger.
Pundit	:	Learned person.
Punji/Panji	:	Yearly Odia calendar/ an almanac.
Punyakoti	:	Name of a cow.
Purana	:	Mythology
Purana Panda	:	Who recites *Purana*/ a reciter of mythological books.
Purohita	:	Priest.
Putana	:	A demoness.
Raga	:	Rhythms/ one of the six modes of music.
Raika	:	Blouse.
Raja Bhoga	:	Chief offerings to the king.
Raja Parva	:	A festival in Odisha held on the first day of the month *Asadha.*
Rajaka	:	A washerman.
Raja-Rani	:	A kind of folk dance.
Ramzan	:	A sacred month of the Muslim calendar
Rana	:	One kind of snake.
Rang	:	Colour.
Rasa	:	Juice.
Rasara Keli	:	One kind of tribal dance.
Rastra Devata	:	State deity
Rathas	:	Chariots.

Rishis	:	Hermits/ sages.
Roza	:	Fasting of Muslims
Rudra mani	:	Name of Lord Siva.
Sabara/Soura	:	A large tribal community of Odisha.
Sadhabas	:	The honest traders engaged in overseas trade.
Sadhana	:	Sincere devotion/ meditation.
Sadhu	:	Saint.
Saga	:	A grass; a pot-herb, greens.
Sagada	:	Cart.
Sahasra Chhidra Ghat	:	An earthen pot taken by the wife of chief devotee/ a pot with thousands of slits or holes.
Sahi Yatra	:	Street festivals.
Sajani	:	Friend.
Sakatasura	:	A demon.
Sakhi	:	Friend or assistant.
Saktibheda	:	Severe injury inflicted by Indrajeet on Lakhmana.
Saktipitha	:	A shrine of the Goddess/ the religious centre.
Salapa	:	Date-palm juice.
Sambhar	:	One kind of deer.
Sandhasura	:	A demon.
Sanju	:	Bullet proof jacket.
Sankhachuda	:	The top of the temple.
Santal	:	The name of a tribe.
Santhaghara	:	House of a mendicant or a saint.
Sapa	:	Snake.
Sapua Kela	:	Snake charmers.
Sapua-Sapuani	:	A kind of folk dance.

Sarangi	:	A kind of musical instrument.
Sarbajana Chadhei	:	A mythical bird.
Sari	:	Cloth worn by woman.
Sathi	:	Friend.
Sati/Sutti	:	Self immolation of a widow who commits suicide jumping herself into the funeral pyre of her husband.
Satyapir	:	A festival which is observed by both the Hindus and Muslims jointly.
Saya	:	A sort of inner under-garment of women wearing saris.
Senapati	:	A commander, a general.
Setu-bandha	:	Construction of a bridge over the sea by Lord Rama to reach Lanka.
Sevatiphula	:	An ornament for the head.
Shloka	:	Invocations.
Shaman	:	Priest of the *Sabaras.*
Shastric	:	Relating to elite or sophisticated people/ Canonic.
Siddha	:	Pure or original; accomplished in holiness.
Siddheswari	:	The name of a Goddess.
Simhasana	:	A royal throne.
Sindura	:	Vermilion.
Sivachitta	:	The mark of three stepped small horizontal lines on the forehead.
Sraddha	:	Death anniversary/ offering of oblation to deceased ancestors, obsequial rites.
Sri Gayak	:	Main singer.
Subha Khunti	:	The pole signifying beginning of the festival/ auspicious pole.
Sunari	:	Goldsmith.
Sunthi	:	One kind of medicine/molasses.

Suryachita	:	Sun-mark on the forehead.
Sutradhara	:	Assistant singer.
Swarna Khadu	:	The golden ornament for the wrist.
Taapoi	:	Daughter of the rich *Sadhaba* family.
Tadaka	:	A demoness.
Tahia	:	Decorative head medal.
Tala	:	Rhythm/ musical time or measure.
Tamaka	:	One kind of musical instrument.
Tamalavana	:	A flower garden.
Tampa	:	A kind of poisonous snake.
Tantra	:	Spell or magic/ the black-art.
Thakurani	:	Village Goddess.
Thakurani Yatra	:	The festival of the Village Goddess.
Thana	:	Police station or seat.
Tilaka	:	Symbol or insignia on the forehead/ a sectarian mark on the forehead or upon the bridge of the nose.
Tithi	:	A lunar day
Tokei	:	Basket.
Triphala Pachana	:	One kind of juice used as medicine made from the combination of *myrobalan, belleric myrobalan* and *emblic myrobalan.*
Tuanya-Tuanyi	:	Twin brothers and sisters of a folktale.
Tulasi	:	Basil plant/ the holy basil, *Ocymum sanctum.*
Tulasi Chaura	:	The container used for basil plant worship/ structure on which *Tulasi* plant is worshipped.
Tunira	:	Quiver.
Turi	:	Musical instrument/ a trumpet.
Ubha	:	Emerge.

Uttarana	:	Apron.
Vahana	:	Vehicle for Gods and Goddesses/ a carriage, a conveyance, a vehicle.
Vaidya	:	A village doctor/ physician.
Vishnu Tilak	:	An insignia mark on the forehead in honour of Lord Vishnu.
Vrata	:	Fasting/ a vow, a religious act voluntarily undertaken.
Yogi/Yogis	:	A hermit, a devotee, a saint.
Zakat	:	Alms
Zari	:	Polythene.

Bibliography

1. PRIMARY SOURCES:

(A) Palmleaf Manuscripts (Sanskrit)

Ratha, Basudev (Somayaji), *Gangabansanucharitam*, Badakhemundi, no date.

Mishra,Haladhar, *Sangita Kalpalata*, (no place, no date).

Rath, Raghunatha, *Natya Manorama*, (no place, no date).

Panda, Rajabali, *Hindu Samskara*, (no place, no date).

(B) Palmleaf Manuscripts (Odia)

Das, Achuyutananda, *Haribansa Purana*, (no place, no date).

Das, Pitambar, *Nrusingh Purana*,(Tanhra, Pitala, 1792).

Das, Iswar, *Jagannath Charitamrita*, (no place, no date).

Das, Mahadev, *Vishnu Kesari Purana*,(no place, no date).

Pattnaik, Raghunath, *Danda Nata*, Jillundi (Ghumusar), no date.

(C) Odia Manuscripts

Anonymous, *Dandanata Bidhi* (preserved in Dandakali Mandira, Kalasandhapur).

Chhotaray, Raja Ramakrushna, *Prahallad Nataka* (preserved in the house of Arjuna Adhikari, a veteran *guru* of *Prahallad Nataka* of village Tentuapada).

Das, Dinabandhu, *Bharata Leela* (*Duari nata*, preserved in the house of Haribandhu Mohanty of Kalasandhapur).

Deo, Biswambar Rajendra, *Radhaprema Leela* (preserved in the village pathagara of B.L.N.Pur near Chikiti).

(D) Reports, Memoirs, Correspondences and Government Publications

The Folk Dance of Odisha, Odisha Sangita Natak Academy, Bhubaneswar, 1995,

Folk Theatre of Odisha, Odisha Sangita Natak Academy, Bhubaneswar, 1998.

Macpherson, S.C., Report upon the Khonds of the Districts of Ganjam and Cuttack, Madras, 1863.

Odisha Cultural Forum, *Odishara Loka Sanskruti*, Cuttack, 1978.

Report of the *Meriah* Agents, 1837-61, Madras, 1865.

Report of William Thackery on Ghumsar Zamindary in Ganjam, Madras, 1819.

Taylor, H.D.(ed.), Memoir in the Ganjam Maliahs in the Madras Presidency, Madras, 1846.

Selections from the records of the Government of India, vol.V, *History of* Rise and Progress of the Operations for the Suppression of Human *Sacrifice,Female Infanticide in Hill Tracts of Orissa, 1836-54*, Calcutta, 1854.

(E) Gazetteers and Manuals

Malley, L.S.S.O', *Bengal District Gazetteer- Angul*, Calcutta, 1909 .

Ramsay, L.E.B.Cobden, *Bengal District Gazetteers- Feudatory States of Orissa*, Howrah, 1950.

Bell, R.C.S, *Orissa District Gazetteers-Koraput*, Cuttack, 1945.

W.Francies, *Madras District Gazetteer-Vizagapatnam*, Madras, 1915.

Maltby, T.J, *The Ganjam District Manual*, Madras, 1892.

Behuria, N.C, *Orissa District Gazetteers-Ganjam*, Cuttack, 1992.

Senapati, N, *Orissa District Gazetteers-Koraput*, Cuttack, 1977.

Manual Administration of Madras Presidency, 3 vols., Madras, 1886.

2. SECONDARY SOURCES

(A) Books

Acharya, P.M., *Odisha Itihasa (*Odia*)*, Cuittack, 1950.

Acharya, Brundaban Chandra, *Odia Sahityara sankhipta Parichaya* (Cuttack, 1975).

A, Thomas & S. Barbara, Folklore- An Enclopaedia of Beliefs, Customs, Tales, Music and Art, California, 1997.

A.H. Siddique, *Bengali Folklore Collections and Studies during the British Period*, 1800-1947, Michigen, 1966

Acharya, Nandikeswar, *Abhinay Darpana* (Sanskrit), Delhi, 1989.

Acharya, Banambara, *Bharata Natyasastra* (Odia), Bhubaneswar, 1963.

Alam Dundas, *Interpreting Folklore*, Bloomington Indian a University Press, 1980.

Alexander, Karpe, *The Science of Folklore*, London, 1970.

Ali, Faruqi, *Lok-git* (Urdu), Agra, 1959.

Anand, Mulk Raj, *Folk-Tales of Punjab*, New-Delhi, 1989.

Archer, Mildred, *Company Drawings in the India Office Library*, London, 1972.

B.Rama Raju, *Folklore of Andhra Pradesh*, New Delhi, 1978.

Bailey, F.G., Tribe, Caste and Nation, Manchester, 1960.

Banerjee, Projesh, *The Folk Dance of India*, Allahabad, 1959.

Bardhan, Moni, *Bangalar Lokanritya O Giti Baichitra* (Bengali), Calcutta, 1961.

Barua, Hem, *Ei Gaon Ei Git* (Assamese), Calcutta, 1961. *Folk Songs of India*, Calcutta, 1963.

Bascom, W.R, *Folklore and Anthropology*, JAF, vol-66, 1953

Behera, Krishna Charana *Odisara yatra o Paramparika Lokapriya Natya Dhara* (Odia) Cuttack, 1979. *Natya Sahitya* (Odia), Cuttack, 1992.

Benerji, B.G, *Folk Illness and Ethno Medicines*, New Delhi, 1988.

Bensor, Wilfrid, *A Bibliography of Folklore as contained in the first eighty years of the publications of the Folklore Society*, London, 1961.

Bhagavat, Durga, *An Outline of Indian Folklore*, Bombay, 1958.

Bhattacharya, N. N., *History of Tantric Religion*, New Delhi, 1987

Bhattacharyya Upendranath, *Banglar Baul O Baulgan* (Bengali), Calcutta, 1957.

Bhattacharyya, Asutosh, *Chhau Dance of Purilia* (Calcutta, 1972). *The Serpent as a Folk-deity of Bengal*, Tokyo, 1965. *Folklore of Bengal*, New Delhi, 1978. *Mask Dances of West Bengal*, New Delhi, 1968

Bhattacharyya. P.N., *'Folk-Custom and Folklore of Sylhet District'*,Mani India, Vol. X (1930).

Biswas, Hemango(ed.), *Folkmusic And Folklore: An Anthology*,vol.1, Calcutta,1967.

Bose, N.K., *Culture and Society in India*, Calcutta, 1967.

Chatterjee, S.K., *The People, Language, Culture of Orissa*, Bhubaneswar, 1986.

Crooke, W., *An Indroduction to the Popular Religion And Folklore of Northern India*, Delhi, 1894.

D.N. Kakar, *Folk and Modern Medicines*, Chandigarh, 1973

D.P., Ghose, *Folk Art of Bengal*, Dept of History Santiniketan, 1977.

Das, Balaram, Jagamohan *Ramayana*, Bhubaneswar, 1995.

Das, Sarala, *Sarala Mahabharata*(Odia), no place, no date.

Das, Surjya Narayana, *Jagannath Mandira O Jagannath Tatwa* (Cuttack, 1966). Odia Sahityara Itihasa (Odia, vol-I, 1963, vol-II, 1965, vol-III, 1966, Cuttack).

Das, H.C., *Folk Music and Dances*, Cuttack, 1988. *Military History of Odisha*, New Delhi, 1986.

Das, J.P., *Chitra Pothi* (Odia), New Delhi, 1985.

Das C.R. (ed.), *Folk Culture and Literature* vol.1, (*Proceedings of the International Seminar on Folk Culture*), Cuttack,1978.

Das H.C. (ed.) *Folk Culture*, vol.IV, (*Proceedings of the International Seminar on Folk Culture*) *(Folk Music andDance)*, Cuttack, 1978.

Das, Birakishore, *Juge Juge Natyasahitya*(Odia), Cuttack, 1981.

Das, Dhiren, *Dandanata* (Odia), Bhubaneswar, 1982.

Das, Gouranga Charana, *Lokanatya Parampara O Kandhei Nacha* (Odia), Cuttack, 1993.

Das, Hemant Kumar, *Odiya Lokanataka* (Odia), Cuttack, 1983. *Odiya Natakara Bikasha Dhara* (Part II), (Odia), Cuttack, 1980. *Odiya Lokanataka,* Cuttack, 1983.

Das, Jogesh, Folklore of Assam, New Delhi, 1991.

Dash, Kunja Behari, *A Study of Odishan Folklore,* Santiniketan, 1953. *Odiya Lokagita O Kahani,* (*Odia*), Santiniketan, 1958. *Folklore of Odisha,* Cuttack, 1991.

Das, Jogesh, Folklore of Assam, New Delhi, 1991.

Dash, Kunja Behari, *A Study of Odishan Folklore,* Santiniketan, 1953. *Odiya Lokagita O Kahani,* (*Odia*), Santiniketan, 1958. *Folklore of Odisha,* Cuttack, 1991.

Das, Raghavananda, *Kathalahari (Utkalakahani Sangraha),* Cuttack, 1901.

Dasa, Jagannath, *Srimmad Bhagavata* (Odia), Cuttack, 1873.

Dasa, Mahadeva, *Vishnukesari Purana* (Odia), Cuttack, 1960.

Dash, K.B and *Folklore of Odisha,* New Delhi, 1979. Mahapatra, L.K.

Dash, Radha Charana, *Utkala Kahani Darpana,* (Odia) Cuttack, 1921.

Dash, Premlata, *Odishara Osha Vrata Katha* (in Odia), Cuttack, 1981.

Dev, Chitaranjan, *Banglar Palligiti* (Bengali), Calcutta, 1966.

Dev, Kishore Chandra *Radhapremalila* (Odia), Cuttack, 1971. Rajendra,

Devendra, Satyarthi, *Meet My people,* Indian Folk Poetry, Ahmadabad, 1951.

Dey, Lal Behari, *Folk-Tales of Bengal,* London, 1833.

Dhar, Somanath. *Kashmiri Folk-tales,* no place, no date.

DhamiJa Jasleen, *Indian Folk Arts and Crafts,* New Delhi, 2002.

Dorson, M. Richard (ed.)*Folklore and Folk life,* Chicago, 1972.

Dundas Alam, *Interpreting Folklore,* Bloomington Indiana University Press, 1980.

Dundas, Alam (ed.), *The Study of Folklore,* Printice-Hall, Englewood, Califf, 1965

Durant, W., *A Story of Civilization,* vol.I, no place, no date.

Duttagupta, Upendra '*Folk-tales of Orissa,* Calcutta, 1923. Narayana, Edgar Thurston, *Omens, and Superstitions of*South *India,* London, 1912.

Enakshi Bhavani, *Folk and Tribal Designs of India* (Hundreds of designs and motifs from folk and tribal crafts of India), Bombay, 1974.

Fiascher, Eberhard, *Folk-tales of Odisha,* Calcutta, 1923.

Fisher, Eberhard & Pathy, *The Murals for Goddesses and Gods,* New Delhi, Dinanath, 1986.

Folk Music & Folklore *Folk Music and Folklore: An Anthology,* Research Institute Calcutta, 1967.

Frazer, J.G. *The Golden Bough,* London,1922.

F.Robins, & Betty, *The Everyday Art of India,* New York, Dashew, 1968.

G.L, Chavunduka, *The Professionalisation of Folk Medicines,* no date, no place.

Gargi, Balwant, *Indian Folk Theatre,* New Delhi, 1991.

Ghose, D.P., *Folk Art of Bengal,* Dept of History Santiniketan, 1977.

Ghose, G.K., *Odisha Dazzel from within,* New Delhi, 1993.

Gibbon, G, *Anthropological Archaeology.* Columbia University Press, New York, 1984.

Goswami, Prafulla Dutta, *Bihu-songs of Assam,* Calcutta, 1957.

Gould, Richard, A., *Living Archaeology.* Cambridge University Press, Cambridge, 1980.

Gupta, Haragovind, *Gaon Ke Git (*Hindi*),* Agra, 1963.

Hand, Waylnd Debs, *Magical Medicine,* Berkeley, 1980.

Harichandan, Niladri *Lokanatya Parampara,* (Odia), Cuttack, Bhusan, 1990.

Honda, Om Chandra, *Pahari Folk Art,* Bombay, 1975.

Islam, Mozharul., *A History of Folktale collection in India and Pakistan,* Bengal Academy, Dacca, 1963.

Jarvis, D.C., *Folk Medicines- A Rural Doctors Guide to Good Health.*

Jenkins, Geraint, *Studies in folk Life,* London, 1969.

Joshi, Om Prakash, *Painted Folk -lore and Folk- lore Painters- A Study with Reference to Rajstan,* Delhi, 1976.

Jain, Jyotindra, *Folk Art & Calture of Gujrat,* Ahmedabad, 1989.

Kakar, D.N, *Primitive Folk and Modern Medicines,* Chandigarh, 1973.

Khanna, Girija, *Home Medicines* - A *Hand book of Folk M e d i c i n e s*, Sahidabad, 1982.

Khuntia, Biswanath, *Bichitra Ramayana,* no date, no place.

Kirklond, Edwin Capars, *A Bibliography of*south *Asian Folklore,* The Hague, 1966.

Krappe, Alexdander, H., *The Science of Folklore,* London, 1930.

Krasa, M., *Odisha Folk Painting,* Prag, 1967.

Kulke, Harman, et.al(eds.), *The Cult of Jagannath and Regional Tradition of Odisha,* New Delhi, 1978

Leach, Maria (ed.), *A Standard Dictionary of Folklore, Mythology and Legend,* New York. 1949.

Mac Cormack, Carol, *Ethnography of Fertility and Birth London,* 1982.

Macpherson, William, *Memorials of Service in India,* London, 1865.

Mahankuda, Padmalochana, *Odiya Jatra Sahityara Itihasa.*Cuttack, 2001.

Mahanti, Manindra, *Paschima Odisara Dhaga-Dhamali,* Cuttack, 1968.

Mahapatra, Sitakanta, *The Rainbow of Rythms,* Jagatsingpur, 2005.

Mahapatra, Syamasundara, *Odiya Lokagathara Parisara O Prakruti* Cuttack,1991.

Mahapatra, Chakradhara, *Utkala Gaunli Geeta (*Odia*),* Cuttack, 1959. *Oria Gramyagiti* (Odia), Cuttack, 1958.

Mahapatra, L.K., *A Hill Bhuiyan Village: An Empirical Socio-Economic Study.*Hamburg University, Ph.D, Dissertation (hectographed), 1960.

Mansingh, Mayadhar, *A History of Odia Literature,* New Delhi, 1962. *The Saga of the Land of Lord Jagannath,* New-Delhi, 1965.

Melville J. Herskovits, *Folklore after a Hundred Years,* A problem of Redefinition, JAF, vol.59, 1946.

Mishra, P.K., *Bharatiya Lok-Myth:Purva Bharat.* Unpublished Ph.D., Dissertation. Visvabharati, Santiniketan. 1969.

Mishra, Mahindra Ku., *Folksongs of Kalahandi,* Bhubaneswar, 1989.

Misro, R.C., *Rural Economy and Society of Ancient Orissa,* Calcutta, 2002.

Misro, R.C.(ed.), *Fresh Light on Early Orissan History, Culture and Polity,* Bhubaneswar, 2009.

Mishra, Gourisankar., *Ganjam Itihasa Paviknama*, Brahmapur, 2003.

Mohanty, B.C., *Patachitras of Odisha*,Ahmedabad, 1980.

Mohanty, Gopinath et.al. *The Cultural Heritage of Ganjam*, (ed.), Bhubaneswar, 2004. *Cultural Heritage of Orissa, vol.IX*, Rayagada District, Bhubaneswar, 2007. Cultural Heritage of Orissa, vol.XI, Koraput District, Bhubaneswar, 2008. *Cultural Heritage of Gajapati*, Bhubaneswar, 2004.

Mohanty, Brajamohan *Odishara Parbaparbani, Osha, Vrata*, (ed.), *Jani Jatra* (Cuttack, 1979).

Mohanty, Banshidhara, *Odia Sahityara Itihasa*, (vol-I, Cuttack, 1970).

Mukherji Ajit Coomar, *Folk Art of Bengal*, Calcutta, 1939.

Mukherji, Sailoz, *Folk Art of India*, New Delhi, 1907 Nagpal, J.C., *Mural Paintings of India*, New Delhi, 1980.

Nayak, Sanyasi, *Kamana Danda* (Odia), Berhampur, 1984.

Nepak, Bhagirathi *Dandanata – Folk Play of Odisha*, Bhubaneswar, 1998.

Pal, Mrinal Kanti, *Catalogue of Folk Art in the Asutosh Museum*, Calcutta, 1962.*Palligeeti Samchayana*. Part I, Santiniketan, 1963.

Panda, Bhagabana,*Prahalladda Nataka*, Bhubaneswar, 1963.

Panda, Aparna, Paralakhemundi, 1923

Panda, Harimohan, *Janabachana*, New Delhi, 2008.

Panda,D.(ed.), Mahima *Dharma and Darshan:Anointer Disciplinary Seminar*, DAV College Koraput, 1957

Pani, Jeevan., *Living Dolls – Story of Indian Puppets*, New Delhi, 1986. *Performing Arts of Odisha*, Jagatsinghpur, 2007

Panikkar, K.N., *Folklore of Kerala*, New Delhi, 1991.

Parmar, Shyam, *Folklore of Madhya Pradesh*, New Delhi, 1986.

Pathy, Dinanatha, *Traditional Paintings of Odisha*, Bhubaneswar, 1991. *Mural Painting of Odisha*, Bhubaneswar, 1991. *Murals for Goddess and Gods*, New Delhi, 1995. *Chitra Bhasha O Chitrita Bhasha (*Odia*)*, Berhampur, 1999.

Patnaik, Naveen, *The Court Costumes of India*, New York, 1995.

Patnaik, Dhirendranath, *Folk Dances of Odisha*, Bhubaneswar, 2000. *Folk Theatres of Odisha*, 1998.

Pattnaik, Sujata,*Folk Legend, Bhagaban Sahu,* New-Delhi, 2006.

Patnaik, Arabinda, *Lokagalpa (*Odia*) in Odishara Lokasanskruti,*Bhubaneswar,

Pattnaik, Kesaba, *Kesaba Ramayana,* Berhampur, no date.

Pradhan, *Krishna* Chandra, *Odia Loka Sahitya O Loka Sanskruti* (Odia),Cuttack, 1995.

Praharaj, Gopala Chandra, *Utkala Kahani in Utkala Sahitya,* Cuttack, 1901.

Ratha, Sibaram, *Osha Kothi,* Berhampur, 2000.

Ratha, A.K., *Daksnina Odisara Pratnatatwika Bibhava* (Odia), Berhampur, 1994.

Rath, Tarini Charana, *Ghumsara Itihasa* (Odia), 1965.

Ray, Girija Shankara, *Odiya Natyakala,* Cuttack, 1967.

Ray, Sarat Chandra & *The Study of Folklore and Tradition in* J.Bors, *India',* Vol. XVIII,.

Raychouddhary, P.C & *Best Loved Folk-tales of India,* New Delhi, Robert, Busseabargar, 1985.

Ramanujan, A.K. (ed.), *Folk-tales from India,* New Delhi: Penguin/Viking, 1993.

Redifield, Robert, *The Folk Society,* JAF, vol.52, 1947.

Roy Choudhry, P.C, *Best Loved Folk-tales of India,* New Delhi, 1985. *Folklore of Bihar,* New Delhi, 1976.

Sahu, Lakshmi Narayana, *Dandanata* (Odia),Cuttack, 1952. *Hill Tribes of Jeypore,* Cuttack, 1942.

Samala, Baishnava Charana, *Odiya Galpa: Gati O Prakruti,* Cuttack, 1974.

Samantaray, Natabara, *Odiya Palli Sahitya (Odiya),* Bhubaneswar, 1970. *Sambalpuri and other Dances of Odisha,* Bhubaneswar, 1997.

Samantaray, Natabara, *Odia sahityara Itihasa,* (Bhubaneswar, 1964).

Satpathy, Santosh Kumar,*Odisara DandaNata.(Odia),* Bhubneshar 1994.

Sengupta, Sankar, *Folklorists of Bengal,* Calcutta, 1965. *The Patas and Patuas of Bengal,* Calcutta, 1963. *Folklore and Folk Life in India,*

Sen, D.C., *The Folk-Literature of Bengal,* Calcutta, 1920.

Sen, Dinesh Chandra *Folk Literature of Bengal.*

Sen, Sukumar, *History of Bengali Literature,* New-Delhi, 1960.

Sharma, Nalivilochan, *Lok-gatha Parichaya* (Hindi), Allahabad, 1959

Stanlley, Margaret, *Ancient Indian Magic and Folk lore,* London, 1921.

Subramanyam, P.R., *An introduction to the Study of Indian Folklore,* Tuticorin, 1972.

Taylore, Edward, *Primitive Culture,* vol.I & II London, 1891.

Temple, R.C., *Legends of the Punjab,* Calcutta, 1844.

Thakur, Upendra, *Madhubani Paintings* (Folk Art of Mithila), New Delhi, 1982.

Thomas, A. Green, & S. Folk lore: *An Encydopaedia of Beliefs,* Barbora, *Customs, Tales, Music and Art,* California, 1997.

Thurston Edgar, *Omens and Superstitions of* south*ern India,* London, 1912.

Tylor, E.B., *Primitive Culture,* London, 1871.

Vatsayan, Kapila, *Traditions of Indian Folk Dances,* Delhi, 1976.

Verrier Elwin, *The Tribal Art of Middle India,* London, 1951. *Folk Songs of Chattisgarh,* Calcutta, 1946. *Bondo Highlander,* Oxford, 1950. *Songs of the Forest,* London, 1953. *Tribal Myths of Orissa,* Bombay, 1954. *Maria, Murder and Suicide,*Bombay, 1943.

Whitehead, Henry, *The Village Goddess of* south *Asia,* New Delhi, 1921

Yagnik, Hasu, *Folklore of Gujarat,* New Delhi, 2002.

(B) Selected Research Articals:

1. Acharya, Sudarshana, *Odiya Lokakatha,* in: Bhanja Souvenir,Vol II, 1979.
2. Bhattacharya, Ashutosh, "Cure Deities of Bengal", in: *Folklore,* vol.III, no.2, February-March, Calcutta, 1962, p.11.
3. Bhattacharya, Ashutosh, "The Cult of Tree deities of Bengal", in: *Indian Folklore,* vol.I, no-4, October-December, 1958, p.7.
4. Bhattacharya, Ashutosh, The Cult of Village-Gods of West Bengal,*Man in India,* vol. XXXV, 1955.
5. Bose, S.K., "Baul Songs of Bengal", in: *Folkmusic and Folklore: An Anthology,* vol.I, Calcutta, 1967, p.46.
6. Chakravarti, N., An Ancient Indian Story in Bengali Vratakatha', *Journal* of *the* Asiatic Society of Bengal, Vol.XXVI (N.S.).
7. Charchi, B., *Bharata Leela* in *Odishara Lokanataka,* Odisha Sahitya Samaja, Cuttack, 1998, pp. 229-32.

8. Chaubey, Ganesh, "Folk-gods of Bihar", in: *Bihar in Folklore Study*, Calcutta, 1972, p.156.
9. Duff, A., "Goomsur; the late war there-the Kandhs of Hill Tribes" in: *The Calcutta Review*, vol.v, no.ix, 1846, p.45.
10. Dutt. G.S., 'Indigenous Dances of Bengal' in *Census of India*,1931, vol.V, Part I- Bengal and Sikkim, Calcutta, 1933.
11. Fisher, P.S., Folk Medicine, in: *West Virginia Historical Society Quarterly*, vol.x, no.4, January, 1997, p.11.
12. Hotta, M.N., "*Phulbani Kandh Sampradayara Lokavidya*" (Odia), in: *Biswabharati Dipika*, vol.VIII, Santiniketan, 1987, pp.15-43.
13. Jain, S.K., "Medicinal Plantlove of the Tribal of Bastar", in: *Economy of Botany*, vol.xix, Calcutta, 1965, p.27.
14. Kar, I.B., *Glimpses of Folk-Theatres*, in: *The Cultural Heritage of Ganjam*, Bhubaneswar, 2004, p. 345.
15. Mahapatra, Sitakanta, "Folk Art of Orissa: Continuity in Visual Tradition" in: *The Rainbow of Rhythms, op.cit.*, p.176.
16. Mahapatra, Sitakanta, "*Saora Icons as Pictograms*", in: *The Rainbow of Rhythms*, Jagathsinghpur, 2005, p.167.
17. Maity, P.K., "Dharm Thakur of Bengal and his Association with Human Fertility", in: *Folklore*, vol.xiii, 3rd March, Calcutta, 1971, p.5.
18. Misro, R.C., *Folk Dance, Drama and Music in the District of Ganjam: An Overview*, in *The Quarterly Journal of the Mystic Society*, vol. 101, no.1, January-March, 2010, p.11.
19. ——————, "Suppression of *Meriah* (Human) Sacrifice in the hill tracts of Ganjam during the 19th century A.D.- A Study", in :*Itihas, Journal of the Andhra Pradesh State Archives and Research* Institute (Hyderabad), vol.xxiv, nos. 1&2, January-December, 1998, pp.109-130.
20. ——————, "Understanding of Folklore in a Regional from Historical Perspectives: The Case of Orissa", in: *Journal of Indian History and Culture* (Chennai), vol.x, March, 2003, pp. 93-104.
21. ——————, "Understanding of Folklore in a Regional from Historical Perspectives: Some Random Thoughts", in M.Krishna Kumari(ed.), *Folklore Studies and Its Bearing on the History and Culture of Andhras*, Vishakhapatnam, 2003, pp. 1-10.

22. ——————, "*Danda Nata*: The Popular Folk Theatre of Ganjam-A Study", in: *Proceedings of South Indian History Congress*, Twentyfifth (Silver Jubilee) Session, Madurai, 2005, pp. 513-517.
23. ——————, "Selected Fairs and Festivals Associated with Siva-worship: A Historical Reappraisal in: *The Quarterly Journal of the Mythic Society* (Bangalore), vol.xcviii, no.1, January-March, 2007, pp. 18-23.
24. Mishra, Sudha, *Performing Folk Arts of* south*ern Odisha (Ganjam)* in *Mardaraja*, Khallikote, 2009, p.157.
25. Mitra, Sarat Chandra, On the Custom of Life Giving Charity in Odisha,*Journal of the Anthropological Society of Bombay*, 1925.
26. Nanda, Somanath, *Odia Tunda Sahitya*, (Odia), *Bhanja Souvenir* vol.II, Bhanjanagara, 1960.
27. Panda, Prahallad, "Folk Dances of Ganjam in *Cultural Scenario of Ganjam"*, p. 36.
28. Panda, Prahllad, "Art and Craft in Ganjam", in: *Mardaraj*, Khallikote, 2007, pp.16-17.
29. Panda, Lakshman Kumar, "*Loka Jeevandhara" in "Odisara Lokasanskruti"*, Bhubaneswar, 1985.
30. Pande, Trilochan, "Bhojpuri Folklore and Folkmusic", in: *Folkmusic and Folklore: An Anthology*, vol.I, Calcutta, p.16.
31. Pani, Jeevan, '*Prahlad Natak: A Theatre of Liberated Reality*', in: *Essays on the Theatre and Theatre Crafts of Eastern India*, Eastern Zonal Cultural Centre, Calcutta, 1989, p. 8.
32. Pany, Remesh, '*Folk Dances*', in: *The Cultural Heritage of Ganjam*, Bhubaneswar, 2004, p. 324.
33. Patnaik, N.R., "Studies in Superstitious Beliefs, Myths, Witchcrafts, Sorcery and Sacrifice of the 19th Century Orissa", in: *Orissa Historical Research Journal*, vol.XXXIII, nos. 3-4, pp.129-130.
34. Patnaik, Kailasha, *Lokakahani* in: *"Konark"*, January, 1996, pp. 35-39
35. Sahoo, A.C., "*Saora* Script and Wall Painting" in: *The Cultural Heritage of Ganjam*, Bhubaneswar, 2004, p.352.
36. Sahu, Bhagabana, '*Kedu* Sacrifies in the Kandh Tracts of Orissa in the second half of the 19th century', in: *Research Journal of the Berhampur University*, vol.IV, December 1984, p.133.
37. Sahu, Bhagabana, *Prahallad Nataka-The Popular Folk Dance of* south *Odisha*, in: *Journal of Odishan History*, vol.XXIV, Dec. 2011, p. 211.

38. Samal, B.C., *Odia Lokanatakara Sanskruti* in: *Odishara Sanskrutika Parampara*, vol.I, Cuttack, 1989, pp. 127-128.

39. Sumabala, P., *Bura Katha and the History of Andhra Pradesh,* in: *Journal of Indian History and Culture*, (Chennai), vol.xv, September 2008, p. 99.

40. Taylor, W., "On the Language, Manners and Rites of the Kandhs of the Goomsar Mountains" in: *Madras Journal of Literature and Science,* vol.v, Jan-june, 1837, p.41.

41. Verrier Elwin, 'The Art of Ikon', *in:* Sitakanta Mohapatra(ed.), *Soura Painting*, New-Delhi, 2009, p.2.

(C) Journals, Periodicals and Newspapers

i. Journals

Indian folklore Research Journal, (ed.) M.D.Muthukumaraswamy, published from Chennai.

Journal of Indian History and Culture, Chennai, September, 2008.

Journal of Royal Asiatic Society of Great Britain and Ireland, vols.VII (1843), XIII (1852), XVII (1860).

Journal of Asiatic Society of Bengal, vol.LII, part-I, 1883, vol.LXVII, 1898.

Journal of Royal Asiatic Society of Bengal, London, 1893.

Journal of Folk-Music and Folklore Research Institute, Calcutta, vol.I, 1967.

Journal of Indian Folkloristics, Journal of Bihar and Orissa Research Society,

vol.II, part-I and part-II, vol.III, part-IV.

Madras Journal of Literature and Science, vol.VI, 1837, vol.VII, 1838.

Folklore (ed.) Shankar Sen Gupta, published from Calcutta-relavent vols.

Proceedings of Indian History Congress, Madras Session, 1944, Aligarh Session, 1961.

Orissa Historical Research Journal, vol.IV, Nos. 1&2, 1955, vol.XIII, No.1, 1965.

Proceedings of Orissa History Congress.

ii. Periodicals(Oriya)

Prajabandhu.................. Relavent volumes.

Ganjam Guna Darpana...... -do-

Hitabadini..................... -do-

Sambalpur Hitaisini......... -do-

Utkala Dipika................ -do-

Konark....................... -do-

Jhankar...................... -do-

Utkala Prasanga............ -do-

Orissa Review.............. -do-

iii. Newspapers (Odia)

The Samaja - Mentioned portions.

Anupama Bharata - Mentioned portions.

The Prajatantra - Mentioned portions.

Index

COLOUR PLATES

Plate 1. A view from the *Danda Nata* performance (*Dhuli Danda*).

Plate 2. A view from the *Danda Nata* showing Kali figure (parabha)

Plate 3. Soura Wall Painting

Plate 4. *Pata Dandua* being tied in the Meru Post

Plate 5. A view from the *Prahallada Nataka* showing Hiranya Kasyapu - the demon king his son Prahallada, wife Leelabati and general Chandamarka.

Plate 6. A view from *Dasakathia* showing *Gayaka* and *Palia* in their traditional attire.

Plate 7. A view from a *Bharata Leela* performance showing Arjuna, Duari, Subhadra and Satyabhama.

Plate 8. A view from *Oshakothi* dance with drummer and *Gahana*.

Plate 9. A view from *Jodi Sankha* performance.

Plate 10. A view from a tiger dance.

Plate 11. Instrumentalists of the *Ranapa* dance.

Plate 12. A view from *Ranapa* dance.

Plate 13. Instrumentalist of the *Demsa* dance.

Plate 14. A view from the *Demsa* dance.

Plate 15. *Soura* wall painting.

Plate 16. A view from the *Thakurani yatra* of Brahmapur (*Ghat Pavi Krama*)

Plate 17. Folk Art *Nabagunjana*

Plate 18. Scene of a *Natha yogi*